The Marriage
Devotional

The Marriage Devotional

365 Simple Ways to Celebrate Your Love

MEERA LESTER

adamsmedia
Avon, Massachusetts

Published by
Adams Media, a division of F+W Media, Inc.
57 Littlefield Street, Avon, MA 02322. U.S.A.
www.adamsmedia.com

Contains material adapted and abridged from *1001 Ways to Do Good*, by Meera Lester, copyright © 2008 by F+W Media, Inc., ISBN 10: 1-59869-474-X, ISBN 13: 9-781-59869-474-1; *The Everything® Guide to a Happy Marriage*, by Stephen Martin, MFT, and Victoria Costello, copyright © 2009 by F+W Media, Inc., ISBN 10: 1-60550-134-4, ISBN 13: 978-1-60550-134-5; *The Everything® Kama Sutra Book*, by Suzie Heumann, copyright © 2004 by F+W Media, Inc., ISBN 10: 1-59337-039-3, ISBN 13: 978-159337-039-8; *The Everything® Law of Attraction Book*, by Meera Lester, copyright © 2009 by F+W Media, Inc., ISBN 10: 1-59869-775-7, ISBN 13: 978-1-59869-775-9; *The Everything® Orgasm Book*, by Amy Cooper, PhD, copyright © 2010 by F+W Media, Inc., ISBN 10: 1-60550-992-2, ISBN 13: 978-1-60550-992-1; *The Everything® Self-Esteem Book*, by Robert M. Sherfield, PhD, copyright © 2004 by F+W Media, Inc., ISBN 10: 1-58062-976-8, ISBN 13: 978-1-58062-976-8; and *The Everything® Tantric Sex Book*, by Bobbi Dempsey with Technical Review by Al Link and Pala Copeland, copyright © 2007 by F+W Media, Inc., ISBN 10: 1-59869-326-2, ISBN 13: 978-159869-326-3.

ISBN 10: 1-4405-0224-2
ISBN 13: 978-1-4405-0224-8
eISBN 10: 1-4405-0858-5
eISBN 13: 978-1-4405-0858-5

Printed in the United States of America.

10 9 8 7 6 5 4 3 2 1

Library of Congress Cataloging-in-Publication Data
Lester, Meera.
The marriage devotional / Meera Lester.
p. cm.
ISBN-13: 978-1-4405-0224-8
ISBN-10: 1-4405-0224-2
ISBN-13: 978-1-4405-0858-5 (ebk)
ISBN-10: 1-4405-0858-5 (ebk)
1. Marriage. 2. Love. I. Title.
HQ734.L3985 2010
306.81—dc22
2010019567

This book is available at quantity discounts for bulk purchases.
For information, please call 1-800-289-0963.

DEDICATION

For my husband, Carlos Jose Carvajal—

You lift me up when I am down, guide me back to reality when I get too crazy, listen patiently when I need to talk, make me laugh when I need to lighten up, hug me when I feel overwhelmed, tease me when all else fails, translate from Spanish when your mother and sisters speak so rapidly that I can't follow what they're saying, and dance with me when you see love in my eyes. My life is richer, fuller, and more meaningful because you, *mi amor*, are in it.

ACKNOWLEDGMENTS

My sincere and deepest gratitude goes to Paula Munier for bringing me such a lovely project in the first place and her unwavering support and insights into how to make the book better.

Thanks also to Matthew Glazer for his professionalism, responsiveness, and attention to detail. I'd like to offer a special thank-you to Laura Daly, development editor, and everyone one else at Adams Media associated with bringing this project to fruition.

Finally, I would like to thank Patricia Rubi and Altagracia D'Antonio for their wise words about marriage, which I've incorporated in this book.

INTRODUCTION

Happily married people live longer, healthier, wealthier lives. What's their secret? They are devoted to each other, practice tender forgiveness, enjoy each other's company, share a vision for their life together, and find ways to keep their sex life spicy. In this book, you'll learn these and many other simple ways that you and your spouse can build intimacy and reinforce your commitment to one another—every day of the year.

With open lines of communication, an ever-evolving and fulfilling sex life, and a mutual respect and admiration for each other, no obstacle will be too great for you two to tackle. Yet amidst harried lifestyles, the responsibilities of careers and children, and financial stress, it's easy to forget to prioritize the health of your marriage. If you need fresh and easy ideas for ways to keep your marriage buoyant, look no further. From impromptu trysts and new sexual positions to couples retreats and joint acts of charity, these are marital tips and tricks that really work—no matter how long you've been married. These proven tips and success strategies empower you to make your marriage the best it can be.

Think of your marriage as the journey of a lifetime with no particular destination—the journey itself is the adventure. There will be exciting moments of new discovery, periods of unforeseen challenges, and delightful experiences. Facing the same direction, making decisions together, and evaluating how your marriage is working for both of you means that at any time you can pinpoint what works and what doesn't. When the two of you decide to embark in new direction to spice up the experience, to learn something new, or to deepen the emotional bonds you share, your journey of a lifetime can bring you both new levels of understanding, commitment, and never-ending joy.

Remember, while neither of you is perfect, you're perfect for each other.

OFFER YOUR SPOUSE PRAISE
AND APPRECIATION

Let's be grateful for those who give us happiness; they are the charming gardeners who make our souls blossom. —Marcel Proust, French novelist, essayist, and critic

Giving praise demonstrates appreciation and high regard for another person. In a marriage, appreciation for what each spouse brings to the marriage matters. All too often, couples can get caught up in their marital routine and forget to notice a gesture of love or some positive action taken by their mates—in other words, all those small, but meaningful acts that say, "I love you."

The secret to getting more of what you both want in your marriage—that is, more of the positives—is to take the time to praise each other. Hold each other in high regard. Overlook minor annoyances. Resist criticizing. Maybe one partner is great at organizing and the other one is sloppy. But the sloppy one is a great cook and the organizer is a workaholic. Nobody is perfect. Nip negative tendencies in the bud and opt for optimism. Praise what you appreciate in the other person—anything from the way your lover looks, tastes, or smells to how neatly he or she writes to-do lists.

— EXTRA CREDIT —

Use one of the 1,440 minutes in the day to praise your spouse for something he or she has said or done. For example, tell him how meaningful it was to hear that you were the center of his universe. Or thank her for bringing you that towel warm from the dryer when you dashed into the house cold and wet from the storm. Love isn't as much about the big romantic moments in life—of course, we all relish those—but rather, rather the thousands of small, ordinary moments that you share every day with the one you love.

KISS AS IF
YOU MEAN IT

Kiss me. Kiss me as if it were the last time. —Ilsa to Rick in *Casablanca*

Philosophers and poets have described the kiss as uniting the souls of lovers. Spouses reveal their love by the way they snuggle up close, embrace, and kiss. Remember that notable phrase from Shakespeare's play Romeo and Juliet? "Let lips do what hands do." Permit your hands always to find each other, but then kiss each other as if it is your first and last kiss. Kissing re-establishes your powerful, intimate connection to each other. Communicate with your kisses that you have given to each other your greatest treasure: the gift of your love.

DAY 2

SEVEN MEMORABLE MOVIE KISSES
1. *An Affair to Remember* (1957), Deborah Kerr and Cary Grant
2. *Breakfast at Tiffany's* (1961), Audrey Hepburn and George Peppard
3. *Casablanca* (1942), Ingrid Bergman and Humphrey Bogart
4. *Ghost* (1990), Demi Moore and Patrick Swayze
5. *Gone with the Wind* (1939), Vivien Leigh and Clark Gable
6. *Some Like It Hot* (1959), Marilyn Monroe and Tony Curtis
7. *Titanic* (1997), Leonardo DiCaprio and Kate Winslet

--- EXTRA CREDIT ---

To really enjoy the rapture of kissing, try sneaking in a passionate "make-out session" during a few stolen moments in the car, between meetings, or when you can grab short bursts of time. Not only will the limit on time add to the excitement, but you will soon realize that kissing can be exciting even when it isn't followed by sex.

REMEMBER YOUR
SPOUSE'S BIRTHDAY

Because the birthday of my life / Is come, my love is come to me.
—Christina Georgina Rossetti, British poet

Birthdays celebrate your entrance into the world. Your birthday is a day to reflect upon how you are sharing the gift of you with others traveling alongside you through the journey of life. Talk with your spouse about how you like to celebrate birthdays. While some people love big flashy affairs, others prefer toned-down versions of fun-filled get-togethers. Perhaps your spouse wants a quiet and simple birthday celebration—possibly just the two of you.

Whether you plan a birthday weekend getaway for two or he orchestrates a blowout surprise party for you that includes family or friends, the important thing is to be thoughtful and considerate of each other's wishes. If your spouse prefers marking that special day without all the fanfare, tone down your plans. Forget the party and instead give him a paper crown or birthday hat. Sing the birthday song to him several times throughout the day.

--- EXTRA CREDIT ---

Rent a rowboat and enjoy a birthday bash for two. Sip sparkling wine or cider from fluted glasses and dine on tea sandwiches and petit fours. Share memories of your favorite birthdays. Read passages of romantic or erotic poetry. Find a secluded place and sample each other's deliciously sweet kisses. Who needs cake?

DON'T HOLD
BACK THE HUGS

———

Millions and millions of years would still not give me half enough time to describe that tiny instant of all eternity when you put your arms around me and I put my arms around you. —Jacques Prévert, French poet and screenwriter

Hugs generate happy, secure feelings that come from the human touch. Author and psychotherapist Virginia Satir noted that humans need four hugs a day for survival, eight hugs a day for maintenance, and twelve hugs a day for growth. A hug can reassure, lift you when you are down, make you happy. Here's how to give the one you love ten hugs a day:

1. After saying good morning
2. As you are parting to go to work
3. After you've returned home at the end of your workday
4. While helping your spouse prepare dinner
5. When you discuss the delicious meal you made
6. When you've both cleared the dishes and cleaned the kitchen
7. While watching your favorite television show together
8. When grabbing dessert or cup of tea before bed
9. After your bedtime ritual of hygiene is finished
10. When snuggling to say the last "I love you" of the day

——— EXTRA CREDIT ———

Hug each other naked. Let the contact between your two bodies, the smell of each other, and the warmth of skin touching skin be the private language that the two of you speak in a moment of amorous intimacy.

DEVELOP DEEP ALTRUISTIC
LOVE FOR EACH OTHER

Love is space and time measured by the heart. —Marcel Proust, French novelist, critic, and essayist

A study by the National Opinion Research Center at the University of Chicago revealed that couples who focused more on each other than on themselves had happier marriages because of their selfless love, or altruism. One possible explanation is that when people show a genuine, self-sacrificing interest in the well-being of their spouses, it triggers a similar altruistic response in their mate. That cycle of positive feelings fuels more of the same, leading to higher levels of marital satisfaction.

—— EXTRA CREDIT ——

Do a random, spontaneous act of kindness for your mate. For example, start a load of laundry before you leave for work. Or drop by the deli on the way home and pick up dinner so she doesn't have to cook. Get his car washed and detailed.

TELL EACH OTHER
YOUR CRAZIEST DREAMS

Sleep hath its own world, and a wide realm of wild reality. And dreams in their development have breath, and tears, and tortures, and the touch of joy. —Lord Byron, "The Dream"

Psychologist Carl Gustav Jung, who closely correlated dreams with myths and archetypal images, opined that modern people would benefit from relying less on logic and science and more on an appreciation of unconscious realms and spirituality in order to have more balance in their lives.

Try sharing with your spouse a dream that defies unlocking. When you access what Jung referred to as the innermost secret recesses of your soul, you will discover that even crazy dreams are often laden with meaning. People who work with their dreams say that dreams can offer clues to the state of your health, solutions to problems, and sometimes even foreshadow the future. If you haven't given dream work a try, invite your spouse to go on a dream exploration with you.

— EXTRA CREDIT —

Buy dream journals for the two of you. Put one on each side of the bed. Write your dreams upon awakening before they quickly disappear, as dreams often do. First, write the narrative of your dream. Then make a list of specific images that appeared in the dream. Use a dream symbol dictionary to extrapolate possible meanings of the symbols, and then rewrite the dream using those meanings. It's been said that only the dreamer can correctly unlock the hidden messages in his or her dream, but analyzing your dreams together can be entertaining.

DATE NIGHT

Walk hand in hand at sunset. Know that your love is warm and intense like the sun that moves across the sky during the day. Watch how the sun slips below the horizon. Stay close while you wait for darkness to come, bringing its gifts, the first stars in the evening sky. The ancient mariners used the stars in the night sky as their guides, but they knew that as surely as the sun set, it also rises. The love you share will soften in intensity and have moments of darkness—every marriage does—but it renews itself in the dawning of each new day.

INCREASE INTIMACY
WITH SOUL GAZING

Life has taught us that love does not consist in gazing at each other, but in looking outward together in the same direction. —Antoine de Saint-Exupéry, French writer and aviator

You've seen your lover's eyes, but have you seen his soul? Eye gazing opens your soul to another, according to ancient Tantric tradition. Gazing into your lover's eyes affords the opportunity to drop your defenses and practice being vulnerable.

When you are physically close to the one you love, the chemicals of love are transmitted more readily. Pheromones, the attraction chemicals your body produces, are transmitted via your breath. Oxytocin, the bonding chemical produced during lovemaking, orgasm, and childbirth, is also produced when you gaze lovingly into your mate's eyes. Love dictates the vision you hold together so that when you turn your eyes from your lover and gaze outward into the world, you and your mate still hold the vision for your love life as you move forward in the same direction. The course of true love may not always, as Shakespeare opined, run smooth, but as you deepen the intimacy between you and your mate, the two of you will be navigating the bumps together.

--- EXTRA CREDIT ---

Increase the intensity of your practice. Sitting comfortably facing each other, gaze deeply into your spouse's eyes while you match your inward and outward cycle of breathing with his or hers. Try a period of soul gazing before slow and sizzling-hot sex.

KEEP ONE
ANOTHER'S SECRETS

Whoever wishes to keep a secret must hide the fact that he possesses one. —Johann Wolfgang von Goethe, German dramatist, novelist, poet, and scientist

Relationship experts say that intimacy is strengthened and marriage bonds deepened when couples regard keeping each other's secrets as a sacred trust. Safeguard the confidences that your partner shares with you. Keeping your word to your spouse makes possible the revealing of vulnerabilities, fears, aspirations, and dreams. A secret can be a wonderful development, such as an upcoming promotion that your partner wants to keep under wraps, or it can be a dark and painful experience or psychological wound that you carry from your past.

When spouses understand that they can always count on their mates to support and love them and keep private the secrets they share, the marriage is strengthened. Love is deepened. Such an intimate sharing serves as a safety valve for both of you. What is not possible or advisable to tell others, you know you can tell your spouse. That is supremely comforting for many married couples.

--- EXTRA CREDIT ---

Think of a secret from your childhood that you would like to share with your mate. It could be that crush you had on your eighth-grade biology teacher or how you slipped away from your Aunt Tillie's ninetieth birthday bash to play games with a friend at the local video arcade.

GENEROUSLY SHARE YOURSELF
WITH YOUR SPOUSE

———————

To see a young couple loving each other is no wonder, but to see an old couple loving each other is the best sight of all. —William Makepeace Thackeray, English novelist

Whether you are newly married or have been married a while and perhaps even have started your family, remember that the love you share is what makes possible everything else, including making babies. It's natural to want to meet the needs of your children, but your partner has needs as well.

Don't just carve out a little time every day; be as generous as you can in sharing your time with the one you love. Sit quietly and talk, or play chess, a board game such as Trivial Pursuit or Monopoly, or a card game such as gin rummy or poker. Watch a favorite television program, discuss a new book that you both have read, or just be playful together. Make it a daily priority to intimately reconnect with your partner in life.

——— EXTRA CREDIT ———

You and your spouse are the leading characters in your own love-story-in-progress. Consider the ways you share yourselves with each other. What would you change about how your spouse shares himself with you? What would make you happier? After both of you have written your answers to those two questions on a slip of paper, switch the papers and read them to each other.

SLEEP LIKE
SPOONS

A good laugh and a long sleep are the best cures in the doctor's book.
—Irish proverb

Drift off to sleep embracing the one you love. You may find that your sleeping position not only reflects your loving connection with your partner, it is conducive to more restful and restorative sleep. And a good night's sleep benefits both of you. The fetal position, many doctors say, is the best choice for a good night's sleep because the position supports the three natural curves in your spine: in the lower back, mid-back, and neck. Curl into the fetal position on your side and snuggle up close to your mate so that your bodies are like teaspoons on their sides in drawer. With one arm cradling your pillow and the other arm draped over your spouse's chest and holding his hand, you both will be in the fetal position for sleep. If your spouse is lying behind you, facing your backside, guide his hand over your heart or cup it under your breast and blissfully drift across that threshold between wakefulness and sleep.

— EXTRA CREDIT —

Try drawing up his knee between your thighs to reduce any space between you. Who needs blankets when you've got each other's body heat for warmth?

SLIP INTO SOME
SEXY LINGERIE

Sex is the point of contact between man and nature, where morality and good intentions fall to primitive urges. —Camille Paglia, *Sexual Personae: Art and Decadence from Nefertiti to Emily Dickinson*

If the last time you bought sexy underclothes was for your honeymoon, it might be time to visit your favorite lingerie shop, especially if your husband likes to see you attired in lacy garter belts, sheer panties, sexy bras, or silky sleepwear. The next time you want to heat things up in the bedroom, dress in a pretty naughty slim-to-nothing that will fire his imagination and put him in the mood for love. Think of yourself as a present. Once you've titillated him into a feverish desire to possess you, he gets to unwrap his present from layers of lace and satin and ribbon.

Don't forget to invite him to slip into those sexy black silk boxers with the tiny red lips emblazoned on the leg or the designer briefs you bought him for his birthday.

— EXTRA CREDIT —

Put on a hot lingerie show just for your man. Show off your catwalk moves as you strut past him with a vampy attitude and slide up against him like a sex goddess seeking her Adonis.

KEEP YOUR
DATE NIGHTS

I love that after I spend the day with you, I can still smell your perfume on my clothes. And I love that you are the last person I want to talk to before I go to sleep at night. —*When Harry Met Sally*

Couples need to reconnect emotionally and physically on a regular basis. If you both have insanely busy lives, the reconnection is vital. Otherwise, the relationship risks becoming sidelined and dwarfed by larger and more pressing demands. Establishing a date night and honoring the commitment to keeping it will help you balance work with your marital relationship.

Your date night can be as exciting as the much-publicized evening out for President Obama and the First Lady, which included dinner and a Broadway show while their daughters Sasha and Malia remained at the White House, or as quiet as an evening of popcorn, *PBS Mystery!* and dessert, which could be just the two of you enjoying the sweetness of a lovemaking session. Date nights provide respite from the frenzy of hectic schedules and enable couples to romantically reconnect with each other. Whether your date night involves a couples cooking class, a long stroll for a latte and a piece of pie, or a movie you both have wanted to see, make the focus be on the two of you.

--- EXTRA CREDIT ---

At the beginning of each month, ask for your partner's input on which nights of that month would be good date nights. Write them into a monthly calendar and tape it onto the refrigerator. That way, the actual date of your date night will never be in question.

DATE NIGHT

Stay at home this evening. Make a batch of popcorn and surf YouTube for the quirkiest, funniest, or most bizarre videos. Consider making your own video and posting it on the video-sharing website.

DANCE WITH HER
IN THE MOONLIGHT

Dancing is wonderful training for girls; it's the first way you learn to guess what a man is going to do before he does it. —Christopher Morley, American journalist, essayist, novelist, and poet

Dreamy and expressive music reigned supreme during the romantic period of music and dance that extended from the 1800s to the 1900s and from which the great waltzes emerged, along with composers like Strauss, Debussy, and Ravel. You can enjoy that music again and even dance to it in the moonlight with your beloved. The moon rises in the night sky during most of the month, so you have plenty of opportunities to pull your lover and best friend out of the house for an impromptu dance under the light of the moon and stars. Grab a portable CD player or iPod speaker so that you can move the instrumental music you need outside. If you can't take music with you, make it yourself. Try humming a favorite tune as you pull her close for your dreamy "one-two-three" waltz steps around the garden.

— EXTRA CREDIT —

Put together a CD of music for the sexiest dances, among them the super sexy samba, passionate rumba, flirty cha-cha, and near-erotic Argentinean tango.

TEXT EACH
OTHER OFTEN

Be still when you have nothing to say; when genuine passion moves you, say what you've got to say, and say it hot. —D. H. Lawrence, English novelist, critic, and poet

In the modern world, text messaging is a rapid-fire way to dispense messages of love between you and your beloved. Send your text messages whenever you find your thoughts turning toward your spouse. When your mate receives your heartfelt words of love, the response can be immediate. Naturally, you and your spouse will find your own secret language to stay in touch, but to find helpful text messaging abbreviations, go to *www.webopedia.com/quick_ref/textmessageabbreviations.asp.* Here are some of the ones most commonly used.

1. 88, hugs and kisses
2. 6y, sexy
3. @TEOTD, at the end of the day
4. CYIMD, see you in my dreams
5. D46? Down for sex?
6. IWALU, I will always love you
7. LH6 and LHSX, let's have sex
8. O4U, only for you
9. PTM, please tell me more
10. TOU, thinking of you
11. TTYS, talk to you soon
12. X, kiss; XOX, kiss, hug, kiss

BE INTERESTED IN
YOUR SPOUSE'S INTERESTS

See, the problem is that God gives men a brain and a penis, and only enough blood to run one at a time. —Robin Williams, American comedian and actor

If your spouse seems to be losing interest in romance and instead directs his passion toward the two ball games via picture-in-picture on the big screen in the living room, you might be tempted to sell the television. Don't. Spouses thrive when mates express genuine interest in their needs, wants, accomplishments, and hobbies. If your separate interests tend to pull you apart, get interested in what interests him.

What do you do if he's a sports nut and you are a theater buff? Or if he loves skating on Rollerblades around the city and you love collecting antique china in small rural towns? To reconnect, you'll have to begin talking about the things you don't understand about baseball or skating. Engage him. Research some fascinating tidbits about player or sports statistics. You may secretly feel thrilled when you hear him bragging to his buddies about how much you know. See where you can find common ground in the hobbies you both love, and try to make the most of it.

EXTRA CREDIT

Take your interest in your spouse's interests a step further. Surprise him with tickets to see his favorite team play or buy him a pair of new wading boots for fly-fishing. Perhaps in turn, he will score opening-night seats for a play that you can't wait to see. When you express an interest in your spouse's passions and invite him to share yours, you strengthen the bonds between you.

TREASURE EACH
OTHER'S FRIENDSHIP

Only your real friends will tell you when your face is dirty. —Sicilian proverb

Put your friendship with your spouse above all others. If your partner comes home angry, frustrated, or distressed, patiently listen to his venting. If her feet hurt from walking all day at the industry trade show, offer to massage them. Anytime your spouse feels overwhelmed, ask what you can do to lighten the load. Best friends give mutual support when it's needed. They listen to and hear not only what you say, but also what you don't say. Here are a few more ways to be your spouse's best friend:

1. Be loyal
2. Be honest
3. Make your friendship with your spouse a high priority
4. Let go of expectations
5. Defend your spouse/best friend if and when it becomes necessary
6. Actively listen to what your spouse tells you, repeating back the words to be certain of the message
7. Be trustworthy
8. Be available when your spouse needs you
9. Protect your mate's confidences like you do your own secrets
10. Praise your spouse when he does something to deserve recognition

--- EXTRA CREDIT ---

Present your spouse with a friendship card on the first Sunday in August, National Friendship Day. Give him or her with a big balloon on which you use a felt pen to write a sexy message, like "How about us friends foolin' around?"

LAUGH AT EACH
OTHER'S JOKES

May those who love us love us; and those who do not love us, may God turn their hearts, and if He cannot turn their hearts, may He turn their ankles that we may know them by their limping. —Irish prayer

Laughter has positive health benefits and also is a rational way to accept the totally irrational aspects of life, including marital disagreements when they arise. Expecting two people to agree all the time is the most irrational expectation you can have. People are prone to asking unanswerable questions and taking life far too seriously. Couples tend to be more accepting when they can view an issue with humor because, let's face it, humor can make everything seem a little bit better. One way to navigate beyond disagreements and lighten things up is to make a little joke and then laugh together at the silliness of it. Self-deprecating humor is also effective in shifting the energy of negativity, darkness, or tension. Don't take yourselves too seriously. Poke a little fun now and again.

—— EXTRA CREDIT ——

Make up a joke about fooling around to share with your mate. For example, try something like this: Adam wasn't banished from the Garden for tasting the apple Eve offered him; no, it was for lusting after the pair she showed him behind the tree.

TALK ABOUT HAVING A
FAMILY BEFORE YOU CONCEIVE

———

A baby is an angel whose wings decrease as his legs increase. —French
proverb

The drive to procreate is biologically programmed into our species. You
may feel an incredible urge to have a child together, but talk about it
before you try to conceive.

Having a baby is an emotional, life-altering decision that imposes
change and stress (both positive and negative) on both of you and upon
your marriage. Consider how conception or adoption and timing could
impact other areas of your life, including finances, careers, home purchase or relocation, health, and other factors.

If having a baby now is right for you, celebrate, get busy in the bedroom, and enjoy the process!

—— EXTRA CREDIT ——

Offer to give a new mom a baby break for an afternoon and evening. It's an opportunity to experience firsthand the joy and work of caring for a newborn infant. The
experience might help you figure out timing for having your own bundle of joy.

DATE NIGHT

Walk to a flower market and view the array of floral offerings. Which flowers do you like; which does your spouse love? Buy some of each and take them home. Look up the flowers' symbolism. What do your choices reveal about you/your love?

CELEBRATE YOUR
LOVE EVERY DAY

They [lovers] are in each other all along. —Rumi, Persian poet and philosopher

Find ways every day to reinforce that special emotional connection you share. Upon awakening, whisper words of love in your spouse's ear. Be animated in your greetings to each other, appreciative of your spouse's uniqueness, and grateful for the experience of finding that special someone to love and marry.

Do little things to honor and celebrate your love as often as possible. Give a Hershey's kiss, a penny for her thoughts of love, a bouquet, or a single, beautiful flower to symbolize and communicate your feelings.

One of the most romantic of all the eras was the Victorian, when men and women elevated the writing of a love letter to a high art, using words like *rapturous, inextinguishable*, or *intoxicating* to describe the object of their passion. The Victorians also were obsessed with the hidden meanings of flowers. Take for example, the rose, the queen of flowers, to which the Victorians ascribed the following meanings:

- **Orange rose:** passionate love
- **Pink rose:** secret adoration
- **Red rose:** romantic love
- **White rose:** innocent love
- **Yellow rose:** friendship

— EXTRA CREDIT —

Create a bouquet containing each color of rose from this list to give to your spouse. Put a note card into the bouquet that describes the meanings the Victorians assigned to each rose color. Let the bouquet express your heartfelt sentiment.

MAKE YOUR BEDROOM
A COUPLE'S SANCTUARY

There is a light that shines beyond all things on earth, beyond us all, beyond the heavens, beyond the highest, the very highest heavens. This is the light that shines in our heart. —Chandogya Upanishad 3.13.7

There are myriad ways for spouses to openly show their love for one another, but to engage in a sexual tryst when the timing is right, most couples want a place of privacy. You and your spouse can create your own special oasis—a place where you can release the upsets and stresses of life, where you shut out others for a while, where you can be intimate. First, remove the items in your bedroom that remind you of work or family responsibilities. Then, make sure the room really is an oasis. Ironically, one of the most neglected rooms in a family's home is often the master bedroom. You can make a few modest changes in the master bedroom to create a place of romantic escape. Try these:

- Light scented candles.
- Move the television out and focus on each other instead of the news or late shows.
- Purchase or make a new duvet (preferably in a luxurious fabric like silk or satin).
- Hang nudes on the walls.
- Move the stereo into the bedroom.

—— EXTRA CREDIT ——

Fill a bedside table drawer with personal lovemaking products, sex toys, lubricants, a couple of wide silk ribbons, and several of his men's magazines. Add a peacock feather, a soft brush, and other such items to stimulate and arouse each other.

EXPLORE THE
OUTDOORS

A mind that is stretched by a new experience can never go back to its old dimensions. —Oliver Wendell Holmes, Jr., American jurist

Blaze some new trails. Do you live near a lake? Help your better half load up the canoe or kayak. If the lake is fully frozen because it's winter, rent some ice skates.

If it is summer and blazing hot, grab a hardhat, helmet light, and spelunking ropes and explore the coolness of a cave with your spouse. Climb a wall at your local outdoor gear shop, or pack your camera and drive to the desert, the beach, the woods, or a mountain to take in the scenic wonders of nature. If your mate loves to fish, spend the afternoon searching for new fishing holes. Plan a camping trip for the two of you to one of America's national parks. Enjoy exploring with the one you love.

— EXTRA CREDIT —

Invite your spouse to join you for an afternoon of berry-picking. Take along a galvanized bucket for the bounty you hope to find. If you don't know of places where wild berry vines grow and aren't up for exploring your local area to find them, visit a farm that has a pick-your-own-berries program.

INVITE HIM TO BE
YOUR SOUS CHEF

The secret of a happy marriage is finding the right person. You know they're right if you love to be with them all of the time. —Julia Child, American cookbook author and television personality

Use your imagination to cook up something wonderful. (It doesn't have to be lamb.) Invite your spouse into the kitchen and give him your sharpest veggie-chopping knife—a santoku or a chef's knife. Standing ever so close, with your hand on his, demonstrate how to hold the knife to safely chop, dice, or slice those veggies. Make sure he knows that speed is not what is needed and that speed increases the chances of cutting a finger. Show him love—soft kisses, a bump of your tush against his, a loving smile—and explain how feelings of love during food preparation makes the resulting meal taste even better.

Of course, if he's the one with the knack for cooking, reverse the roles and you do the work of the sous chef. With all those chopped veggies ready to drop into something, why not prepare some shrimp or chicken in an Asian stir-fry? All you'll need to add is some rice or noodles and a pot of hot tea.

DAY 25

—— EXTRA CREDIT ——

Turn up heat in the kitchen with a wink and smile at him as he endeavors to do the prep just the way you like it. Savor the meal you created together. While you wash and wipe the dishes, offer up a kisses and bring out some fortune cookies into which you've slipped your own X-rated predictions such as, "You're beginning to move up and you'll like the new position" or "Keep your equipment in good operating condition and fortune will soon smile on you."

ENGAGE IN A
WRESTLING MATCH

You know what I'm thinkin'? Two words . . . RE - MATCH. —The
Wrestler

DAY 26

Remember rough-housing when you were a kid? If you haven't tried it now that you are all grown up, you might be happy to learn that it's still fun. Wrestling can start simply enough with a challenge, a tickle, or a tease. Regardless of how it starts, that bodily contact of getting physical can get your heart pumping, your mood elevated, and your muscles warmed up. Go ahead, grunt and giggle as you try to wiggle out of the takedown position.

All that maneuvering and laughter provide great health benefits such as lowering blood pressure, strengthening the immune system, increasing pain tolerance, and reducing stress. So let the competitive spirit of your inner child come out and engage your spouse in a wrestling match. Imagine the heat you'll be generating, that skin-to-skin contact, and the release of all that energy and tension.

— EXTRA CREDIT —

Do a little research about wrestling's basic moves. (Here's a little to get you started: 3,000 years before Christ, ancient peoples near the Nile drew hieroglyphics in the temple tombs of Beni Hasan, Egypt. Their images depicted wrestlers in many of the positions that are still used today.) Share the knowledge and the fun as you practice your maneuvers with your favorite playmate. Could that be a whole new level of respect he's showing you?

PLANT SOMETHING
AND WATCH IT GROW

The secret of improved plant breeding, apart from scientific knowledge, is love. —Luther Burbank, American botanist

Get dirty together in a garden and plant some seed. It's a great way to grow your own grub or create a living tapestry of seasonal flowers, fruits, trees, herbs, vines, and shrubs. During those dreary long days of winter the two of you can cozy up together on the couch to pore over the seed catalogs. You don't have to agree on everything, but together decide what to plant for year-round seasonal interest and beauty in the garden. You'll have untold hours of talking and dreaming.

Perhaps that's what Vita Sackville-West and husband Harold Nicholson did in the 1930s after buying Sissinghurst Castle in rural Kent, England. The grounds and garden they designed and created reflects the dazzlingly hot reds, oranges, and yellows of the roses and other plants that Vita loved and the masculine geometrical designs that appealed to Harold. Today, visitors from all over world travel to Sissinghurst to see the gardens that are now maintained by England's National Trust. Check out their garden at *www.invectis.co.uk/sissing/*.

— EXTRA CREDIT —

Why wait to create your own landscape of love? Try gardening on a smaller scale. Fill a few pots with planting mix, sprinkle in some herb or vegetable seeds, and add water until thoroughly moistened. Then move the pot into a warm area with lots of light, and allow nature to take her course.

DATE NIGHT

Every country in the world has cookie recipes. With your spouse, choose a country you both would like to know more about. Research your chosen country and find a cookie recipe beloved by the people of that place. Whip up a delectable batch. While you and your honey-babe devour cookies hot from the oven with a glass of cold milk, share what you've learned about your chosen country—its culture, history, traditions, and people.

DAY 28

PLAY A
GAME TOGETHER

Happiness never decreases by being shared. —Gautama Buddha

Choose a competitive game such Wii golf, tennis, or bowling; a board game like chess, mahjong, Scrabble, dominoes, or backgammon; or even cards. In games of chance such as poker, you can follow established rules or modify them.

Or, get really creative and design your own romantic board game in which you include fill-in-the-blank statements about your past along with true or false questions, multiple-choice questions, and actions that each of you must do (for example, kiss the other person, fondle the other person's most private area, find the lifeline on the other person's hand). Use a roll of the dice to move forward designated pieces such as a heart and an arrow representing the two of you. Wrong answers mean the player doesn't advance forward. Decide as a couple whether or not you will make bets to up the ante.

Friendly competition can increase your enjoyment of a game, but don't let the spirit of competition push you apart. The point is to draw closer together in the process of playing something that you both enjoy.

—— EXTRA CREDIT ——

Add the element of stripping to the game. Most games lend themselves to incorporating the advance or retreat element that translates to you adding or removing your clothes. Getting naked is always fun, and upping the stakes of the game with the possibility of playing in the nude just kicks the fun up a notch.

TAKE AN
EDUCATIONAL FIELD TRIP

Whoso neglects learning in his youth, loses the past and is dead for the future. —Euripides, Greek dramatist

Many colleges, universities, museums, and independent organizations sponsor educational trips with scholars and others who are experts in a particular academic discipline. For example, you could accompany an ornithologist on a trip to the Amazonian rain forest to study birds, a Lewis and Clark expert while you're on a white-water rafting trip on the Colorado River, or a working archeologist on a dig of ancient ruins in Turkey. Traveling with educational experts and researchers like archeologists, historians, and others working in a wide variety of disciplines can be an enjoyable way to experience and learn about a culture or subject firsthand.

Travel tours offered by Smithsonian Journeys (*www.smithsonianjourneys.org*), for example, features experts leading tours to many world heritage sites. A program known as Exploritas (*www.exploritas.org*), formerly the non-profit Elderhostel program, offers 8,000 programs in all fifty U.S. states and more than ninety countries. One of the notable aspects of Exploritas is the emphasis on lifelong learning. And remember, the best part of an educational trip to an exotic location is that you'll be traveling there with your best friend and lover.

--- EXTRA CREDIT ---
Talk with your spouse about what the two of you would like to learn from a particular destination. Make a poster of that place by gluing a map of it to poster board. Attach pictures of that location that you've clipped from magazines. Add printed recipes and other items that will intensify your desire to make such a trip happen.

CURL UP TOGETHER
AND READ THE SUNDAY PAPER

If you don't read the newspaper, you are uninformed. If you do read the newspaper, you are misinformed. —Attributed to Mark Twain, American humorist and writer

For some couples, Sunday just wouldn't be the same without time to leisurely read the Sunday paper. And what could be sweeter than snuggling together on the couch or in a love seat reading and sharing your favorite sections of the paper?

Think of it as a weekly ritual that strengthens your relationship as a couple. Work the Sunday crossword puzzle together or giggle over the funnies. Share tips from a travel article or resolve to cook a recipe from the food section. Clip sale coupons or use the ads to talk about purchases for your home. If you don't own your home, take out the real estate section and start dreaming. If all that reading makes you tired, put aside the paper, snuggle closer, and take a nap together.

--- EXTRA CREDIT ---

Read a newspaper that you don't normally pick up to expand your awareness of what's going on beyond the boundaries of your neighborhood, perhaps one from outside of your region or state. Or, choose an English-language newspaper from another country, for example _The Brussels Journal_, the _Prague Daily Monitor_, or the _Sunday Times_ (London). It doesn't even have to be the Sunday edition.

INVITE HIM TO SOAK
IN YOUR BUBBLE BATH

There must be quite a few things that a hot bath won't cure, but I don't
know many of them. —Sylvia Plath, American poet and novelist

At the end of a long, stressful day, nothing quite compares to the long
soak to relax and de-stress. Perhaps you love hot steamy baths. Or maybe
you prefer dry heat followed by a cool shower. The use of steam in the
bath, according to some sources, predates the ancient Greco-Roman
bathing pools. Steam baths, so favored by the Greeks, soon became popular with Romans before spreading throughout Europe. But there were
also those who loved the dry heat of the Turkish bath. After a period of
sitting in dry heat, the bather would enjoy a quick immersion in a cool
pool. Then the body would be hygienically washed and massaged.

Today, most modern master bathrooms have some combination of
tubs and showers. Try bathing together as an exercise in hedonism.

--- EXTRA CREDIT ---
Carry the pleasures of the bath into the bedroom. Put scented oils and scented
soaps within easy reach of your bath. Set out cold drinks that you and your partner
can sip while soaking. Add some romantic music and a candle or two for the perfect
ambiance. Dry off with fresh, thick towels and then take turns massaging each other
with your favorite scented oil.

MOVE THE TREADMILL
NEAR THE TV

I don't exercise. If God had wanted me to bend over, he would have put diamonds on the floor. —Joan Rivers, American comedienne

Most likely, you enjoyed running around as a child, playing tag, kick the can, soccer, and all kinds of other outdoor activities. In fact, if you were like most other kids, you probably preferred running, skipping, or hopping to walking. But walking was preferable to having to sit still, like in church or when your great-aunt or some other family dignitary came by.

Perhaps it's when we leave the exuberance of childhood behind that we began to forget how great it feels to move the body and all its parts. But an exercise routine started when you are young and maintained throughout your adult life can contribute to your longevity and quality of life. The introduction of televisions into households has had an insidiously addictive effect on husbands and wives, luring them into a sedentary lifestyle and a dangerous complacency about their health. But if you move the treadmill over to where you can see the television, you can exercise for an hour or more and not miss a thing.

— EXTRA CREDIT —

Don't have a treadmill? Try walking in place. You can even do it with two-pound weights. Or, you can shop for a treadmill at a sporting goods store or recycled sporting goods shop. Look at the cost as an investment in your health.

UNPLUG
FOR A DAY

At the touch of love, everyone becomes a poet. —Plato, Greek philosopher

Most couples need a respite when their lives feel overwhelmingly full and chaotic. That's the perfect time to take a break. Unplug from as much sensory input as possible. Turn off all the electronics—that includes computers, digital assistants, cell phones, radios, and televisions. Put away the newspapers and take a news break as well. Retreat from all the messages that the world blares at you 24/7. Shun the insistent neon brightness and the frenetic energies that clamor for your attention, and find a place of silence and solitude that you can share with your spouse.

When just the two of you find ways to move in a quiet rhythm for a twenty-four-hour period, you both can let go and empty yourselves of the sensory overload your bodies and minds have accumulated. You can then begin to soak up peace. The peacefulness found in such deliberately chosen moments is actually always available to you, but it gets covered by noise and activity. You can almost feel the energy of love moving between your two hearts as you enjoy solitary moments together.

--- EXTRA CREDIT ---

After a day of unplugging, light candles, which have been used for centuries to beckon peace and to call forth a sense of the sacred. Sit in comfortable chairs and meditate together for a while or just sit and share a glass of wine or sparkling apple cider. There is nothing to do but be still and enjoy each other's presence in that moment. "To fill the hour,—that is happiness; to fill the hour, and leave no crevice for a repentance or an approval," was the counsel of Ralph Waldo Emerson in "Experience," *Essays: Second Series* (1844).

DATE NIGHT

Rent and watch the video of *Man of La Mancha*, the 1972 film that featured Peter O'Toole, James Coco, and Sophia Loren. After enjoying the story about the delusional but enchanting and chivalrous dreamer Don Quixote, discuss your dreams with each other.

DAY 35

MEET IN
THE DREAMTIME

The dream was always running ahead of me. To catch up, to live for a moment in unison with it, that was the miracle. —Anaïs Nin, French-born American author

The aboriginal people of Australia believe in two types of time—one is the time that we are aware of taking place continually during our waking, conscious moments, and the other is the time that exists in an infinite sacred realm known as the dreamtime. The aboriginals believe that what happens in the dreamtime informs the waking consciousness. Their creation myth begins in the sacred time—before time—during which all of creation came to be formed by the work of totemic beings or our ancestral spirits. Their dreamtime includes the past, present, and future.

Ask your spouse to meet you for a dance in the dreamtime. Assume that when you both have made the commitment to enter each other's dreams, upon falling asleep you will. All it takes to meet for that slow, dreamy dance is for both of you to consciously think of it as you drift off to sleep. Prepare yourself for bed as though you were going to incubate a dream. Eat lightly if at all, bathe, and prepare to sleep between clean sheets with your head upon a pillow inside a fresh pillowcase.

--- EXTRA CREDIT ---

Make an aromatherapy pillow by filling a small sachet bag with dried lavender. Tuck the filled sachet bag into your pillows before going to bed.

DON'T PERMIT SOCIAL NETWORKING
ACTIVITIES TO LIMIT SPOUSE TIME

We waste time looking for the perfect lover, instead of creating the perfect love. —Tom Robbins, American novelist, *Still Life with Woodpecker*

Your spouse loves social networking/micro-blogging via Twitter, and he both follows and has followers. He sends his tweets out into the universe as often as he can, while you like to spend great chunks of time reading your friends' comments and silly proclamations about being stuck in a lobster trap or reaching a new level in Fishville.

According to Neilsen findings published on CNET in February 2010, Facebook.com has 400 million or so users. In addition, Neilsen found that worldwide, the average social networking user spent more than five and a half hours surfing social networking sites during the month of December 2009. Keeping up with your photos, videos, groups, links, notes, and pages on social networking sites can be time-consuming. Or maybe your job requires you to do media work online, like getting your name, product, or service before the media and millions of others. But if you don't have the luxury of a lot of time to spend with your husband or wife, make it a point to use your time wisely. Invest in the marriage, even if it means cutting back on the web-based social networking.

—— EXTRA CREDIT ——
Use the old-fashioned tools of a calendar and clock to limit time spent on social networking. Make social networking activities into a sort of business activity to be accomplished during a given length of time between certain hours of the day or evening . . . and no more.

SOAK UP SOME
CULTURE TOGETHER

Culture is the widening of the mind and of the spirit. —Jawaharlal Nehru

Attend a rock 'n' roll concert, an opening night at the opera, an evening at the symphony, the performance of a work by a local playwright, or even an open-mike session of poets at the local coffee shop. Choose a cultural event that you and your spouse would both enjoy. If an event is out of the question, consider spending an afternoon at a museum, visiting a nearby historical site, attending an art gallery opening, or taking in a talk by a local author or artisan.

Exposure to cultural events can stimulate your minds, engage your senses, and spark interesting conversations. More important, you are enjoying each other's company as you share the experience.

—— EXTRA CREDIT ——
Present your lover with some culture coupons—IOUs to cultural venues that he can cash in whenever he feels so dulled down that only a dose of culture can cure him.

NEVER LIE
ABOUT MONEY

A lie can travel halfway around the world while the truth is still putting on its shoes. —Mark Twain, American humorist and writer

Good marital relationships have three essential components that qualify them as superior: trust, honesty, and effective communication. While men may lie about income, women may lie about spending. Lying about money is an issue of both trust and communication. You and your partner are each other's helpmates and best friends for life. Finding the courage to be truthful with each other means you put your heads together to come up with solutions for financial dilemmas or creative ways to deal with financial concerns.

During difficult times, two carrying the load together lightens it. If it helps, sit down as a couple to share a glass of wine to unwind and relax before broaching the subject of finances. Keep in mind that relationships shrink and die when dishonesty and distrust prevail, but in an environment of truthfulness and transparency, relationships grow into their highest potential.

— EXTRA CREDIT —

Have a heart-to-heart confession with each other. Ask your mate not to react but to simply listen. Confess your most recent secret purchase. Tell your mate what you bought. Truthfully reveal how much the item cost and how you paid for it (cash, credit card, or check). Then listen without reacting while your spouse confesses to a recent secret purchase. By not flipping into a knee-jerk, emotional reaction, you both are making it safe for each other to tell the truth.

INVITE HER TO YOUR
FAVORITE SPORTING EVENT

Commonsense is the wick of the candle. —Ralph Waldo Emerson, American essayist and poet

Your wife might not know the rules of the NFL, the difference between baseball's American and National leagues, or that hockey pucks are made of vulcanized rubber, but she might love learning about interesting sports facts and trivia from you. Inviting her to a game shows her that the passion for sports that you have doesn't usurp her place in your life. (There's the risk that she might feel that way if you frequently go to sporting events with the guys.)

Instead of asking your buddies to join you for a sports outing for which you've scored tickets, invite your wife. It's just common sense that doing so might make her feel less like a sports widow.

— EXTRA CREDIT —

Amplify the sports outing experience for her by inviting her to a baseball game and taking her to lunch at the stadium club beforehand. Fill in the blanks of her knowledge about the teams scheduled to play, history of the long-standing rivalry between the two, and notable players. Make it special, and you might just have a new baseball buddy.

CREATE A FIVE-YEAR PLAN
FOR YOUR MARRIAGE

All you need is the plan, the road map, and the courage to press on to your destination. —Earl Nightingale, American author and motivational speaker

Did you know that spouses' brain chemistry changes, depending on how long they have been in love? Anthropologist Helen Fisher, PhD, professor and human behavior researcher at Rutgers University and author of *Why We Love*, says that biological programming is why people get antsy after about four years of marriage. The drive for a couple to remain together to see a child through its infancy (or about four years) dates back millions of years.

Whether or not your marriage has passed that four-year threshold, invite your spouse to brainstorm a five-year-plan for your marriage. Envision the two of you well on your way into a long and happy married life. With your spouse, discuss what your life will be like. How many children do you have? Where do you live? What are your careers? What traditions do you keep? How do you have fun together? Does your family attend religious services and if so, where? How will your family portrait look then?

—— EXTRA CREDIT ——

Relax with your mate over a cup of hot tea, a glass of cider, or a flute of bubbly and discuss ways to celebrate the accomplishments of your five-year plan as you achieve each one.

DATE NIGHT

Sample another culture's cuisine. Indulge your taste buds, for example, by dining on couscous and Moroccan lamb accentuated with caramelized prunes and toasted slivered almonds. Wash the lamb down with sweet and fragrant mint tea and breathlessly whisper in your spouse's ear, "Je t'adore," French for "I adore you." Finish your delectable meal with slices of baklava drizzled with melted chocolate.

If you can't find a Moroccan restaurant, try cooking the meal yourself. The good thing about eating out is that you won't have to do the belly dancing yourself . . . although that could be fun, too.

DO A CHARITABLE
DEED TOGETHER

Never doubt that a small group of thoughtful, committed citizens can change the world. —Margaret Mead, American cultural anthropologist

Take a cue from the many Hollywood celebrities as well as successful artisans, musicians, politicians, and others who support a favorite charity, and get involved. If you feel inspired to do a random kind act or make a charitable donation that could change the life of someone else, talk about it with your lover. Decide together what appeals to the both of you and how much time, money, and commitment that together you could pledge.

Booker T. Washington once said, "If you want to lift yourself up, lift up someone else." For example, work in a soup kitchen, be hospice volunteers, or host a fundraising party for your favorite cause. You don't have to follow in the footsteps of Angelina Jolie, with her United Nations work, or Susan Sarandon's support of Heifer International. Whether you choose to help a local family or organization or work on the global scale, you and your spouse will be earning good karma.

--- EXTRA CREDIT ---

With your spouse, spearhead a fundraiser. Throw a dessert buffet or sit-down dinner and sell tickets to family members and friends. Give the money to charity.

TAKE AN
EDUCATIONAL FIELD TRIP

Education is an ornament in prosperity and a refuge in adversity. —Aristotle,
Greek philosopher

Take advantage of the learning opportunities around you. Choose an educational trip that appeals to you and your spouse. For example, if you love French cooking and he loves medieval architecture, sign up for a field trip that takes couples through the south of France to see arched Roman bridges and medieval villages. Side trips might include visits to markets where you can shop for local, fresh fruits, cheeses, vegetables, locally pressed olive oil, and wine. Practice saying to each other "I love you" in French: "Je t'aime." Alternatively, if he enjoys poring over old manuscripts and you love art, combine your interests by taking a class that focuses on historical illuminated manuscripts.

—— EXTRA CREDIT ——

Indulge your appetite for learning by extending your stay for a week or two to visit the places where Van Gogh and other Impressionist painters worked, taste the foods of the south of France, discover how perfumes are made and where lavender is grown, or take the train from Nîmes across the French border with Spain. You might also head to the French Riviera and Monaco for a romantic respite with your spouse.

WAIT FOR HIM
BETWEEN SILK SHEETS

———

Women are silver dishes into which we put golden apples. —Johann
Wolfgang von Goethe, German dramatist, novelist, poet, and scientist

Get ready to experience sensual hedonism with your partner. Become
the queen, awaiting her king in their royal bed. Replace your cotton or
polyester sheets with natural hypoallergenic silk sheets in his favorite
color. Thousands of years ago, the Chinese perfected the art of making
silk, using filaments from the cocoons of silkworms. Today, some of the
most luxurious bedding is lightweight, ultra-soft silk in a dizzying array
of exquisite colors. Be creative in enticing him to join you between the
sheets. Let your imaginations go wild in discovering new positions to
wrinkle those new sheets.

—— EXTRA CREDIT ——

Pack a spa basket full of scented oils, whipping cream, body frosting, and an assort-
ment of brushes, feathers, and sex toys. Place it near the bed within easy reach when
you both are ready for that special hedonistic experience.

SEEK PROFESSIONAL HELP
WITH ESTATE PLANNING

Taxes are paid in the sweat of every man who labors. —Franklin D. Roosevelt, U.S. president

The stress of financial concerns on a marriage can be alleviated through estate planning. With your estate plan mapped out, the two of you can feel more positive about your financial future. Your estate size might not be as large as you'd like, but nevertheless you want to preserve it. A good estate planner is extremely knowledgeable about estate tax laws and can preserve your wealth by helping you:

- Determine if you need to prepare a will, assign power of attorney, write a health directive, determine a health-care decision-making proxy, and/or create a living trust
- Evaluate and inventory your assets to figure out the best place to start an investment plan
- Establish a trust for those who will inherit your estate
- Understand federal and state tax implications
- Decide whether or not you'd prefer to leave your estate in a charitable trust
- Determine whether or not it is wise to leave all your assets to your surviving spouse

— EXTRA CREDIT —

Ask your friends, family members, and business colleagues for recommendations of books about estate planning. Read them, and then discuss key points and strategies with each other. Keep in mind that you are planning not just for the two of you but also for any children you have and offspring that they might have someday.

CHOOSE TO VOLUNTEER
IN A COMMUNITY GROUP

Only those who have learned the power of sincere and selfless contribution experience life's deepest joy: true fulfillment. —Anthony Robbins, motivational speaker and popular self-help author

The problems of America's communities are great. The planet is in trouble because collectively we have not been good stewards. The rift between the haves and the have-nots has continued to widen. Wars go on despite popular opinion against them. There are still hot spots in the world where warlords and thugs commit genocide, where every five seconds a child dies of hunger or a hunger-related disease, and where people are still being forced into forms of slavery.

For these and many other reasons, you and your life partner might feel powerless to bring about change, but the truth is that each human being has some power. Aligned with others, a couple, a community, or a country can change the status quo. Perhaps you start by focusing on ways to become the best you can be and then by volunteering to work with a community group to change your town or city for the better. To shift a paradigm, it only takes one person, one good intention, and one act of generosity at a time. Just imagine what a group, a nation, or an international coalition working together could do.

--- EXTRA CREDIT ---

Fight hate in your community. Help the Southern Poverty Law Center teach tolerance and seek justice for victims of hate crimes. To learn how you and your spouse can become involved in the movement, go to *www.southernpovertylawcenter.org*.

SHARE THE CARE
OF HOUSE PLANTS

Flowers really do intoxicate me. —Vita Sackville-West, English poet, novelist and designer of England's Sissinghurst Castle Gardens

Flowers and indoor plants add touches of nature to home interiors and help make your living space a place for a marriage to prosper. Cut flowers or healthy plants are welcoming in the foyer. Pretty pots of blooming African violets on a windowsill brighten a dining room or kitchen. A bamboo or money plant in your home office can serve as a reminder of good fortune and prosperity. But plants also can improve the air quality in your home by removing the carbon dioxide and releasing oxygen and also increasing humidity levels. Some plants have medicinal value; for example, a piece of aloe vera can soothe a minor burn, leaves of mint can be used to create a mouth rinse, and the scent of lavender in soaps, sachets, and essential oils has been used to reduce stress.

But houseplants, like humans, need food, water, and light to live. Some need less light, it's true, but all will need to have dead leaves removed, an occasional misting, dusting, and occasionally new soil, a larger pot, or both. If neither you nor your spouse wants the sole responsibility of caring for your plants, explore how you might share the load. Perhaps one spouse takes care of the feeding and watering for one month and you do those tasks the next.

—— EXTRA CREDIT ——

Visit your nearest botanical garden and learn about the plants you and your spouse most enjoy. Support the garden by purchasing one or more for your home. Just be certain that you both understand how to care for the plant in order to keep it alive and looking good for a long time.

DATE NIGHT

Send a text message to your spouse to join you on a journey back to ancient India. Set up the *Kama Sutra* board game in your bedroom and get ready for some sexy fun. You may get so hot and bothered that you forget your place on the board or won't finish the game, but you can always pick up where you left off on your next date night.

DO TANTRIC YOGA'S
HAPPY HUG

The sexual embrace can only be compared with music and with prayer.
—Marcus Aurelius, Roman emperor, philosopher, and author of *Meditations*

Partnering to do yoga poses is also an exercise in bonding. It establishes togetherness, promotes trust, and fosters deeper levels of communication between you and your mate. Some yoga poses are specifically designed for couples. These poses, or asanas, increase your awareness of your partner, increase the flow of energy between the two of you, and heighten the spiritual awareness that goes along with love and sex.

To do the Happy Hug, stand facing each other with your toes touching. Now hug, releasing yourself into your partner's arms. Take five deep breaths in unison with your partner. Let the air fill your abdomen and then slowly exhale all of it, releasing your tensions, fears, and stress. Take turns rubbing each other's back for a minute or two.

--- EXTRA CREDIT ---

Who needs flowers, champagne, or chocolates to convey to your mate how you feel about him or her? Buy book of sexual positions for lovers that includes yoga positions. Highlight those positions in the book that you would like to try with your mate. Don't be shy. Take the lead and soon you both may feel a synergistic rising of sexual energy and temperature rising even as your bodies are bending, stretching, curving, undulating, and thrusting.

WEAR THE
PERFUME HE LIKES

Ointment and perfume rejoice the heart: so doth the sweetness of a man's friend by hearty counsel. —Proverbs 27:9

More than two millennia ago, fragrant anointing oils and spices were commonly used, and while the word "perfume" rarely appears in biblical passages, sweet incense and specific scented oils like oil of myrrh, calamus, cinnamon, cassia, and olive are often mentioned in the Bible. Bring ancient times into the modern era by making a point to choose a scent that your partner enjoys.

A splash of your signature perfume can make you feel sexy and confident while inspiring romantic feelings in your spouse. How do you find the one scent best suited to you? A survey by *Glamour* magazine revealed that of all the perfume scents worn by modern women, it is the fresh and natural girl-next-door scents that men prefer. If your man likes it when you wear perfume, by all means wear the perfume he likes. Choose to spray or dab it on wrists, earlobes, elbows, back of knees, neckline, and even your inner thighs. For best results, apply perfume to your naked body after you have recently showered and dried off.

--- EXTRA CREDIT ---

Spend the afternoon perfume shopping with your spouse. Find a scent that he loves on you. Choose a new scent for him that makes you want to lay claim to him all over again. Just remember that your nose can handle only about four scents before it experiences overload.

CAREFULLY NAVIGATE EMOTIONAL MINEFIELDS IN BLENDED FAMILIES

Love me when I least deserve it, because that's when I really need it. —Swedish proverb

Modern parenting roles do not necessarily adhere to the traditional model of previous generations, in which the mother did most of the child care and the dad stepped in when a strong authority figure was needed to enforce the rules. Today, many married couples must parent children they created with a previous partner. Perhaps the new marriage has created a new child or children. Maybe there's a large disparity between the ages of the children—for example, teens and newborns.

If your marriage has created a blended family with stepchildren, there inevitably will be emotional minefields to navigate as you shepherd your children through the transition period linking their former family living situation with your current one. Regardless of their ages, children will question their status in the new family, as well as their roles. It can be a time of confusion, fear, doubt, worry, anger, hurt, and possible feelings of alienation for them. They are likely also grieving the loss of the divorced parent.

There is nothing worse for a child than to feel unwanted and unloved. The best tool you have for negotiating such issues is to love, love, love them, and then love them more. Healing takes time, patience, and understanding, but you can rest assured that the adjustment can and will happen eventually.

— EXTRA CREDIT —

Buy packs of note cards that are appropriate for the ages of the children in your blended family. You and your spouse can use the cards to write personal notes to each of the children. Give a note to praise, express love, thank, encourage, celebrate an accomplishment, or seek forgiveness.

REVERSE YOUR
SEXUAL ROLES

If a woman hasn't got a tiny streak of harlot in her, she's a dry stick as a rule. —D.H. Lawrence, English novelist, poet, and critic, "Pornography and Obscenity"

Falling into habitual patterns of behavior and the same old routine leads to boredom in the bedroom. Try spicing things up in your seduction and lovemaking department by doing role reversals.

Are you the one who waits for your hubby to initiate the sex? Or do you usually make the overtures? If the former, become the harlot. Take the position of the initiator. Practice the gentle art of seduction. Offer to rub his back and then permit your hands and fingers to freely roam and explore. If you are usually the aggressor, take a more subdued tack and permit him to have his way with you. Radically changing the way you engage in foreplay can result in both of you becoming bewitched, bothered, and breathless . . . and loving every minute of it.

—— EXTRA CREDIT ——

Take your role-playing public. Offer to meet him at the neighborhood bistro bar for a drink. Wear a wig or scarf that conceals your real hair color. Put on your finest little black dress and a pair of dramatic sunglasses and prepare to pick him up.

REMEMBER NOW
THERE ARE TWO

Marriage, n. The state or condition of a community consisting of a master, a mistress, and two slaves, making in all two. —Ambrose Bierce, *The Devil's Dictionary*

Now that you've legally and emotionally thrown your lot in together by getting married, make clear joint agreements concerning household management, time together versus time spent apart, and, perhaps most important, finances. A common mistake newlyweds make is taking on too much debt in the form of a home mortgage or high rent before they're ready, or without planning ahead to a point in the near future when one income might go away. This brings immediate money pressures and makes for an even more difficult first year of marriage. You will be happier if you stay well within your financial means and allow yourselves the time and lack of pressure that comes with keeping your overhead low.

—— EXTRA CREDIT ——

Subscribe to newspaper or magazine that focuses on finances and wealth. Become a fiscally responsible, wise investor.

SLOWLY UNDRESS
EACH OTHER

Venus favors the bold. —Ovid, Roman poet

The sensuous, seductive way that you undress each other can heighten sexual anticipation. Think of the process as foreplay.

For wives, stand behind him and unbutton his shirt, undo his jean or trouser button and zipper, and slide your hand down his inner thigh, pushing along the fabric of his trousers. Let your fingertips trail over all parts of your spouse's body as you inch his pants lower. Lean in close for soft, smoldering kiss against his neck or back.

For husbands, unzip her dress or undo the buttons of her shirt. Pull her close in her half-dressed state and kiss her tenderly. Don't hurry the process. Remove each garment as if each deliberate movement increased your desire and excitement. Don't hurry the process. When she's standing in her undergarments, draw her close and tell her how beautiful she is. Take time to enjoy the tactile sensation of clothing coming off and hands and lips touching each other's flesh. You want a slow sizzle, not a fast burn.

--- EXTRA CREDIT ---

Put together a playlist of music to set the ambiance for clothing removal. You might choose music that crosses genres or stick to the kind of tunes you and your spouse most enjoy. The right music can get you in the mood for prolonging the pleasure.

DATE NIGHT

Consider the idea that your body and that of your spouse is a personal territory with its own hills and valleys, peaks and crevices—in short, a fleshly landscape for your own personal exploration. Be bold, take your time, and explore wherever your curiosity leads you, you adventurer, you!

SERVE DINNER DRESSED IN
A TEENSY-WEENSY APRON

Tita was more worried about saving her skin than about anything else. —Laura
Esquivel, *Like Water for Chocolate*

An imaginative way to get the sparks quickly flying between you and
your spouse after work is to serve him a hot meal attired in a bit of fabric
that serves as an apron. Make it easy on yourself and purchase Japanese
sushi takeout on your way home. When your spouse comes through the
door, the meal is ready to serve.

Take your time setting the stage for dinner. Carry in the paper plates
and chopsticks wearing only a teensy-weensy bit of fabric that ties behind
your back and barely covers your torso. While the takeout food might
charm his palate, the sight of you will be an unexpected visual delight
that could shift the direction of the whole evening. Suffice it to say that
his thoughts might not remain long on the food.

--- EXTRA CREDIT ---

Serve mochi, a ball of strawberry, chocolate, vanilla, or mango ice cream rolled in
rice flour dough, for dessert. It's sensuous on the tongue and cold. You can then use
your cold tongue to touch or lick sensitive areas on his hot body.

STICK A SEXY NOTE
ON HIS MIRROR

Imagination grows by exercise and contrary to common belief is more powerful in the mature than in the young. —W. Somerset Maugham, *The Summing Up*

You know the spot on the mirror where he looks when he shaves in the morning. That's the perfect place to stick a note with an imaginative sexy message. Invite him into the shower to try a new body wash with you. Or offer to dry him off with a towel you just fetched from the dryer. Or, write a more explicit, yet open-ended, message. Here are a few to get you started:

- What is it about sex toys . . . ?
- I've got some reproducing equipment I'd like you to check out . . . and I don't mean the copy machine . . . .
- Slip out of your underwear while I prepare my surprise . . . I won't be long . . . .
- I've heard big mirrors give a better view; do you like to watch . . . ?
- Bikini wax . . . Brazilian wax . . . au naturel? Which do you like best?
- Ever experienced lip balm on your nipples or the most private parts of your body . . . who'd know it would feel so soft and sensuous?

--- EXTRA CREDIT ---

Put a small note pad near the bathroom mirror that's accessible to both you and your spouse so that there's no impediment for either of you to write and post imaginative, sexy notes for each other whenever the muse inspires you to do so.

FIND SOMEONE ELSE TO
SHARE YOUR JOINT GOALS

Dream as if you'll live forever. Live as if you'll die today. —James Dean, film actor

Maybe you and your partner share a big dream of having a vacation home where you can truly retreat from the world. However, given your financial situation, you're beginning to think that your dream is an impossible one—out of reach now and possibly always.

If that is what you are thinking, stop right there. Rather than discounting the worthiness of your dream or giving up on it, contemplate how to make it happen . . . perhaps by investing in a time-share property or working out creative financing on a small rural house or beach cottage. There are almost as many ways of working a deal on a piece of real estate as there are people to make those deals. Get creative and talk about your options. Involve a creative-minded broker to help you. Don't say that a goal is impossible, but rather think of how you can possibly manifest it.

--- EXTRA CREDIT ---

Start searching on real estate websites to find your dream home or a vacation bungalow where you can shack up together alone for days or even weeks. The world can wait while you and your beloved reconnect and rediscover the joy of simply being a twosome hiding away from the world.

ESTABLISH BOUNDARIES
FOR YOUR CHILDREN

The father who does not teach his son his duties is equally guilty with the son who neglects them. —Confucius, Chinese thinker and social philosopher

Pediatricians and child psychologists have long noted that children do best when their lives have structure. The world can be a very scary place unless boundaries are in place to render a sense of security to children and teens. As teens go through the process of individuating, they push up against and even test the rigidity of parental and societal boundaries.

As parents, you are responsible for establishing boundaries for your children, including setting curfews, time frames, and limits that are acceptable for doing homework, eating meals, going to bed, getting up in the morning, dressing for school, staying over at a friend's house, and having friends visit in your home. In addition, assigning your children duties or chores teaches them perseverance, time management, and sense of purpose—all necessary for success in life.

—— EXTRA CREDIT ——

Have a family meeting to go over curfews and other boundaries, as well as to review each child's duties and responsibilities. Make sure everyone knows what the limits are. Praise the good. Avoid focusing on negatives and use gentle redirection, as necessary.

USE LIPS, TEETH,
AND TONGUE TO EXCITE

As soon as she commences to enjoy pleasure, the eyes are half closed and watery; the body waxes cold; the breath after being hard and jerky, is expired in sobs or sighs; the lower limbs are limply stretched out after a period of rigidity; a rising and outflow of love and affection appear, with kisses and sportive gestures; and, finally, she seems as if about to swoon. —The Ananda Ranga, *Sir Richard Francis Burton, Translator*

Read the ancient texts of the *Kama Sutra* or the *Ananda Ranga* and you'll soon discover that many parts of the body have erogenous zones. It is obvious that the genitals are the first regions to come to mind when you think of erogenous zones. In most people, when even slightly touched, the genitals react immediately with warmth, then a change of color, and then swelling. However, do not ignore using your lips to kiss, your teeth to make little love bites, and your tongue to stimulate erogenous areas of your partner's body. Gently rake your fingers through your partner's hair or along the chest area or down the back. Love bites leave the wearer with a remembrance of the erotic activity that produced them. Nibbles, bites, and gentle slaps are all a little difficult to comprehend unless you are of a passionate nature and in the moment of pleasure that masks the intensity of the initial mark. Endorphins, chemical substances in your body that are enhanced when you are sexually excited and that cause euphoria, can mask any pain that occurs during receiving the marks. The reminder comes a bit later.

— EXTRA CREDIT —

Use your lips and tongue to explore and stimulate his erogenous zones. Allow your tongue to warm and moisten sensitive areas of his body, then blow to cool them. Invite him to reciprocate on your body.

SAVE MONEY
REGULARLY

A penny saved is a penny earned. —Benjamin Franklin, American author, inventor, and politician

Saving for the proverbial rainy day makes good sense, especially if you and your spouse are just starting out on the lifelong adventure of marriage. Or, perhaps you've been married long enough to have witnessed and weathered the cyclic changes in the economy. You know that in life, stuff happens. When you have money in a savings account for when there's an unexpected job loss or illness or major appliance failure, the crisis won't be nearly as stressful on your marriage.

Having cash set aside for good surprises is advisable, too. Try to deposit the same (or more) amount every month into a different savings account and forget about it until you need it. When your spouse comes home to tell you he's been promoted and you'll be spending the next winter in Paris, you can feel jubilant and go shopping for a warm coat.

—— EXTRA CREDIT ——

Involve your spouse and the entire family in saving. Establish savings accounts for your preteen and teens; give piggy banks to your toddlers and school-age children and teach them how to use them.

DATE NIGHT

Get in touch with the sensuality of nature. Walk barefoot outside. Feel the sensuous warmth of the sun against your face and body, the delicate caress of the breeze upon your skin, the hard sun-baked earth and soft, cool grass under your feet. Breathe deeply and draw into your body the subtle energy of the earth, sun, and wind. Consider how alive you now feel.

ABSTAIN TO
REIGNITE THE FLAME

Absence makes the heart grow fonder. —Thomas Haynes Bayly, English novelist and poet

DAY 64

Suppose you love toasted marshmallows. Forget associating the treat with childhood camping and ghost stories. Consider how great a perfectly toasted marshmallow tastes. Now, think of having sex in the same way as indulging your taste for that sugary white confection, heated to a moist, soft perfection. You indulge your desire for it, have your fill, and when your craving is satisfied, you don't want any more . . . at least for a while. The longer you refrain from indulging your craving, the stronger the craving again becomes.

In the same way, your sex life can sizzle after a period of imposed abstinence. You and your spouse get to decide how long you will refrain from having sex. Waiting in anticipation of when you can make love again can call up a seemingly insatiable appetite in both of you, heighten your expectations, and intensify the enjoyment of the magical moment when it arrives.

— EXTRA CREDIT —

Go camping. Take along a bag of marshmallows. Toast marshmallows on long sticks and take turns feeding them to each other. Don't worry if your kisses get a little sticky; it's part of the fun.

SCRATCHING
AND MARKING

If it can lick, it can bite. —French proverb

The *Kama Sutra* sex manual gives specific techniques for scratching and marking during sexual encounters. Marking goes beyond what most Westerners might be used to, but it is titillating nevertheless. The *Kama Sutra* lists eight ways to use your fingernails against your lover's body:

1. Sounding—your lover's body hair stands on end from the soft touch or stroke of your nails.
2. Half moon—the impression left when the nail presses against buttocks, breasts, or thighs.
3. A circle—the impression of two half moons made together in opposite directions.
4. A line—the line is drawn with the nail upon the lover's body.
5. A tiger's nail or claw—a line drawn on the lover's breast.
6. A peacock's foot—the impression made in the skin with the five nails together.
7. The jump of a hare—the five-nail impression made tightly together close to the nipple.
8. The leaf of a blue lotus—an impression created on the hips or breast that resembles a lotus (which has large, flat leaves that are rounded or oval and notched).

--- EXTRA CREDIT ---

During lovemaking, imaginatively create your own artistic mark on the body of your lover, preferably in a place where your signature mark, when seen, will be a reminder of the pleasures you experienced together.

DECIDE ON YOUR
IDEAL FAMILY SIZE

A father is a banker provided by nature. —French proverb

Perhaps you were raised in a noisy household with several siblings and, now that you are married, would like a large family. Your partner, however, was an only child and thinks having one or two children is the perfect family size. What's most important is that you two talk about it ahead of time so you have some idea of where you're headed.

It may also interest you both to know that the cost of raising a child from cradle to college is high, and will likely rise with inflation. For a middle-income family, the cost to raise a child born in 2008 through the age of 17 is roughly $221,000, according to a 2008 government study released by the U.S. Department of Agriculture's Center for Nutrition Policy and Promotion. You might not think about the financial aspect while you are happily making a baby, but it's an excellent idea to give it due consideration before you increase the size of your family.

— EXTRA CREDIT —

It isn't enough to just know that a baby has a huge financial impact on a family's budget; it's equally important to gather financial information and make important decisions before the baby is born. For example, check the medical insurance coverage for prenatal care that your company (or your spouse's) might offer. Draw up a budget based on a single salary. Find out if your company or your spouse's business covers maternity/paternity leave. Ask yourselves if you can afford to start a family right now and, if so, whether you could handle multiple babies (for example, twins or triplets).

FLASH HIM WEARING
ONLY A RAINCOAT

After a debauch of thunder-shower, the weather takes the pledge and
signs it with a rainbow. —Thomas Bailey Aldrich, American author and poet

If the period when you were making love like rabbits in springtime has
past and you've now settled into an established routine that's comfortable, if not a little boring at times, shake things up by doing something
he won't expect. Choose a day when you feel a little unsettled, perhaps
like the weather. Strip, shower, and slather on body butter to perfume
and soften your beautiful skin. Slip your naked and recently hydrated
body into a raincoat. When your spouse comes home from work, flash
him as he steps in the front door. This will have the effect of putting
a smile on his face and a spring in his step as he begins to chase you
through the house. It's totally up to you as to when and where you let
him catch you. Inside a dark closet could be fun, especially if it's car-
peted, except that there he won't be able to see the splendor of your
smile, like a happy rainbow after a wild storm.

— EXTRA CREDIT —

Go for a walk in a rainstorm with your lover. Let him know you remembered the
umbrella and raincoat but forgot your panties.

GET A CPA TO HELP YOU
DO FINANCIAL PLANNING

All the Congress, all the accountants and tax lawyers, all the judges, and a convention of wizards all cannot tell for sure what the income tax law says.
—Walter B. Wriston, U.S. banker and former chairman of Citicorp

A certified public accountant (CPA) can help you and your spouse implement plans to accomplish financial goals. A CPA can provide analytical thinking skills to help you do your financial planning. Ask friends and family members for a recommendation.

First, you and your spouse need to figure out what you are looking to accomplish with financial planning. For example, do you need comprehensive investment strategies, budget advice, tax information, strategies for dealing with credit card debt, advice about insurance policies and coverage—or all of the above, some of the above, or something else? Your financial planner will also want to know what level of risk you feel prepared to take on. You may be asked about risk levels on many different occasions while working with a CPA, as your level of risk usually changes over a lifetime.

—— EXTRA CREDIT ——

Make sure you and your spouse understand the specialty designations of CPAs. For example, a CPA with a designation of PFS is a personal financial specialist. A CPA with a designation of CFP is someone who is also a certified financial planner. The specializations mean that the CPA has had to go through extensive training and pass a rigorous examination. There is no licensing requirement for these specializations, but CPA specialists do adhere to a code of ethics.

MAKE UP EROTIC
STORIES TO SHARE

The truly erotic sensibility, in evoking the image of a woman, never omits to clothe it. The robing and disrobing; that is the true traffic of love. —Antonio Machado, *Juan de Mairena*

The art of storytelling has practically disappeared today. Just think about how thrilled you are with the rare fiction writer who can take your breath away. There is a small but growing segment of contemporary erotic writers who are capturing our imagination with their writing. Check online or at your favorite bookseller for erotic stories to read with your lover. Trust and develop your own skills as a storyteller. Practice the art of telling stories to your partner and see where it takes you both. Creating stories is a great way to fan the flames of sexy feelings.

—— EXTRA CREDIT ——

Try your hand at interactive erotic storytelling. Start your story with a character or two and then, with words, paint them in their world. Take them on an adventure and make their travel difficult in some way. When you've painted them into a corner, let your spouse continue the story. Don't forget to make it sexy and titillating for both of you.

DATE NIGHT

Take a bike ride. Drop in to your local ice cream parlor for a frozen yogurt. Savor the cool, smooth sensation of the frozen concoction on your palate. Ask your partner which hot spots on his body are clamoring for the cool caresses of your tongue.

SHOW RESPECT
DURING DISAGREEMENTS

Without feelings of respect, what is there to distinguish men from beasts?
—Confucius, *Analects*

Showing respect to one another during any kind of dispute can keep the two of you on a positive track toward resolution. You both have brought to your relationship the expectation that you'll work things out. This is the basic definition of commitment. The relationship must provide a safe container within which conflicts can be resolved.

Requesting an appropriate time for dealing with a disagreement is respectful and shows your commitment toward finding a resolution for the problem. Give your spouse advance notice of a "clearing the air" session. That way, you both can carefully consider the issue prior to discussing it. You might also ponder how to couch your remarks so they are thoughtful, logical, and respectful. Be open to what unfolds, and don't come with a preconceived notion of what the resolution or compromise is going to be.

DAY 71

--- EXTRA CREDIT ---

Use words of endearment and pet names to help keep the rhetoric disarming, polite, and civil during the disagreement.

DON'T CARRY
EMOTIONAL BAGGAGE

Nothing vivifies, and nothing kills, like the emotions. —Joseph Roux,
Meditations of a Parish Priest

Leave behind old emotional baggage when engaging in a discussion about a current issue of contention with your spouse. Don't bring up points of contention that have triggered arguments in the past with your mate or in your previous relationships. If, for example, you want to have a baby but your husband wants to wait, it's a good idea to acknowledge that the subject makes you feel emotional because having a family has always been important to you. Be prepared to own and share your own emotional baggage if necessary, but avoid emotional outbursts since they fan the flames of emotional upheaval and may lead you to saying things that you did not intend to say.

--- EXTRA CREDIT ---

Put the Golden Rule into practice. Genuinely try to see your spouse's point of view and yourself through his eyes. Treat him as you want to be treated.

GET CREATIVE IN
RESOLVING CONFLICTS

Marriage is three parts love and seven parts forgiveness of sin. —Langdon Mitchell, *The New York Idea*

Instead of allowing the gulf between you and your spouse to grow wider over some crisis, get creative in resolving the conflict. Sometimes couples have to stand in one another's shoes to fully comprehend what has happened between them. It's not always easy to figure out what to do or say when emotions are flooding your brain, but taking a time out, writing about it, researching what other couples have done in dealing with a similar situation, or talking to a trusted friend or even your minister or priest can be instrumental to putting your marriage back on a happy track.

Forgiveness of your mate and also yourself can help initiate the healing process. So can understanding that you both are unique and are meant to be different. The way your brains work is different. Only after you have accepted the fact that the two of you just see the problem differently can you get truly creative to find a way to bridge it.

— EXTRA CREDIT —

Find answers you seek. Calm your mind. Ask yourself what you need to know to understand the problem and for the solution to arise. Then wait for it to emerge. If it doesn't, let go and try again at another time.

PRACTICE
DIPLOMACY

Lofty words cannot construct an alliance or maintain it; only concrete deeds can do that. —John F. Kennedy, U.S. president

Think of diplomacy as the art and application of negotiation without arguments or other expressions of heated conflict. Many couples have happily discovered that phrasing a request or couching a complaint in a certain way has its benefits. In other words, try to find just the right way, the right words, to phrase a problem or ask for a partner's help in finding a solution. Outbursts or confrontations—decidedly undiplomatic—result in hurt feelings and bruised egos.

You married each other to share in the joys and sorrows of a life together; you need to maintain that connection even when the situation is sticky. "When two people love each other, they don't look at each other," said Ginger Rogers, but rather, "they look in the same direction." A diplomatic husband might answer his wife's question, "Does this dress make me look fat?" with an answer like, "When the curves of such a beautiful woman are all in the right places, who notices the dress?"

—— EXTRA CREDIT ——

In a tough situation where neither you nor your spouse can find a way to talk about the problem, try "shuttle diplomacy." It is practiced by many nations of the world when a conflict has escalated, increasing the challenges of finding a solution. In shuttle diplomacy, a third party acts as mediator to carry ideas, communication, and proposals back and forth between the conflicted parties. Ask a friend you both trust to be your diplomatic shuttler.

SET THE RIGHT TONE
FOR A NEW MARRIAGE

There is nothing half so sweet in life as love's young dream. —Thomas Moore, English lawyer, author, scholar, and statesman

Newlyweds can be so deeply in love that they can't imagine a need for scheduling time to discuss emotional difficulties or problems. However, newly married or not, it's a good habit for couples to regularly meet for the express purpose of presenting practical and emotional issues that need to be aired. Honesty and trust must exist for the process to work. Couples in vibrant and healthy marriages regularly communicate about the agreements they've made to each other.

Just as a well-functioning business has regular meetings to make certain all the employees work as a team, a good relationship practices the same procedure. For some reason, too many couples don't see the necessity of having such meetings at home, while they easily accept this practice as a given at work. However, as it goes in business, so it goes (or doesn't) in a relationship. Turn off the cell phones, and ensure there will be no interruptions (children, pets, neighbors) or distractions. Within this period for communication, each of you can state feelings or ask questions while the other listens and then answers. Questions can include these:

- What have you not communicated that you want to talk about?
- What haven't you been acknowledged for that you want me to recognize?
- What's not working? What's working better?

--- EXTRA CREDIT ---
Pencil these meetings into the family calendar or program them into your electronic devices so they become officially scheduled. See the meetings as important as health checkups, necessary for the health of your marriage.

KEEP YOUR WORD
TO YOUR FAMILY

But I have promises to keep, / And miles to go before I sleep. —Robert
Frost, American poet

Couples who do what they say they will do and who follow through
when they say they will are seen by their spouses and family members
as dependable and trustworthy. Keep your promises, and your partner
as well as other family members will know that they can always count
on you.

Endeavor not to break your promises, but if you must, then at least
be honest and forthcoming about why you made the promise in the first
place and the reason or reasons why you couldn't keep your word. Marriages are hurt by a pattern of broken promises. You can ensure that your
relationship stays healthy and buoyant by keeping your word.

—— EXTRA CREDIT ——

Write your promise on a piece of paper and tape it to your computer. It's a constant
reminder. Do what it is you promised to do and do it quickly. That way it won't hang
over you like a duty. Knowing you haven't yet kept your promise is a burden that
becomes harder to bear each day.

DATE NIGHT

Visit a local jazz club. Then stop off at a neighborhood bistro or an upscale restaurant for dessert such as decadent tiramisu and a glass of port or brandy. Focus on feelings of happiness and be fully present while talking, listening, or just being with the one you love.

TRY TO SEE YOUR
SPOUSE'S POINT OF VIEW

He who sees all beings in the Self, and the Self in all beings hates none.
—Isha Upanishad

Each spouse necessarily views situations and circumstances that arise in the marriage from his or her point of view and personal concerns. That's not wrong; it's just the way it is. Men and women's brains often see things differently, so it's a good idea to at least try to see your spouse's point of view. Consider the following example.

DAY 78

You ask your husband if his consulting business could spare him long enough to fix the leaky faucet in the kitchen because the water bill is straining the family budget. He agrees to try to fix it first thing Saturday morning. When Saturday comes, he instead takes off for the golf course for a round with a potential new client. You believe that he has totally forgotten his promise to fix the faucet. All day, you listen to the drips, steaming with anger. When he comes home, you let him have a piece of your mind. But what if, instead of criticizing and judging him, you try to understand his point of view? You might arrive at the conclusion that he saw the potential new client as a means to increase his income, a choice that would greatly benefit the family finances, and the means with which he could hire a plumber to do something that he isn't sure he knows how to fix.

— EXTRA CREDIT —

Ask him to share his ideas about how best to solve a particular problem. Hear him out as he explains his take on it. If you rush to judgment, criticism, and rejection, he will likely shut down and tune you out. Show him whenever possible that you can not only see but also appreciate his point of view.

SEE POWER-SHARING
AS A PROCESS

Equality consists in the same treatment of similar persons. —Aristotle, *Politics*

With today's new normal of equal marriage translating into multiple breadwinners paying the bills, and divvying up housework and childcare on an ad hoc basis, there's a great deal of confusion about how to handle it all. How long should a new mother (or father) stay home with a newborn child? How much "help" with household or parenting should be expected of the spouse who works outside the home? Who makes sure the bills are paid on time? Who decorates the house? How are buying decisions made?

For better or worse, there are no fixed answers to any of these questions. So, if you're feeling overwhelmed and unsure of how to share power in your marriage, first, take a breath—you're not alone. Second, honor the emotional support you give each other no matter how well or not so well power-sharing is going in your marriage. Know that power-sharing will be a process of negotiation that will last as long as your marriage.

Your emotional support is the foundation for the discussions and negotiations that will be necessary in order to reach agreement about how to share power as you structure your day-to-day lives together. When you have this unbreakable emotional bond, each of you knows that no matter how difficult your disagreements may be, both of you are committed to seeing the process through.

--- EXTRA CREDIT ---

Write a contract for the division of labor in your household. In this contract, make two columns after each chore: One column records who does the task presently; the second reflects the product of your negotiation: who agrees to take on that task in the future. Beyond the everyday tasks, don't forget to list child-care assignments, checkbook balancing, paying bills, and dealing with health insurance paperwork.

UNDERSTAND THAT DIFFERING
VIEWPOINTS ARE HEALTHY

The ultimate test of a relationship is to disagree but to hold hands. —Alexandra Penney, *How to Make Love to a Man*

The best marriages are ones in which you can be supportive of your spouse, respect his or her point of view, but also express your individuality, including your opinions and ideas. Differing viewpoints not only stimulate interesting discussions but also provide an alternative lens through which to view life, politics, sex, religion, and even relationship issues.

See disagreements between you and your partner as a place to start a discussion. Agree on how to disagree. It's healthy for your relationship for you to share divergent viewpoints, talk about them, and grow and evolve together as a result. Clear communication is the key.

—— EXTRA CREDIT ——

Have a long discussion about something about which you don't agree. Keep it friendly. Let it get heated, but don't let it get so personal that tempers flare. Then switch positions on the topic. The point is to discover how much fun it is to disagree.

DON'T ACCIDENTALLY
HUMILIATE YOUR SPOUSE

No one can make you feel inferior without your consent. —Eleanor
Roosevelt, U.S. First Lady and humanitarian

When you feel the urge to lash out in a hurtful way, stop and ask yourself whether humiliating your partner will make the situation better or
worse. Humiliation is such a destructive verbal weapon that the only
reason a person would use it is to vent pent-up anger or rage.

Why not instead tell your spouse exactly what he or she did to upset
you and how that action resulted in your feeling hurt, anger, or resentment? Explain that you don't like feeling that way and it's hurtful and
destructive to your relationship. Talk about positive and productive ways
to disagree without resorting to insults and personal attacks, which only
serve to sabotage a marriage.

--- EXTRA CREDIT ---

Shift the paradigm. Choose a behavior different from the pattern of behavior you
normally exhibit when you are arguing with your mate. Psychologists say that it only
takes one person to shift the paradigm. Only one of you has to make choices that are
different from your usual behavior patterns in order for everyone in the paradigm to
change their respective behaviors. Give it a try with your spouse and/or your children
and see for yourself. It works.

TALK ABOUT
YOUR DREAMS

This is the day, Sancho, on which will be seen the boon my fortune is reserving for me; this, I say, is the day on which as much as any other shall be displayed the might of my arm, and on which I shall do deeds which shall be written in the book of fame for all ages to come. —Don Quixote character, Miguel de Cervantes, *The Ingenious Hidalgo Don Quixote of La Mancha*

Could there be any better time to reveal your dreams to your spouse and for him to share his with you than when you are lying in the dark in each other's embrace engaged in pillow talk? There may be many reasons why one or both of you have not be able to speak of your dreams, but when you feel safe, loved, and protected as you do in bed together, use those moments to divulge your private dreams about yourself and your life and your goals.

Perhaps you are a lawyer who wanted to be an artist, a writer who wanted to fly planes, or a real-estate executive who dreamed of becoming an ambassador. If your logical mind has always dictated your course in life and silenced you when you wanted to give voice to your dreams, it's time to share those dreams with your spouse.

— EXTRA CREDIT —

Start the discussion by asking your spouse to think back to the time in his childhood when he decided what he wanted to be when he grew up. Then ask him to share with you all the reasons that dream never came true. When it's your turn, speak openly and truthfully about why your dreams never materialized either. Perhaps there are now ways to help each other achieve such dreams.

SEEK
COMPROMISE

It's better to lose the saddle than the horse. —Italian proverb

Compromise can work well in marriages as an effective method for settling disputes. The greatest value of compromise, other than providing a way through a seemingly impassible blockage, is that it can restore household harmony and peace and enable your relationship to get back on track. There are four areas where problems are likely to occur and where growth is possible:

1. Self and Boundaries. Maintain your individual identity as you create an interdependent, not dependent, relationship with your spouse.
2. Money. Create a productive financial partnership with your spouse, not using money as an instrument of power but as a foundation for mutual fulfillment.
3. Sex. Restore a fulfilling, respectful sexual union, making sex the basis of an emotional and spiritual connection in your relationship and a foundation for self-growth, rather than allowing it to be a bargaining chip in a marital power game.
4. Family. Build safety, nurturance, and boundaries for your children, living in community with your extended family, friends, and neighbors.

--- EXTRA CREDIT ---

The next time communication gets sticky or blocked over some issue in your marriage, figure out an equitable solution in which you both agree to accept something less than what you had originally wanted . . . and move on.

DATE NIGHT

Lie together in a hammock. Gaze upon each other as if no one else in the world existed. Imagine that you can depend on only each other for protection, care, and love. What wouldn't you do for each other? Think of how you could show your appreciation to your helpmate, and then do it.

LISTEN WITHOUT
INTERRUPTING

Give every man thine ear, but few thy voice. —Shakespeare, *Hamlet*

Being able to finish each other's sentences is a wonderful indicator of how close you've become, but resist the temptation to do it. Listening to your partner, even when she takes the circuitous route to the point, shows that you are patient, considerate, and appreciative of what she has to say. Knowing when to chime in and when to remain silent is a skill that you can learn with a little practice. You don't have to be a silent partner, just one who understands when to speak and when to be quiet . . . at least until it's your turn to talk.

Active listening requires that you not only listen, but also interpret and evaluate what you have heard. In other words, you are alternately taking in information, processing it, repeating it back to make sure you have understood correctly, and expressing your own ideas in relation to the information you've been given.

--- EXTRA CREDIT ---

Ask your spouse an open-ended question (not one that can be satisfied with a yes/no answer). Then practice your active listening skills. Give her your full attention. See how active listening improves the communication between you two.

KNOW THE
OUTCOME YOU WANT

We can't solve problems by using the same kind of thinking we used when we created them. —Albert Einstein, German-born American physicist

In a dispute with your mate, the payoff you seek may not be the one you end up getting. So before you take up your adversarial position, consider the possible outcomes. For example, let's say you replaced the washer and dryer ahead of the schedule that you and your spouse agreed on. You expected that he would see the logic in your point of view about how much it was costing to run the dryer through two or three cycles to get the clothes thoroughly dry. What you didn't anticipate was he would agree with you about the need and the cost, but not the timing. The money you spent on the appliances was money he had allocated for a surprise trip to Aruba. Now the trip must be postponed. Instead of being happy about the new appliances, you feel dejected—not the outcome you expected.

Spouses who often bicker over marital issues face many challenges in their relationship. What can possibly thrive in an atmosphere of negativity? It takes time, patience, and a willingness to sort out the problem and know the optimum outcome for all involved before you begin to work through the disagreement, deal with the emotional turmoil, and seek resolution. When you have achieved a healthy, harmonious, and happy marriage, you'll realize that working through the tough stuff made it worthwhile.

--- EXTRA CREDIT ---

If you find you can't get to a resolution acceptable to both of you, seek help from a professional marriage counselor to gain clarity about your particular problem or situation. Sometimes a trained professional can provide much-needed insight in as few as one or two sessions.

SET BOUNDARIES
WITH IN-LAWS

Please all, and you will please none.—Aesop, Fables

Establish and safeguard healthy boundaries in your marriage, including with your in-laws, to ensure that you and your spouse are each other's first priority. Here are some suggestions for how to manage an overeager in-law:

- Regulate in-law visiting times and frequency (visits end at a specific time and don't continue for days, weeks, or months).
- Limit topics of conversation (forbid discussing subjects that always seem to end in argument or involve your spouse or children).
- Control the frequency of telephone contact (one call each week or whatever you decide).
- Make clear the rules for when the in-laws baby-sit or visit your children (for example, take away the junk food given to your toddler, explaining to your child and your in-laws why you don't allow it in your house, and also insist on certain bedtimes for your children when they stay over at their grandparents' homes).

Having clear boundaries that everyone understands and then enforcing them can make your married life more satisfying and enjoyable. It also ensures that your children have a healthy and satisfying relationship with their grandparents.

--- EXTRA CREDIT ---

Make time for the two of you as a couple and set boundaries that safeguard your time with your spouse even if it means making certain that in-laws and every one of your relatives and friends knows which night is your date night. Make no exceptions.

DIVIDE HOUSEHOLD
CHORES FAIRLY

No man will ever make love to a woman because she waxed the linoleum . . . "My God, the floor's immaculate. Lie down, you hot bitch." —Joan Rivers, American comedienne

Most married couples keep their house relatively clean. But which one of you does the chores depends on your joint ideas of household roles and work. In some marriages, the couple will decide that the spouse who makes the dinner does not have to do the dishes and cleanup because the other spouse will take care of it. If they make dinner together, both have to share in the cleanup and associated chores such as taking out the garbage and putting away the linen and dishes.

Many couples also designate a certain day to do the general house-cleaning and other chores. Children, from toddlers to teens, can and should help with household chores as well. You and your spouse can choose to compensate them with allowances or other rewards. The point is to get everyone to pitch in to help keep the family home and pets clean and cared for.

—— EXTRA CREDIT ——

Create a chore chart for each member of the family. Alternatively, search the Internet and find chore charts and lists already compiled and ready to download. You can personalize them with photos, affirmations, or quotes.

FIND A DIFFERENT WAY
TO VERBALIZE A PROBLEM

Next time I see you, remind me not to talk to you. —Groucho Marx, American comedian

All married couples fall into habitual ways of talking—sometimes at each other instead of to each other. To avoid the defensive posturing or response from your spouse, find another way to say what's on your mind with "I" statements that describe the problem in a nonjudgmental way. Language is an amazing tool. Use different words and a different tone to express them and your statement is received in a different way.

For example, instead of saying "you always fly off the handle every time I bring up your lavish spending," try saying, "I feel angry and fearful when you spend money and forget to enter it in the checkbook." Make it about the problem and your own feelings and reactions in relation to the problem. Remove the "you" from the statement, and rephrase. Take your time. Breathe. Ask your partner to repeat back to you his or her understanding of what you have said. This way of communicating can help defuse hostilities and make you both more mindful of what you are feeling and why.

—— EXTRA CREDIT ——

Be mindful of how often you use certain words that your spouse might consider to be big turnoffs—words like "never" and "always," which you might most often use when making an accusation. Try to minimize their use, if not excise them altogether from your vocabulary.

KISS AND
MAKE UP

Let him kiss me with the kisses of his mouth: for thy love is better than wine.
—The Song of Solomon 1:2

Although it seems contrary to modern belief, disagreeing with your spouse, even when it involves heated exchanges, doesn't necessarily do permanent harm your marriage. Sometimes it just clears the air and allows both of you to release your pent-up emotions over some disagreement. Afterward, of course, you both may need time to feel grounded and connected.

At some point when you've reestablished your emotional equilibrium in order to forgive each other, you might want to make up with a kiss. If it comes too soon, it might not feel genuine. But how and when it comes doesn't really matter as much as the fact that you both know being friends and lovers is far more important than any screaming match over a difference of opinion. So go ahead and kiss each other. It's the best part of making up.

—— EXTRA CREDIT ——

Kiss, but don't stop with just one. Kiss him for choosing you to be his life partner, for being a father to your children (even if they are as yet unborn), for being a good provider, for being a lover and a poet and a dreamer. For the myriad reasons you love him, kiss him again and again.

DATE NIGHT

Visit a quiet bookstore where you can share a coffee and browse through magazines or books that have nothing to do with children or finances or other everyday issues. This is time for the two of you to indulge in your hobbies and interests.

DON'T GO
TO BED MAD

It is a new road to happiness, if you have strength enough to castigate a little the various impulses that sway you in turn. —George Santayana, *Winds of Doctrine*

Make an iron-clad rule that even if you're so angry you can't stand even speaking to each other, you have to kiss before bed, no exceptions. Take anger out of the bedroom for a self-imposed period of separation. Think of the things you like about being married to your spouse. Return to the bedroom and give each other a goodnight kiss. That mandatory kiss must last for a slow count of ten. With your lips touching, you reconnect emotionally and physically.

The problem or issue you got so heated over will still be there in the morning, but so will your marriage. Resting and recharging will enable you both to avoid ultimatums and to talk less emotionally another time, on another day.

--- EXTRA CREDIT ---

After you both have crawled in bed for the night, inch your foot under the covers and over his ankle. That simple overture might be enough to draw you physically closer. If he doesn't respond right away, try lightly moving your thigh over his. You won't remain apart for long.

TAKE A
PARENTING CLASS

Some are kissing mothers and some are scolding mothers, but it is love just the same, and most mothers kiss and scold together. —Pearl S. Buck, "To You on Your First Birthday," *To My Daughters, with Love*

If you are like most parents, your parenting skills are limited to what you have learned from your parents. Early-childhood experts say there are several keys to being a great parent. The following list includes some of them:

- Allow your child to explore his or her universe.
- Tailor your parenting style not to your own parents' style, but to your child's personality.
- Be a good role model for your child.
- Have structure in your child's life by setting clear boundaries.
- Express lots of love to your child.
- Create strong, loving bonds by spending time with your child (make it regular and emphasize quality).

EXTRA CREDIT

Read with your spouse a parenting book relevant to your child's age to understand the development stage your child might be experiencing. Try some of the activities suggested by the author. Discuss your concerns as a couple and talk with your child's pediatrician for other ideas and insights into good parenting.

BE HIS SOUNDING
BOARD FOR NEW IDEAS

When you realize that there is nothing lacking, the whole world belongs to you. —Lao-tzu, Taoist sage

When your spouse shares his bright, new idea with you, resist the urge to respond right away and, instead, consider his tone. Is he animated, excited, happy, pleased with himself? Or, does his tone suggest fear and uncertainty? His tone indicates the emotion he's feeling.

Do you usually nod affirmatively and listen closely to his concept and specific details—or do you interrupt, anticipate what he's about to say, or shut him down with a dismissive phrase like, "that'll never fly" or "hasn't it already been done?" Evaluate his mood, before automatically reacting or jumping to conclusions. Give him and his idea your full attention. Support his emotional energy (if he's down, lift him; if he's happy; be joyful with him). Above all, practice patience and positive thinking. When you show him that you are his receptive, considerate wife, with a warm smile and words encouragement for him, he feels safe enough to share his wild, crazy ideas with you, his sounding board.

— EXTRA CREDIT —

Know the cues of nonverbal communication. Silence, for example, can indicate deception, distrust, and moodiness; fidgeting reveals impatience; a clenched fist shows tension, anger, and frustration; and arms crossed over the chest suggest a closed-off, defensive posture. On the other hand, open palms, a direct gaze, and smiles and nods affirm openness and a sense of security and trust.

VISIT AN AMERICAN
NATIONAL PARK

I remember as a child reading or hearing the words "The Great Divide" and being stunned by the glorious sound, a proper sound for the granite backbone of a continent. —John Steinbeck, *Travels with Charley*

Head out with your spouse to visit a national park and expand your knowledge of American history. Finding a park won't be a problem, since there are literally hundreds of options in America's national park system. Each one has a unique history. For example, if you live in California, you might take a boat out to Alcatraz Island, located in the middle of the San Francisco Bay. Alcatraz was chosen as the site of the first lighthouse as well as the first U.S. fort on the West coast. On the other side of the country, you and your spouse could choose to walk a piece of the Appalachian Trail, a scenic footpath that stretches 2,175 miles from Maine to Georgia, crossing through fourteen states. Or, you might visit any number of the national historic sites or battlefields in Pennsylvania. For a really wild adventure, venture down to the Everglades National Park in south Florida to see various endangered species of wildlife indigenous to that subtropical wilderness. For a complete list of America's national parks, go to *www.nationalparks.org*.

— EXTRA CREDIT —

Grab the popcorn and curl up with your hubby to watch *The National Parks: America's Best Idea*, a six-segment documentary by Ken Burns. The DVD, book, and CD are all available at *www.shoppbs.org*.

SORT OUT DIFFERENCES
IN PARENTING STYLES

What we are teaches the child far more than what we say, so we must be what we want our children to become. —Joseph Chilton Pearce, American author

You and your spouse may not have had the same kind of parenting when you were growing up. Before you take on the job of parent, it's important to review your personal history and take stock of the emotional baggage you may be carrying (everyone has some) from your parents' successes and failures. Why? Because in parenting, as in other areas of life, it is normal to rely upon past experience to shape your future expectations. Most people enter marriage believing their parents' marriage and the child-rearing style by which they were raised is the right model to follow with their own kids. Many times this is true. The opposite situation is just as common, if you grew up with parents who had a bad marriage and an equally poor parenting style.

Sit with your partner and share your views on how to raise your children, what values to instill in them, what types of discipline will you use, what the structure of your family life will be, what rules will you put in place, and other parenting topics.

--- EXTRA CREDIT ---

After discovering where you and your spouse agree and disagree about parenting issues, decide together on how you will discipline, teach your values to your child, and also in which religion your child will be raised. In short, get together on a parenting game plan for your family.

SHOW GRATITUDE
TO EACH OTHER

There is more hunger for love and appreciation in this world than for bread.
—Mother Teresa, Albanian Catholic nun, founder of the Missionaries of Charity

After a long day, both of you can feel frazzled and frustrated. Words of appreciation and thoughtful actions can lengthen a short fuse or dampen a hot temper. When you are appreciative and acknowledge his contribution, you get more of the same in return.

For example, resist the impulse to impatiently yell at your partner because you've had a long day with the children and he feels too tired to make dinner, even though it's his turn. But be grateful and communicate it if he offers to pick up the cluttered living room or feed and burp the baby or do a load of laundry and the dishes while you make the dinner.

Treat each other the way you want to be treated. That contributes to a healthy marriage. It also demonstrates to your children how husbands and wives show appreciation and gratitude to each other.

--- EXTRA CREDIT ---

On a card or piece of writing paper, jot down a heartfelt message of appreciation to your spouse for all the hard work he or she accomplishes daily. Leave the card on his pillow or near her toothbrush. Ideally, the message will be read in private, not amid the clatter and chatter of a busy household.

DATE NIGHT

Visit a carnival and let your inner child come out to play. Have funnel cakes, nibble on roasted corn on the cob, or share a candied apple. Hold hands, experience the thrill of a ride on a roller coaster or Ferris wheel, and feel the pulsing energy and excitement of the carnival as if you had just fallen in love.

INSTILL SPIRITUAL
VALUES IN YOUR CHILDREN

Train up a child in the way he should go: and when he is old, he will not depart from it. —Proverbs 22:6

Your spiritual values guide your behavior in the world throughout your life, including in business dealings and family relationships. When you impart your spiritual beliefs to your children, you help them understand the moral positions of right and wrong. You give them a code of behavioral conduct to live by and help them understand the place of religion and spirituality in human life. The work of teaching your children about spirituality takes patience and consistency.

By the time children are ready to start school, their moral and ethical values are already ingrained. But that doesn't mean your work as a parent and as your children's primary spiritual adviser ends. As your children grow and become even more inquisitive, you will have the opportunity to reinforce the spiritual values that have guided you. Have family discussions about situations and answer questions that concern your children. Doing this provides a great opportunity to put the discussion in a larger context, because by helping your child grow spiritually and morally, you will be helping them to establish moral families. That's good for society as well.

— EXTRA CREDIT —

Establish a short list of consequences in the event your child violates the core values held by you and your partner. For example, devise appropriate options for dealing with the discovery that your child has lied to you or stolen something from a friend, the school, or a store.

SHOW KIDS HOW PARENTS
AGREE AND DISAGREE

———————

Nature has given us two ears, two eyes, and but one tongue; to the end
that we should hear and see more than we speak. —Socrates, classical
Greek philosopher

As a happily married couple, you are in a perfect position to demonstrate
for your children how the two of you sometimes agree and at other times
disagree. They are taking cues from you all the time, whether you realize it or not. You don't have to always temper or modulate your tone of
voice. It's okay for your children to see you animated when debating
some topic you are both passionate about but about which you disagree.
General George S. Patton once stated, "It's better to fight for something than live for nothing." But disagree with dignity; avoid screaming
matches, name-calling, and physical altercation.

You want to instill in your children good judgment, high purpose
and ideals, an appreciation for meaningful discourse, and possibly even a
sense of humor. Each of these can be reflected during disagreements with
your spouse. You can use your differences of opinion to demonstrate for
your children how to reason through differences with others in a demo-
cratic style. That's a gift they may not easily get elsewhere.

——— EXTRA CREDIT ———

Stop disagreeing long enough to choose a sexy French movie (with English subtitles,
if you don't speak French). Sink into comfortable seats in the darkened theater,
munch on chocolates, and enjoy the film. Alternatively, you could just French kiss
through the entire show.

MAKE LOVE LIKE YOU'RE
GONNA GET CAUGHT

Virtue and vice, evil and good, are siblings, or next-door neighbors, /
Easy to make mistakes, hard to tell them apart. —Ovid, Roman poet, *The
Remedies for Love*

If the idea of making love in places where you might get caught appeals
to you, ask your spouse if he likes the idea, too. In the movies, people
make love in all kinds of places: the backseat of parked car in a public
lot, the bathroom of an airplane, a nightclub's dark alleyway, in the surf
along a beach, the floor of a host's home, a closet, or even the kitchen
counter. In real life, too, people make love in lots of places where they
could potentially be discovered during the act. The risk of being discovered ups the tension and fear but also heightens the experience.

However, you don't have to actually risk having the police tap on
your car window with a nightstick. Use your wild imagination to con-
vince yourself that you're gonna get caught and then make love as if the
danger were real and you have only moments before you are in the glare
of police spotlights.

—— EXTRA CREDIT ——
Invite friends over for an old-fashioned Western cookout. Then, a few minutes
before your guests are due to arrive, attired only in your cowgirl boots and hat and a
serape to cover your naked body, invite your partner to saddle up the ride of his life.

DON'T BEND OVER BACKWARD
FOR YOUR SPOUSE'S EX

The thing that impresses me most about America is the way parents obey their children. —Edward, Duke of Windsor

You may be facing a number of challenges if you have recently married a man who has children. If you're very lucky, the ex-wife may encourage her children to give you an opportunity to build a loving, warm relationship with them (the best possible situation). Unfortunately, many ex-wives won't be so generous, even though it's good for everyone involved. Both internal and external forces may be undermining your positive efforts and intentions to step into the role of spouse and supportive parent. His children might may feel possessive of their father, see you as the interloper, and believe that liking you means they are somehow betraying their biological mother.

Psychologists say that you can't give in or give up, and advise parents to use the authoritative style of parenting—give lots of love and understanding and warmth, but do so with a lot of control. Give children the gift of time to adjust.

— EXTRA CREDIT —

Attend a lecture on blended families. Learn about possible pitfalls and how to avoid them. Learn what you have to do to gain the trust of stepchildren and how adjustment can differ in each age group.

GIVE HELLO AND
GOODBYE SMOOCHES

Happiness is like a kiss. You must share it to enjoy it. —Bernard Meltzer,
radio host

The habit of smooching as an expression of love is a great habit for couples to cultivate, whether or not you are newly married. A kiss can ease
your mate into a rough Monday morning or end the day on high note.
Give a little peck on the lips, cheek, head, neck, hand, nose—virtually
anywhere on your spouse's body when you feel like expressing an "I love
you" without saying it. A smooch is a great way to convey "Good morning, Sunshine" or "See you later, Sugar," or "Meet you in bed, Sweet-
heart." You have a lifetime of reasons to give smooches, but you really
don't have to have a reason, just the desire.

— EXTRA CREDIT —

Grab his tie, belt, shirtsleeve, or hardhat, and pull him close for a slow, smoldering
smoochathon. Once you've awakened the giant in him, let him take the lead to
ravishing you once more before he leaves for work.

TALK ABOUT YOUR
DREAMS AS A COUPLE

Two souls with but a single thought; two hearts that beat as one. —Baron
Eligius Franz Joseph von Munch-Bellinghausen, Austrian dramatist

Your love has united you, and your hearts perhaps now are united in sharing a dream. Maybe it's the dream of owning your own home . . . or buying a larger house, or one in a different type of neighborhood. Or, maybe
you desire a vacation home in a warmer, cooler, or drier climate. For the
dreams you share as a couple, take the necessary time to allow your minds
to separately explore various aspects or elements of your shared dream.
Then come together and talk about the dream, first in general terms, then
in specific detail.

For example, where and when do you want to start looking for that
new home or vacation retreat? What is the price range you'd be willing to
pay? What specific features do you require? Allow your shared dream to
ripen. You won't have just one conversation about that dream, but rather
many. Expect the dream to evolve, along with myriad ideas about how
to begin manifesting the dream.

—— EXTRA CREDIT ——

Schedule time into your daily planner to daydream. Encourage your spouse to do
the same thing. Daydreaming is not just a pleasurable activity; it serves the purpose of
clarification so that the dream can manifest.

DATE NIGHT

Head off to the local culinary academy for a late lunch or early dinner and treat your taste buds to the day's culinary delight, created by students under the watchful eye of the head chef or teacher. Linger over dessert and coffee.

AVOID PUSHING EACH
OTHER'S HOT BUTTONS

For two people in a marriage to live together day after day is unquestionably the one miracle the Vatican has overlooked. —Bill Cosby, American comedian

You likely already know what your spouse's hot-button issues are, and your partner probably knows yours. For many couples, hot-button issues often involve children, money, religion, pets, lack of time spent with the family, previous relationships, in-laws, and politics, to name a few. A hot button is a stimulus/response behavior. It's the thing that someone says or does that pushes you into conflict. Or, you say or do something that pushes your partner into an emotional place where he doesn't want to be. He feels vulnerable and in order to feel safe again, he reacts (or, probably more correctly, his inner child reacts). When you are reacting in response to someone pushing your hot button, you become less creative, organized, efficient, happy, and productive.

Avoid targeting each other's vulnerabilities. As individuals and as a couple, explore what triggers you to feel so upset. Try to understand why (an intense reaction often relates to something that has happened in the past). The goal is to find a way to maintain your mental and emotional equilibrium and to restore happiness.

--- EXTRA CREDIT ---

Make a list of your hot-button issues and ask your partner to do the same. Trade lists. Consider those topics taboo . . . at least until they are no longer provocative.

SEE COMMUNICATION AS A
LIFELINE TO A LONG MARRIAGE

I dunno, she's got gaps, I got gaps, together we fill gaps. —Rocky Balboa, *Rocky*

The leading character in the Rocky films wasn't an eloquent or particularly articulate speaker—his style was direct and to the point. He and wife Adrian had their problems, but they communicated well with each other because they both listened with ears, minds, and hearts. That is really the secret to good communication—saying what you have to say clearly, without ambiguity, and listening with full attention to your spouse. Excellent communication skills are perhaps the most important tools that married couples can have. In many cases, it is the glue that holds a marital relationship together when the marriage must navigate through rocky times, no pun intended.

If you and your mate seem more like adversaries than partners; if your ordinary conversations often escalate into disagreements or shouting matches, communication (or lack of it) might be the problem. Seek help as necessary and return to the work of building a strong, healthy marriage to last a lifetime.

--- EXTRA CREDIT ---

Find out more about men's and women's communication styles. Read books, attend classes, search the Internet for appropriate articles, and apply what you learn to your marital relationship. Good communication skills will serve you well in all your relationships, but especially in your marriage and in your job or career.

AVOID FIGHTING IN FRONT
OF YOUR CHILDREN

My husband and I have never considered divorce . . . murder sometimes, but never divorce. —Dr. Joyce Brothers, American psychologist and advice columnist

If you missed episodes of television personality and clinical psychologist Dr. Phil McGraw discussing why parents should get real and stop fighting in front of their children, you might not realize the impact that parental fighting can have on kids. It's like living in a war zone, and the damage it does to children is often evident in their later relationships as teens and grownups. They may exhibit symptoms of low self-esteem and feel insecure, guilty, helpless, and lost. Worse, when they become parents themselves, they are likely to repeat the pattern of fighting they witnessed while growing up.

Dr. Phil advocates leaving the room instead of fighting. Let you partner know by some visual cue that you're upset and a fight's about to start. Take the discussion to a private place out of earshot of your children. Even better, work at having a happy marriage and show your children what that looks like so when they grow up, that is the multigenerational family pattern they repeat.

--- EXTRA CREDIT ---

Let your pugnacious tendencies and competitive spirit come out in a healthy way. Play the "Beat the Parents" board game. Or try the game "Kids Battle the Grown-Ups." Find out who are the most competitive smarty-pants in your family.

EAT MEALS TOGETHER
AS A FAMILY

It is illegal to give someone food in which has been found a dead mouse or weasel. —Ancient Irish Law

It's important that you and your spouse be united about your family eating at least one meal together every day, if possible. Busy schedules often mean eating fast food and on the run. Plus, you may find mealtimes with children to be exasperating. Getting kids to eat what's good for them is a common issue that couples face.

Seemingly infinite patience along with the establishment of an unbreakable rule about eating together has its rewards. Nutritionists and food experts suggest that eating meals together not only helps strengthen family bonds, it also is associated with improved diets later in life. A report in *Science Daily* linked the frequency of family meals during adolescence with a better diet when those children grew into adults. They consumed more foods with key nutrients, including dark-green and orange vegetables, more fruit, and fewer soft drinks. Use patience with your children who may be finicky eaters, but put a priority on structured meals to ensure that they eat better as young adults.

--- EXTRA CREDIT ---

Take out a subscription to a culinary magazine. If your spouse doesn't like cooking, encourage him or her to learn about pairing wine with food. You might even purchase a subscription to a wine magazine for him or her.

TRUST ENOUGH TO
SHOW VULNERABILITY

And the day came when the risk to remain tight in a bud was more painful than the risk it took to blossom. —Anaïs Nin, French-born American author

If you and your spouse have not yet been able to discuss each other's emotional vulnerabilities, the lack of such communication could be indicative of a lack of trust between you. To be an intimate team in which you are free to play out erotic and sexual scenarios, the two of you must earn each other's trust. Only then will you feel courageous enough to risk opening yourself to your mate to reveal your deepest vulnerabilities and to support him in revealing his.

Pulling back the layers that hide your core fears, secret desires, and emotional vulnerabilities, and sharing them with each other, can be accomplished only in an environment of implicit trust. When you are able to share those innermost parts of your psyche, your intimacy levels can deepen, enabling your marriage to flourish.

—— EXTRA CREDIT ——

Since vulnerability and fear register much the same way—a need to survive (in the case of vulnerability, it is the need to allow yourself to feel possible wounding), choose some detail that is perhaps less frightening than your deepest fear but nevertheless scary. Trust your spouse to keep your revelation private. Trust your spouse to support you and to love you in spite of the revelation. Reveal it.

DEVELOP EMOTIONAL
INTIMACY WITH YOUR SPOUSE

Your task is not to seek for love, but merely to seek and find all the barriers within yourself that you have built against it. —Rumi, Persian poet and philosopher

Psychologists say that emotionally healthy people who thrive in strong, committed relationships may have had the advantage of having healthy relationships modeled for them. Their interpersonal relationships include such elements as respect, boundaries, truthfulness, and transparency. Those who don't seem to be able to make successful relationships may have had less nurturing models or choose bad partners because they are driven by psychological factors (such as the need to rescue, seek father figures, or date bad boys or divas) rooted in low self-esteem.

You can develop and deepen emotional intimacy with your partner by sharing in an emotionally honest way your sexual truth—what excites you, what you fantasize about when you're being pleasured or pleasuring yourself, and what concerns you have about sex. You have to feel absolutely safe about revealing your innermost self with your partner, but such sharing can deepen your love for one another.

—— EXTRA CREDIT ——

Set an example of openness. Ask your spouse to share his deepest fear with you. Be tender and gentle with his revelations. Create a safe and accepting atmosphere for personal fears and vulnerabilities to be openly discussed.

DATE NIGHT

Visit a local planetarium for an hour or two of lofty stargazing with your spouse and later blast out of orbit in a star-struck lovemaking session.

DISCUSS
GENDER ROLES

This gender thing is history. You're looking at a guy who sat down with Margaret Thatcher across the table and talked about serious issues. —George H.W. Bush, former U.S. president

The views that you and your spouse hold about gender and the responsibilities associated with the roles of husband and wife likely are derived from your respective families. But deviation from traditional gender roles can be a source of friction in many marriages, especially if husband and wife have been raised in different cultures and thus have different ideas about roles and responsibilities of men and women.

The traditional role of a wife as the homemaker, taking care of the home and children, while the husband earns the money isn't necessarily the best model for all families. Gender roles are now negotiated between couples. Sociologists call it "model of double burden." The gender roles and duties of husbands and wives are negotiated as part of their ongoing relationship. Talk about it frankly with your spouse. There's no right or wrong way about how you divvy up family responsibilities—just what works best for you.

--- EXTRA CREDIT ---

Grab your spouse, a bag of popcorn, and watch *Tootsie*, the 1982 movie starring Dustin Hoffman, Jessica Lange, Teri Garr, and Charles Durning. Hoffman's character is an actor who auditions for a woman's role on a daytime soap when he is unable to otherwise find any acting roles. The movie explores gender roles and male/female differences.

UNDERSTAND HOW CORE VALUES
CAN HELP YOUR MARRIAGE

The unexamined life is not worth living. —Socrates, classical Greek philosopher

Your values have been with you since childhood . . . that's when most of us acquire them from our parents, teachers, and religious leaders. Values are those principles, such as honesty, resourcefulness, loyalty, and perseverance, that we adhere to as we live our lives.

But sometimes values can be a source of friction. For example, let's say your spouse is outgoing and gregarious; he places a high value on social interaction and sharing. Yet you value quiet and solitude and associate those things with a sense of the sacred. It's your husband's nature to engage in playful, flirtatious interaction with everyone, especially women and while you accept this as who he is, you feel threatened when he visits friends, including women, on social networking sites or texts. This increases the tension between you.

It's good to remember that you are both individuals and a couple. Discuss your feelings and talk about your values. Knowing the core values that both you and your spouse hold dear can empower you to shape your relationship and clarify how certain values might help either strengthen or create conflict in your marriage. The most successful marriages are those in which spouses share common values, beliefs, and attitudes.

— EXTRA CREDIT —

Sit together and make a list of all the core values you can think of that you hold dear and then choose five or six that best represent those values from which you derive your strength. Ask your spouse to make a similar list. Compare your lists; discuss the values each of you chose and talk about the impact of those values on your marriage.

SEND YOUR SPOUSE A
NAUGHTY TEXT MESSAGE

I'm the kinda girl who works for Paramount by day, and Fox all night. —Mae
West, *Sextette*

Sending a suggestive sexy text by cell phone has come to be called "sexting." Try sending your spouse short, sexy messages to tease and titillate him. Tell him, for example, "I'm in the shower, care to join me?" "I'm alone with nothing on . . . want to play?" "Your kisses turn me on." "I'm thinking of you . . . feeling hot and bothered." "You make me want to kiss you all over." You could also send an erotic poem, a joke that has meaning for just the two of you, or a steamy observation about love. See for yourself how sexting can get him through the door faster than pushing "send" on your cell.

Keep in mind, however, that if your spouse is at work, sexting may not be a good idea. If he is going into an important meeting with the foreign delegation, asking his boss for a raise, directing traffic, or working on a dangerous jobsite, for example, you might want to hold off transmitting that sexy text. It's also not a good idea to send nude pictures, even if you blur your face and strategically crop the photo. You never know when something will end up in cyberspace.

— EXTRA CREDIT —

If you can't resist sending a digital picture when you are sexting your spouse, choose one that has special significance for both of you and that will evoke a sexy memory that you share.

SPEAK OPENLY
ABOUT YOUR GOALS

You are never too old to set another goal or to dream a new dream.
—C.S. Lewis, Irish-born British novelist

Once you know that your dreams are safe with your spouse until you are ready to unveil them to the world, speak openly with your partner about your goals for achieving those dreams. Figure out the best way to align your dream with the Law of Attraction to manifest it. The law is not wishful thinking, daydreaming, or a momentary flight of fancy, but rather brings you what you desire when you (1) are clear about what you want; (2) energize your desire for the item with thoughts, emotion, visual imagery, and a strong conviction that it is coming to you; and (3) feel and express gratitude for what you already have and what is in the process of coming to you, even if it hasn't arrived yet.

—— EXTRA CREDIT ——

Write an affirmation to remind yourself of your dream or goal. Tape it to your refrigerator, computer, bathroom mirror, or even the dashboard of your car. The point is to be able to remind yourself frequently that your dream is worthwhile and that you must keep it in the forefront of your mind if you want to manifest it.

FIND ANSWERS IN YOUR
SPIRITUAL BELIEFS

We come nearest to great when we are great in humility. —Rabindranath
Tagore, *Stray Birds*

When your heart is heavy because you cannot figure out the best solution to a relationship problem, turn to your spiritual beliefs. It's been said that every problem has an answer, and often the right answer is the simplest and the one most overlooked.

TRY THE FOLLOWING THREE STEPS:
1. Think about the problem and give it over to a higher power, according to what you believe.
2. Ask for the answer to come to you as inspiration.
3. Then, stop analyzing and let it go. Expect the answer to reveal itself.

In that way, you are also working in alignment with the Law of Attraction. Those who believe in the way the ancient law works say that your thoughts attract everything that comes into your life. If your relationship nurtures you and your spouse, it's likely that your positive thoughts will bring positive solutions to issues that may arise.

—— EXTRA CREDIT ——

Attend your favorite house of worship, be it a synagogue, church, temple, mosque, meetinghouse, or other type of place where you can find the answers you seek in an environment that provides a spiritual vibe.

PRACTICE THE
ART OF FORGIVENESS

You have to be very fond of men . . . very fond of them to love them.
Otherwise they're simply unbearable. —Marguerite Duras, French author and
film director

Spats happen. Something one of you said or did set the other spouse's
emotions on a negative trajectory. If the two of you had different cultural
upbringings, you may have cultural as well as psychological minefields to
navigate. That will require patience, understanding, and special communication skills. Start with forgiveness and try to reach an understanding.

— EXTRA CREDIT —

Apologize to your partner for something you did and only you can fix. Be clear that
you are reaching with love and forgiveness and not with some ulterior motive. Be
prepared for the possibility that your mate might need more time to come around.

DATE NIGHT

Feed each other finger foods, sip wine from the bottle, and make love on
the rug, even if it's amid throw pillows, the dog's chew toys, and a baby
shoe or two.

STAND UNITED
ON FAMILY RULES

Free the child's potential, and you will transform him into the world. —Maria Montessori, Italian physician and educator

Your work as a parent is to take a child from total dependency to independence in eighteen years. If you're lucky, you will have freed the genius inherent in that child to manifest in the world. If you do your job well, the child will be a well-adjusted, productive member of society, well-equipped to deal with whatever problems and challenges life brings. But while young, inevitably every child will push up against parental boundaries—it is both normal and natural.

Parenting styles run the spectrum, from authoritarian to permissive and everywhere between the two. In the authoritarian style, parents establish rules and expect them not to be challenged. Children make few, if any, of their own choices. When rules are disobeyed, the parents take punitive action. In contrast to "you will do this" messages from parent to child, permissive parenting tends to go in the opposite extreme. Parents provide very little structure or boundary setting, ostensibly to encourage a child's creativity. For many couples, the most workable model is one that gives a child autonomy and encouragement to learn self-discipline while allowing parents to set limits and ground rules for the ways their children behave in the household. You stand firmly united as a couple, but also have some flexibility.

— EXTRA CREDIT —
Research on the Internet to learn about different styles of educating children, including the Montessori philosophy and model.

DAY 120

120

UNDERSTAND THAT
LOVING IS ACCEPTING

I believe that we are solely responsible for our choices, and we have to accept the consequences of every deed, word, and thought throughout our lifetime. —Elisabeth Kübler-Ross, Swiss-born psychiatrist

Completely unconditional love is an ideal no one can achieve. However, there are aspects of unconditional love that are very appealing. Perhaps the best statement defining a realistic version of unconditional love is, "I love you for who you are, and for who you are not." It acknowledges that the one offering love has judgments and requirements that they're attempting to minimize, or go beyond. This acceptance is one of the most beautiful qualities of love. And perhaps that is the best we can ever achieve. Acceptance of who the other person (your spouse) is means you recognize that he has free will and that his choices may not always be what you desire—and yet, you love him.

—— EXTRA CREDIT ——

Create a "Celebration of Our Love" poster or giant card. Choose photographs to stick on your poster board that reveal you and your spouse enjoying poignant, happy, funny, sad, and celebratory moments in your life together. Write catchy phrases under the pictures. Add positive messages about loving unconditionally. The poster makes a great Valentine's Day or wedding anniversary present.

LET THE PAST
STAY IN THE PAST

If you want the present to be different from the past, study the past.
—Baruch Spinoza, Dutch philosopher

Allowing unresolved hurts, issues, and conflicts from previous relationships to surface in your current marriage can damage marital harmony. Watch for triggers that bring up those old feelings, doubts, and insecurities. You must first accept responsibility for your own happiness and then embrace the process of growing together as an individual and a couple. Here are five ways to release and let go of your past.

1. Reconnect with it through art, letter-writing, or meditation in order to honor your memories as the first step in releasing them.
2. Re-experience it through remembering. You may feel the old hurt, sadness, or anger, but allow the feelings to flood into your heart and mind. Experience the feelings until they no longer bother you, then count backward from ten to release.
3. Redirect your memories and thoughts. Don't give the past any power over the present.
4. Allow adequate time for your broken heart or traumas to heal and for calm thinking to guide you forward.
5. Choose new directions, new friends, and new opportunities to pursue today and tomorrow and leave the past behind.

--- EXTRA CREDIT ---

Resist asking your spouse about old lovers. Also, honor your own memories but let them remain in the past. Constantly bringing up references to previous lovers or spouses may alienate your current partner. Focus on the love you currently share.

HONOR YOUR
RIGHT TO PRIVACY

"If everybody minded their own business," the Duchess said in a hoarse growl, "the world would go round a deal faster than it does." —Lewis Carroll, *Alice's Adventures in Wonderland*

You and your spouse might prefer different levels of privacy. Your needs could range from a measure of personal privacy within your marital relationship to a fairly constant state of emotional and physical connectedness between the two of you. This can become a problem if you are married to someone who has needs very different from yours. The different needs for privacy can lead to friction and blaming.

The first step to managing this difference in needs is to cease making the other person feel wrong for his opinion, and stop judging this difference between the two of you as evidence of dysfunction. Less verbal communication is not necessarily bad, unhealthy, or wrong; it is merely less verbal communication.

--- EXTRA CREDIT ---

Buy a small, locked security safe and use it to keep safe and private your most personal papers and diary or journals. Give your spouse one for his personal or valuable items.

MAKE TIME FOR
COUPLE TOGETHERNESS

He who is fixed to a star does not change his mind. —Leonardo da Vinci,
Notebooks

You have a busy schedule, and so does your spouse. If you have children, their schedules can wreak havoc on yours. With such harried lives, it's equally important to schedule time for solitude and also time to be together with your committed partner. Many couples do this best by sharing a common adult interest that they do together regularly, be it golf, the symphony, motorcycle riding, or birding. This is not the same as attending children's sporting activities or recitals together, as that falls into the category of family time.

The important thing about couple togetherness is to make sure this time is solely about sharing something you enjoy doing as a couple. Make it fun for both of you; then it will be easy to keep it up as a habit for life.

— EXTRA CREDIT —

Time is best kept with a calendar or a clock or both. If you keep the family schedule, be sure to insert your couple time and resist the urge to change it or release it. It is just as important as your child's soccer game or the dentist appointment.

HONOR YOUR SPOUSE'S BACKGROUND

All truths are easy to understand once they are discovered; the point is to discover them. —Galileo, Italian scientist, astronomer, and mathematician

When people from vastly different backgrounds, races, cultures, or religions marry and start their lives together under one roof, matrimonial discord can sometimes rear its ugly head. If you are married to someone of a different race, religion, or ethnic group, undoubtedly you will face many challenges. Problems can arise from the different definitions of "normal" that you and your spouse as well as your respective in-laws have for a variety of situations and circumstances.

You won't always see through the same racial, religious, or cultural lens, but it is important to honor your spouse's truth and for your spouse to honor yours. When you manage your differences well, you are the recipient of many blessings.

— EXTRA CREDIT —

Take a great quote or saying about truth and have it made into a personalized decal or, if you are crafty, incorporate the saying into a beautiful piece of wall art. For example, the Bible verse "The Truth shall make you free" (John 8:32), or some other verse about truth that provides a supportive, uplifting, and inspirational message.

DATE NIGHT

Appreciate the spell that the moon casts over lovers all over the world. Whether or not there's a full moon, sweep your spouse into your arms and dance spontaneously down the street under the stars as you explore a local art and wine festival.

TALK TOGETHER
ABOUT TABOO TOPICS

When one door of happiness closes, another opens; but often we look so long at the closed door that we do not see the one which has been opened for us. —Helen Keller, American author, political activist, and lecturer

Everyone is emotionally vulnerable and insecure at certain times and junctures of their lives. In a healthy marriage you understand your partner's areas of vulnerability and do not hit below the belt by saying things to intentionally trigger these vulnerabilities. Each spouse needs to let his or her partner know exactly where the belt line lays. When you are in harmony, you understand that some topics require special handling.

Some typical "no go" areas of discussion with which you may begin your list include former lovers and spouses, criticisms of parenting styles (particularly when the children are from a former marriage), weight and other aspects of appearance, and any blanket statements that inflame the discussion. This does not mean you never discuss any of these or other below-the-belt areas. It just means you do so with great care, respect, tenderness, and love.

--- EXTRA CREDIT ---

When you sense your partner is feeling vulnerable, let a comforting touch of your hand to his convey the message that you and he are emotionally connected and together you can get through anything. You don't have to speak a word for him to understand.

DON'T LIE

Three things cannot be long hidden: the sun, the moon, and the truth.
—Siddhartha Gautama (Buddha)

Keep the facts straight; don't bend them, twist them, or paint them into white lies. Cultivate an atmosphere of transparency in your marriage so that you speak the truth and expect your spouse to do the same. Sadly, research shows that many people, even married couples, lie to each other. Most people lie as often as once or twice a day. Such falsehoods can be lies of omission, exaggerations, or twists of the truth to impart a false impression. Lying most often occurs during phone calls rather than face to face.

Married couples don't lie as frequently as the rest of the population, but their lies—for example, hiding a financial splurge or an act of infidelity—can impart huge consequences. In good marriages and happy relationships, couples at least try to stick to the truth.

— EXTRA CREDIT —

Go for a half day without telling even a little white lie or a lie of omission. If you are able to do it for a half day, then try it for a full day and see how rich life becomes for you. The truth is always exciting, author Pearl S. Buck once noted. She advised to speak it often because without truth, life is dull.

FOSTER
INTERDEPENDENCE

He who is being carried does not realize how far the town is. —Nigerian proverb.

There are many different relationship styles—independent, dependent, codependent, and interdependent. Interdependent is the healthiest, for it is characterized by the interplay of mutual need and support. The interdependent relationship is never destructive, but rather nurtures and nourishes both partners.

In this context, interdependence means that you and your spouse depend on each other for some, but never all, of your needs. That type of relationship, in turn, guides marriage partners into a deeper realization about themselves (increasing self-esteem) as well an understanding of the world and how it relates to them, and how they relate to it.

—— EXTRA CREDIT ——

Embolden yourself to try to do something new that you ordinarily would just ask your mate to fix. For example, try to fix a broken sprinkler head, change out a light fixture, replace your garbage disposal, or change your flat tire. If your spouse doesn't cook or do laundry, be his assistant and encourage him to try. You both might feel newly empowered.

MAINTAIN COUPLE HARMONY

If we have no peace, it is because we have forgotten that we belong to each other. —Mother Teresa, Albanian Catholic nun, founder of the Missionaries of Charity

Marriages today are challenged by a variety of stressors. For example, the birth of a baby, though welcome, nevertheless puts added strain on a marriage. Likewise, crises such as a death in the family, job loss, sudden illness, and even moving to a new locale are stressors that challenge household harmony. There also are some things couples do that almost always disrupt the peace and harmony of their home life—for example, if you:

- Pursue your own interests, relationships with friends, and personal destiny to the exclusion of your spouse's.
- Bicker over every little annoyance and aggravation.
- Focus on your job more than your family and marriage.
- Stop communicating with your spouse.
- Seek *all* meaning for your life outside of your marriage.

Finding ways to restore balance can tax the emotional and intellectual resources of both partners. It takes resiliency on the part of the couple along with the desire to re-establish peace, safety, and security.

— EXTRA CREDIT —

If you can't carry on a meaningful conversation with your spouse about each other's bickering, seek the counsel of a trusted friend or clergymember. Assess what you might be doing to inflame the situation. Then stop doing those things, and reach out to your mate. When your spouse knows you are trying to re-establish harmony by fixing yourself first, she likely will be more willing to examine her role in the problem.

SEEK PROFESSIONAL
HELP, IF NECESSARY

I am a success today because I had a friend who believed in me and I didn't have the heart to let him down. —Abraham Lincoln, U.S. president

If you want to improve communication with your spouse, deepen the bonds you share, or probe some emotional/psychological wound, seek professional counsel with a qualified therapist. A marriage counselor or qualified mental health professional can give you the tools to resolve conflicts, help you see and understand opposing views that you and your partner may hold, enable you and your spouse to work through an issue that has hurt the marriage (such as infidelity or an addiction), or assist you in probing the reasons behind the decline in caring for each other. Couples counseling can help you and your spouse not only save your marriage but transform it into a better, happier, more buoyant relationship.

--- EXTRA CREDIT ---

Get out of your head and into your body. Invite your spouse to set aside your relationship issues for a while to join you for a morning of horseback riding, lunch in a quaint, nearby town, and an afternoon of exploring. Reach for his hand. Share tender kisses. When you feel brave, dare to explore uncharted spaces that exist between you.

MAKE DINNER WHEN
SHE'S WORKING LATE

Little Jack Horner sat in a corner, /Eating his Christmas pie: He put in his thumb, and pulled out a plum, /And said, what a good boy am I! —Old English rhyme

Lend a hand on the nights that your wife must work late. Even if the only cooking you do is opening a can and heating the contents in a bowl, most likely it will be appreciated. Throw together a salad. Put out a loaf of French bread with bottles of dipping oil and balsamic vinegar, and you'll score extra points. If you know your way around the kitchen and see cooking as an extreme sport, go all out and prepare osso buco Milanese and saffron risotto with a Caprese salad.

How about a chocolate opera cake or fresh pears steamed in port for dessert? Okay, that might be a little over the top. You don't want her thinking the worst—for example, that you broke her antique china platter or wrecked the car and are trying to butter her up, as they say, to soften the news.

— EXTRA CREDIT —

Make double quantities of five different casseroles, such as lasagna, Mexican tamale casserole, tuna noodle casserole, hamburger pasta, or other type of meal for each day in the work week and freeze them. You can defrost and reheat for quick, delicious entrée during the week. You'll discover that it's a great time management strategy and takes the guesswork out of figuring out dinner.

DAY 132

DATE NIGHT

Take her bowling for half the price. Find deals online or contact your local bowling alleys for special deals. Some include a pitcher of beer and a couple of games. What could be more fun than to work on your game with the love of your life? Later you might even offer to show her a little jaw-dropping action at home.

WORK ON YOUR
BILLS AS A COUPLE

Money is in some respects like fire; it is a very excellent servant but a terrible master. —P.T. Barnum, *The Art of Money Getting*

Paying bills might seem like a one-person activity, but when your spouse is in the dark about the family finances, the end result can be stress, confusion, and money issues in your marriage. If talking about finances is more difficult for you and your spouse than talking about sex, try working on your bills together. Even if only one spouse is responsible for paying most of the bills, it's important for the other spouse to know where the money is going.

Also, the person in your marriage who handles the finances may feel unduly burdened, whereas sharing the concerns and the financial commitments you've made together can ease that strain. You'll both feel reassured to know that as a couple you are sticking to your budget. Paying bills together can provide a way to strengthen your financial goals and ensure that you and your spouse both understand your current financial picture and have a sense of what your future financial situation might be.

> ── EXTRA CREDIT ──
>
> Track your spending for two weeks. At the end of that period, schedule a time when the two of you can talk frankly about your bills, the budget, and saving for the unexpected.

LEARN DISCIPLINE
STRATEGIES

The real menace in dealing with a five-year-old is that in no time at all you begin to sound like a five-year-old. —Jean Kerr, "How to Get the Best of Your Children," *Please Don't Eat the Daisies*

Legislate that golden rule, "Do unto others as you would have others do unto you" to guide the discipline strategies in your home. Successful discipline of children requires a strong commitment to a family culture of absolute, inviolable respect for each member's safety and well-being. This commitment to assuring that everyone in your family gets the same level of physical and emotional safety translates into a zero tolerance for verbal or physical assaults made to or from anyone in the family. The unbreakable commitment to respect and safety must first be lived by parents within the marital relationship. Here are a few other pointers.

- Don't give up your authority or bargain with your children.
- Don't discipline your children until you are calm and without anger.
- Set clear limits.
- Make simple, clear statements.
- Emphasize the positive.

Remember that parental discipline leads children to self-discipline; eventually they will be empowered by their own self-control.

--- EXTRA CREDIT ---

Good behavior can also be reinforced in children through the books you read to them and with them. Find age-appropriate books that reinforce the message of respect and good behavior and read them with your children.

HUNT FOR
BARGAINS

Shopping is a woman thing . . . the noisy crowds, the danger of being trampled to death, and the ecstasy of the purchase. —Erma Bombeck, American humorist and newspaper columnist

Don't keep all the shopping fun to yourself. Turn your search for a bargain into a treasure-hunting adventure with your spouse. Explore the yards of the families participating in a block sale. Dig through the contents of cardboard boxes at a garage sale. Paw over tables at a church white elephant sale. Attend a farm auction. Or drop in on a twins' club exchange for parents of multiples, where they trade or sell the furniture and clothes that their babies or toddlers have outgrown. Or, clip coupons and head to the nearest department store to locate that special discounted item. Surf the Internet for the item you seek.

While you are focusing on that one special bargain, the real treasure will be the time that you carve from your busy schedules to do something fun together. Whenever possible, consider recycled items from consignment shops, church charity thrift stores, and city flea markets.

--- EXTRA CREDIT ---

Check out *www.freecycle.org*. It's an organization that focuses on reducing waste that goes into landfills and instead provides the means for people to get recycled products from within their own communities. Membership is free.

TAKE A NUTRITION
CLASS TOGETHER

In cooking you've got to have a what-the-hell attitude. —Julia Child,
American-born cookbook author and television personality

As married couples age, they are likely to put on the pounds together.
Learning how to eat intelligently is akin to learning how to care for your
car; your body is the vehicle in which you travel through life. You and
your spouse undoubtedly want each other to be around for a long time.
To do that, you have take care of yourselves and maintain a healthy
immune system.

Know what is in the modern packaged food products. They often
have many different additives to preserve, enhance flavor, maintain or
alter texture, and are fortified with vitamins and minerals. It's likely you
don't even know what you've put into your body if your food sources
aren't fresh but rather packaged and otherwise preserved. Understand the
nutrition your body needs to stay fit and healthy as well as the nutrient
values of all types of food, such as sources of protein, vegetables, fruits,
nuts, legumes, and fats? It might be time to think about signing up for
a nutrition class offered at a local hospital, community college, or even
through a park and recreation department.

— EXTRA CREDIT —

Subscribe to an online group that focuses on nutrition and other health issues. Forum
users can post questions and receive responses from subscribers of specific user
groups on the worldwide online bulletin boards. Google makes it easy with many
group topics, such as health/fitness, health/medicine, conditions and diseases, and
several on nutrition. See http://groups.google.com.

POSTPONE ORGASM TO
HEIGHTEN ANTICIPATION

Speed passion's ebb as you greet its flow, —To have,—to hold,—and,—
in time,—let go! —Laurence Hope, India's Love Lyrics, "The Teak Forest"

A good way to extend and heighten your sense of pleasure during sexual intercourse is by delaying orgasm. Although the experience of orgasm is highly individualistic from one person to another, the duration of an orgasm always depends on the amount of neurotransmitters released in the brain. Like water that spurts out of a suddenly punctured bottle, there is a finite amount of neurotransmitter supply that can be released.

In the pre-orgasmic period of lovemaking, couples can slow the tempo to increase their pleasure and heighten anticipation of that eventual release. Some men have a more difficult time having an orgasm than others. This is great for prolonged sex, but not very satisfying for the man who feels as though he can't let go into the orgasmic bliss. For this man, use positions that feel empowering and experiment with new, exciting positions, too. Touch your mate lovingly and use your hands to brush the sexual energy into his heart area to remind him that he is loved and that he can relax and let go.

—— EXTRA CREDIT ——

The ultimate is to have orgasms together, at the same time. This is something that is difficult for most couples and is not necessary for a healthy, exciting sex life. Still, in the adventure of sex, it is something that can be easily accomplished if you are seasoned lovers and take the time to develop the capacity for it.

MAKE A FAMILY
BUDGET

Life is a progress from want to want, not from enjoyment to enjoyment.
—Samuel Johnson, English critic, poet, and essayist

Creating a budget may not sound like much fun, but try to see past the work to the completion of it. Think how happy you'll feel knowing that as a couple you have a bible to follow to control family finances and ease any financial stresses your marriage may be suffering. Make sure that it works for day-to-day and month-to-month money management in your household.

Include the following items from the "Yours," "Mine," or "Our" money pots: Mortgage or rent payment, food, transportation expenses (car loan payments, gas, maintenance, and car insurance, as well as public transportation), home or renter's insurance, utilities, health and dental insurance and expenses, taxes, student loan payments, and savings (child's education) or retirement plan contribution. Add other items as necessary.

Hug and kiss each other when you're done. You've just taken the first big step in controlling your financial future.

— EXTRA CREDIT —

Have some fun with your spouse in creating a budget for your next family vacation. Include categories such as hotel, gas, meals, entertainment, shopping, tips, and the like. Encourage each family member to be responsible for sticking to the budget.

DATE NIGHT

Invite your spouse to join you in playing a money-related board game like Monopoly, Cashflow 101, Modern Art, The Game of Life, or Acquire. Although they all are relatively simple to play, each imparts financial lessons that can be applied to real life. So grab a plate of fruit, popcorn, or other favorite snack and spend the evening playing smart with your sexy other half.

NEGOTIATE THE
LOWEST PRICE

You must be fully prepared to lose a great deal to make a great deal.
—Anonymous

Discover how to get great prices on just about everything through the art of haggling. If you and your spouse have never tried negotiating for the lowest possible price on something you wanted, it's never too late to get started. The dollars you save could lighten your heart and feed the family cookie jar. And having more financial freedom can ease stress on a marriage.

Remember to always be nice and avoid an audience of other buyers who might be near enough to hear you asking the seller to come down in price. In department stores and outlets, start by looking for imperfections and damaged goods and asking for a deal on them. Don't be embarrassed. Stay focused. Do your homework to see what the competition's price is for the same product. Try asking, "Is that the best deal you can give me?" or "Is that your absolute lowest price?" or "Can you lower the price if I give you all cash, right here and now?"

--- EXTRA CREDIT ---

Remember the answer is always no until you ask, and that you have to ask in order to find out whether or not you might actually get a better deal. Practice the art of haggling (negotiating) first with your spouse, then try it out on a merchant. The merchant might not budge on price if he or she senses reticence on your part. On the other hand, you might just receive a bigger discount than you expected.

ESCHEW
ULTIMATUMS

The love we have in our youth is superficial compared to the love that an old man has for his old wife. —Will Durant, American historian and writer

Before issuing an ultimatum to the person you love, consider whether or not it builds marital trust or in any way fosters a sense of teamwork. Marriage is about partnering. Ultimatum issuers are not thinking about the power of their togetherness but rather demanding something they want. If the other spouse doesn't conform, for example, to the change desired by the spouse issuing the ultimatum, neither spouse will be happy, and that doesn't build trust or love. It's as if your spouse has become your adversary instead of the other half of your team.

Learn to negotiate, bargain, and resolve conflict in other ways, but avoid demanding that things be "either/or." Find some way to reconnect with each other and to get down to the business of making the marriage work better for both of you. Marriage relationship expert Barbara De Angelis has noted that "the real act of marriage takes place in the heart . . . and it's a choice you make, not just on your wedding day, but over and over again . . . reflected in the way you treat your husband or wife."

— EXTRA CREDIT —

Apologize for something you've said or done that you know has hurt your spouse's feelings. Retrench from an intractable position that you secretly assumed. Show your spouse over and over again that you deeply love him or her and that your marriage is as important today as it was on your wedding day.

LET HIM HAVE
A MAN CAVE

All marriages are happy. It's the living together afterward that causes all the trouble. —Raymond Hull, Canadian playwright, television screenwriter, and lecturer

Back in the day when cavemen, hunting for food, found a wild beast, they clobbered it with their clubs and dragged the animal back to their caves to devour it. In modern times, men still want their caves—exclusive spaces in their home just for them—where they can hang out and do what they love. Some retreat to the man cave to watch weekend sports shows on a big-screen television. A small refrigerator or bar stocked with snacks and beverages is often de rigueur in a man cave. Other men don't care about the bar; they want a place to display trophies they acquired playing football, baseball, basketball, volleyball, golf, tennis, or something else that involved guys and games. Some men just use the man cave to play their guitars and drums in a soundproof music room, work out on a punching bag, lift weights, enjoy movies in a home theater, or indulge a lifelong love of collectibles.

No matter what his interests, encourage your husband to create his own man cave and help him. He'll likely invite you into his cave to watch a movie, have a brew, or hear the latest rock 'n' roll tune he's mastered. You just might discover he's happier and more fulfilled having that man cave than before he had it. The two of you could be on your way to creating some fantastic memories. Just think of the happiness shared by Fred and Wilma Flintstone.

—— EXTRA CREDIT ——

Surf the Internet for visual images of man caves. Get more ideas from the DIY (Do It Yourself) network. It regularly airs a show about man caves and how to create them. See www.diynetwork.com/man-caves/show/index.html.

WORK WITH A CREDIT
COUNSELING FIRM TO END DEBT

A small debt produces a debtor; a large one, an enemy. —Publilius Syrus, Latin writer

The average American family with at least one credit card carries roughly $10,700 debt with a double-digit interest rate, according to a 2010 report on CNN Money.com. As people in debt are usually worried about it, reducing your debt will help the two of you relax and enjoy life. Here is how you can manage spending and debt:

- Limit spending.
- Know exactly what your money is spent on.
- Pay down your debts with the highest interest rate first.
- Plan ahead for the unexpected and save enough to live on for several months.
- Seek professional guidance quickly when you are in trouble.

Consider enlisting the help of a professional credit counseling organization—a third party to help you. Make sure the company you work with is a nonprofit and that no fees are required upfront. Avoid companies that tell you they will settle your debt for pennies on the dollar.

— EXTRA CREDIT —

Request your credit score from one of the three reporting companies—Experian, Equifax, or TransUnion. Your credit score is used by banks and other lenders to determine the interest rates they will offer you when issuing a mortgage or credit cards. A copy of your credit score costs $15, but copies of your credit reports are free.

SHARE PARENTING
CHORES

There was never a child so lovely but his mother was glad to get him to sleep. —Ralph Waldo Emerson, *Journals*

It's vital to agree on how you are going to share the work of parenting, because it is a 24/7 job requiring teamwork. You and your spouse are both going to be tired at the end of the day, whether you both hold down jobs or one of you is staying home to care for your child. The issue of a fair way to share parenting chores inevitably comes up.

Studies show that marital satisfaction drops significantly after the birth of the first child. This is mainly due to a lack of mental and emotional preparation, especially on the part of the husband, who doesn't realize (until he's feeling neglected and miserable) that it is entirely normal during the first six to twelve months after a new baby arrives for the husband to move into the number two slot in his wife's attentions and affections. Fortunately, this situation usually balances out again as your child gets older. Parenting while also finding time for each other is a balancing act that you and your spouse will have to work through, and you will. Just give yourselves the twin gifts of time and understanding.

— EXTRA CREDIT —

Buy your wife flowers and fold the baby clothes that are in the dryer or the clean clothes basket. Give your husband the gift of a long nap. Such small appreciative acts can shift attitudes in a house of overworked, overtired parents.

CONSIDER HUMANITARIAN
RELIEF WORK

For those who wish to climb the mountain of spiritual awareness, the path is selfless work. —The Bhagavad Gita

Couples who engage in charitable work or service make themselves and the world a better place. If you and your spouse feel the urge to help others, perhaps less fortunate than you, don't hesitate to get involved. The earthquake in Haiti in January 2010 spurred people all over the world to help in any way they could. Perhaps you and your spouse were among those who made donations.

Many societies have a history of religious and cultural traditions that include charitable giving or personal sacrifice for the good of someone else without seeking recognition for it. Find some charity or charitable work that has meaning for you both and get involved. Two people, a couple, whose hearts beat as one, sharing a common vision, can make a huge difference in the lives of others. Indeed, they are sharing a part of their lives with others, perhaps people they don't even know.

—— EXTRA CREDIT ——

Look up the meaning of "humanism." You will find that it is a moral philosophy that places emphasis on humans helping humans, in contrast to relying completely on a higher power or supernatural authority. Humanists rally around issues of human rights, reproductive rights, gender equality, and social justice.

DATE NIGHT

Go to the video store, rent several comedies on DVD, and pick up a pizza.
Spend the evening curled up in bed with your mate. Laugh heartily. Medical researchers and scientists say that laughter causes the brain to release
certain "feel good" chemicals that strengthen the immune system and lower
blood pressure. So laugh yourselves silly—it's good for you.

SEEK PROFESSIONAL ADVICE
WHEN BUYING A HOME

I long, as does every human being, to be at home wherever I find myself.
—Maya Angelou, American poet

Buying a home together is one of the happiest, most exciting things you will do as a couple. However, the process can put you on an emotional roller coaster, not just because it is one of the most expensive purchases you will make as a twosome, but because there are so many aspects of it that can get complicated. Seek the advice of a professional real estate agent or broker and engage the services of a licensed home inspector to examine the house for any problems with the construction, foundation, roof, and major systems such as electrical, plumbing, and heating/air conditioning before you buy. Becoming knowledgeable about the process will lessen the opportunity for misunderstandings and confusion that can lead to arguments.

Certainly, factors such as price and what you are getting for that price will necessarily influence your decision to buy. To learn more about the process, go to *http://portal.hud.gov/portal/page/portal/HUD/topics/buying_a_home.*

FLIRT MORNING,
NOON, AND NIGHT

All women are flirts, but some are restrained by shyness, and others by
sense. —François de La Rochefoucauld, French author

If you have ever visited Miami, the Gateway to Latin America, you know
that there's just something sexy about Latin American men and women,
young and old alike. Many exhibit such self-confidence in their own
sexual appeal that you have to admire their lack of inhibition and their
seemingly innate ability to flirt. You see young men flirting with women
young and old; old men flirting with their wives.

Flirting doesn't have to stop just because you're married. Couples
who've been together for a while develop a kind of shorthand to tele-
graph to each other their interest or sexual desire. It could be a certain a
look, a lifting of an eyebrow, a deep sigh, a mischievous smile, or some
other way, using body language. If sex isn't on your mind, but lighthearted flirtation is, go ahead and get your game on. It lets your spouse
know that he or she still finds you attractive, interesting, and desirable.

—— EXTRA CREDIT ——

Flirt with your spouse in places he or she doesn't expect it, for example, at church
or in the supermarket. Rub up against him in the aisle of Home Depot and say in
your sexiest, playful voice, "I could go for you in a big way. Care to do some heavy
petting right here, right now?"

BUILD SPOUSAL TRUST
FOR FINANCIAL DECISIONS

Money is better than poverty, if only for financial reasons. —Woody Allen, American screenwriter

It's fairly common in many marriages for only one spouse to handle the family finances, even though the big decisions usually are made together. It's a good idea that the one who doesn't handle the finances stays fully apprised of how much money is coming in, how much is being spent, and how much is being saved or invested. That way, you're on the same page about your financial present and future. Jointly preparing your business profit and loss statement, your personal tax documents, balancing the checkbook, or working on the family budget can spark discussions about finances.

Build spousal support and trust for the financial decisions that one of you (or both) makes by having regular discussions about money. Learn to do online banking. Discover how to check balances in your accounts whenever you want. Ensure that family financial information is transparent and accessible to both spouses at all times.

—— EXTRA CREDIT ——

Assemble a family financial binder. Insert pages with tabs to section off monthly statements from banks, credit card companies, and investment accounts. Although you will want your spouse to have access to bank account numbers, security questions, passwords, and information on how to log on to your online accounts, keep that information private in locked drawer, file cabinet, or safe.

MAKE YOUR SPOUSE CHICKEN SOUP WHEN HE'S SICK

Worries go down better with soup than without. —Jewish proverb

It turns out that the advice mothers and grandmothers have been dis-
pensing for generations—actually since roughly the twelfth century—
about chicken soup being good for you when you're sick with a cold is
true. Research suggests that the soup may actually reduce inflammation
associated with the common cold. In addition, the steam can soothe
irritated throats and stuffy noses. Finally, soup is a source of fluid for an
ailing body fighting infection. So give your spouse a generous helping of
love in the form of a steamy bowl of chicken soup the next time allergies,
a cold, or the flu takes hold.

--- EXTRA CREDIT ---

For really great chicken soup, drop a whole chicken (rinsed and patted dry) into a
large soup pot along with enough water to cover it. Add chopped carrots, celery,
and onions, salt, pepper, and a bit of chopped fresh Italian parsley, and simmer for
several hours. The chicken will fall off the bone. The vegetables and chicken will
produce a lovely stock and the strained soup will be both fragrant and tasty.

STAY HOME FROM WORK TO
BE WITH YOUR SICK SPOUSE

Heaviness in the heart of man maketh it stoop: but a good word maketh it glad. —Proverbs 12:25

You know how awful it is to catch the nasty bug that's been going around the office. So when your spouse gets sick, consider taking the day off to care for him. When your body is suddenly laid low by an infection, the warm, fuzzy feeling imparted by the kind words and loving attention of a spouse is better than a shot of brandy or a warm pair of cashmere bed socks.

While you're home, tidy up the bedroom, stack magazines he enjoys next to the bed, and be sure to stock up on Kleenex!

The following list itemizes things you and your spouse can do to minimize the risk of getting sick:

- Wash your hands frequently; it helps to stop the spread of germs
- Eat a well-balanced diet
- Exercise
- Get plenty of rest
- Encourage people who are coughing to cover their mouths so droplets are not spread

> ## —— EXTRA CREDIT ——
>
> Encourage your spouse to join you in getting the flu shot each year to avoid contracting the flu. If you do get it, even though you've had the shot (and some people do), it is likely that you will only suffer a mild case of it.

TREAT HIM
TO A PEDICURE

The real sin against life is to abuse and destroy beauty, even one's own—
even more, one's own, for that has been put in our care and we are
responsible for its well-being. —Katherine Anne Porter, Pulitzer Prize–winning
American writer

You love to be pampered and so does your man, whether he admits it or not! Think of how you both can get what you enjoy. Book an appointment for pedicures for yourself and your mate at your favorite nail salon. Pick up coffee on the way there. While the salon's staff go to work on your feet, you two can chat together, sip your coffee, and even get a shoulder and back massage if your salon has that type of chair. Or, you can flip through magazines, sharing tidbits of news and interesting information or just hold hands and relax into the experience. Once he shares the experience with you, it's likely he will want to make his-and-her pedicures a regular thing.

—— EXTRA CREDIT ——

Invite your hubby along for an afternoon at the spa with you. Encourage him to get the works—a facial, manicure, and a long, relaxing massage. Who doesn't love being the center of attention? If he's been working a lot and not taking time for the two of you or even himself, retreating from the world into the spa with you for an afternoon will be a much deserved and welcomed break.

DATE NIGHT

Draw a warm bath. Undress your spouse and yourself and crawl into the tub together. Wash each other's hair, massage each other, and soak until your body feels totally relaxed and refreshed. Shower off, dry off each other, and put on fresh pajamas before crawling into bed for the night. Sleep in.

REVEAL YOUR
SEXUAL EXPECTATIONS

Sooner or later, the truth comes to light. —Dutch proverb

Women crave intimacy and are more influenced in their desire for sex by cultural and social factors, whereas men have a stronger sexual desire than women and think about sex more often than women, according to study after study of men's and women's sexual differences. Physicians, psychologists, and sex therapists seem to agree that the first step to achieving your full sexual potential is a no-holds-barred frank discussion about sexual expectations with your partner. Yet, even though many couples desire deeper intimacy, talking about it often proves to be difficult.

Even if you don't talk about your expectations, it's a good bet that you and your spouse fantasize about your sexual desires, so why not skip the guesswork and ask the question, "What arouses you?" and "How often do you want to have sex?" Sex talk can be fun. Dirty sex talk can even get you hot. You might start a frank sexual discussion by asking, "Do you want to have sex once a day or several times a week?" Relationship stress increases when one partner wants sex and the other one doesn't. Understanding what excites each of you and sharing that information with each other can help with arousal issues.

--- EXTRA CREDIT ---

Research books, articles, and Internet sites that focus on the sexual aspects to having a thriving marriage. Share what you've learned with your partner. Marriage and family therapists say that the first step to having a great sex life is finding healthy and positive ways to talk about your partner's and your desires. Open the conversation with an interesting fact as a point of departure into discussion, or even write out a questionnaire for you and your spouse to complete. Discuss your answers with each other.

HELP YOUR SPOUSE
TO THE SHOWER

But a $6,000 shower curtain? Even if cleanliness is next to godliness, isn't that kinda steep? —*Los Angeles Times* (August 9, 2002)

If your spouse is returning from a long flight, getting over the flu, or just needs a moment of pampering, help him take a shower. You can turn on the shower until the temperature is warm (but not too hot), put soap and shampoo in reach, fetch some fresh towels and a washcloth, and set out clean underwear and pajamas or clothes.

When he's finished bathing, offer to rub him down with a warm towel and dry his hair. Of course, he may feel up to doing those things himself, but more than likely he'll be secretly delighted that you offered.

—— EXTRA CREDIT ——

Depending on how he feels after his shower (alert or tired and sleepy), set the programming on the radio, television, or CD player to material that either interests him or will help him relax.

FIND CHARITY WORK
YOU LOVE TO DO

Do something wonderful, people may imitate it. —Dr. Albert Schweitzer, German humanitarian, physician, and theologian

Set the example for your children and others through charity work. Perhaps, if you are like some couples who enjoy volunteering together, the two of you volunteer at a local soup kitchen during Thanksgiving and Christmas each year. Or you pack boxes of food for Second Harvest to be given to needy families. Perhaps you walk for the American Heart Association to raise money for research. Whatever you do, you are both eager to change a bleak present into a bright future for others. That is the noble work of Bill and Melinda Gates and their charitable foundation. In his annual letter, Bill Gates noted that in times of economic downturns, the neediest suffer the most.

Volunteering in charity work that you both love is another thread that renders a meaningful pattern in the tapestry of your married life. Volunteering gives your lives meaning and purpose. There are a million reasons why you should do it, but few that justify not volunteering if you can. An added benefit is that your children may be inspired to emulate your endeavors.

—— EXTRA CREDIT ——

Read books on how to turn your passion into profits, products, services, humanitarian aid, or change in the world in some way. Check out the book *1001 Ways to Do Good* (Adams Media). It is full of ideas about allowing your passion to do good works, including some that cost you nothing but that can make a big difference to others.

EXPLORE SEXUAL
THOUGHTS AND FEELINGS

Love is a cunning weaver of fantasies and fables. —Sappho, ancient Greek poet

Imagined in the minds of lovers, powerful fantasies can be the prelude to incredible sex. Indeed, the mind may be the most erogenous zone of all. Some people report being capable of having orgasm solely through fantasizing, without any accompanying physical stimulation. If you haven't been using your mind to help get you turned on, you should consider giving it more focus. This is particularly true if you have any difficulty sustaining arousal or achieving orgasm. Sexual thoughts and feelings come in many forms. Here are a few:

- Being in love or lust and thinking about the object of your desire.
- Mental images of something or someone that turns you on.
- Fantasies of something erotic happening to you.
- Fantasies of witnessing something erotic.
- Anticipating sexual touch by yourself or another.
- Anticipating a sexual encounter with someone you lust after.

— EXTRA CREDIT —

Crawl between the sheets before bed while your lover is in the shower and begin your fantasy. Use any or all of the six items from this list to shift away from the cares of the world into a magical, sensual, erotic fantasy world. When your spouse slips into bed beside you, keep the fantasy going while playing it out to completion with him or her.

MASSAGE YOUR
SPOUSE'S ACHING MUSCLES

It is in moments of illness that we are compelled to recognize that we live not alone but chained to a creature of a different kingdom, whole worlds apart, who has no knowledge of us and by whom it is impossible to make ourselves understood: our body. —Marcel Proust, French novelist, critic, and essayist

If your spouse works a difficult manual job or has just completed an afternoon of tough yard work, he might be suffering from muscular aches and pains. If so, offer to give him a massage. Ask your spouse if it would be okay to use some massage oil, perhaps one associated with mood elevation, such as lemon oil, or relaxation, such as lavender. Since long before biblical times, fragrant oils and spices were used for healing. Twelfth-century mystic Hildegard von Bingen wrote about herbs and medicinal plants in her book *Physica* and used their oils in healing. Your partner might even start feeling a little frisky during the massage. And while you want to finish the massage you started, a little fooling around couldn't hurt . . . could it?

— EXTRA CREDIT —

Set the mood for a long, sensuous massage by dimming the lights or using candles and putting some relaxing instrumental music on the iPod. Put your scented massage oils or body butters in a basket within easy reach. Warm the palms of your hands by vigorously rubbing them together before touching your lover's body. Keep the parts of his body that you are not massaging covered with a sheet so he doesn't get the shivers, which will cause his muscles to tense. You want him nice and relaxed.

SUPPLY INTERESTING
READING MATERIAL

The mind, once expanded to the dimensions of larger ideas, never returns to its original size. —Oliver Wendell Holmes Jr., American jurist

Sometimes you read a newspaper article or a magazine feature that makes you think of your spouse. Instead of letting the connection fall by the wayside, take a moment to be sure you share that story with him or her—either e-mail a link or cut out the story. If you hear a book review that would pique her interest or learn of a new magazine that's right up his alley, take the initiative to give the book or subscription as a gift. When you stimulate each other's intellectual curiosity and show interest in your spouse's interests, the scope of the conversation between you enlarges.

—— EXTRA CREDIT ——

Make her a hot toddy or tea toddy to sip while your spouse looks at the reading material. Find recipes for the hot toddy (often made with honey, hot water, lemon juice and whiskey or other type of alcohol), tea toddy (made with tea), and endless variations on the Internet. A good-quality bourbon will impart a vanilla sweetness to a hot toddy. Brandy, scotch, and rum (as in hot buttered rum) are other good choices for a relaxing hot drink mixture.

DATE NIGHT

Take her out for a smoothie. She can choose from any number of heavenly blended drink combinations, based on fruits and also vegetables with added ingredients such as honey, ice, frozen fruit, frozen yogurt, and various combinations of other healthy ingredients, including herbs, vitamins, protein powder, and other nutritional supplements.

TOLERATE YOUR
SPOUSE'S COMPLAINTS

When you have no choice, mobilize the spirit of courage. —Jewish proverb

Everyone does it sometimes. Cut her some slack. Maybe she had a bad day at work, the cashier at the grocery store was rude, or the kids have been under her skin all day. She may snap, bark, moan, groan, and complain about everything under the sun. Resist the urge to point it out to her. It's not likely to remedy the situation. It could even make things worse.

Best bet? Just relax, tune out what you can, and let it go. You knew at times she could turn into a Wendy Whiner, but you loved and married her anyway.

--- EXTRA CREDIT ---

Suggest that your spouse utilize her mind/body connection and entertain ideas of robust health and happy times rather than think about how angry she feels.

REPLACE "YOU" MESSAGES WITH "I" STATEMENTS

It takes two to quarrel, but only one to end it. —Spanish proverb

Using "you" messages (such as, "You always forget my birthday!" or "You're so sloppy!") can come across to your spouse as blaming, and they will have the effect of putting your partner on the defensive. Moreover, as you utter the statement, you may actually feel that you are somewhat defenseless.

It's better to try to replace those "you" messages with "I" statements such as, "I feel _____ (name an emotion, such as hurt, anger, frustration, resentful) when you _____. I want _____ (state behavior change you seek from your partner)." Your partner should clearly understand your emotion, why you are feeling it, and what he or she can do about it.

— EXTRA CREDIT —

If you have trouble verbally expressing your concerns using "I" statements, use a different tack to communicate your issue with your spouse. In a note or letter, clearly state the problem as you see it. As succinctly as possible, explain the emotions you feel as a result of your mate's attitude, action, avoidance, or inaction.

DON'T GOSSIP ABOUT YOUR SPOUSE'S FRUSTRATIONS

Loose lips sink ships. —World War II slogan

During World War II, there were many sayings and slogans warning people to be discreet with information that could be seen as vital to protecting American interests. In the same way, it's also important for marriage partners to keep the trust their spouses have placed in them. You are your partner's most trusted ally; your spouse can feel safe in venting or discussing job frustrations with you and knows it won't go any further. Interestingly, according to some studies, business leaders who face difficulty at work value trust over objectivity when turning to their spouses for insight and feedback. The business leader's spouse doesn't even have to possess technical knowledge or business expertise.

We live and work in worlds populated by friends, acquaintances, family members, and coworkers, and those people often are separated only by degrees. It really is a small world. Although a friend or relative might want to know all the latest gossip, don't share your spouse's frustrations with his or her job. That's no one else's business.

— EXTRA CREDIT —

Give your spouse the gift of mindfulness. Be attentive to every aspect of your relationship with him. Notice how you listen, how you speak, whether or not you thoughtfully choose your words or just utter whatever your mind is thinking. Do you ever remain silent or think about silence as a good thing and the best response in certain situations? When you practice mindfulness, your focus is on only one thing at a time.

ENSURE A SMOOTH
RUNNING FAMILY

Drag your thoughts away from your troubles . . . by the ears, by the heels, or any other way you can manage it. —Mark Twain, American humorist and writer

When you are fearful or stressed out, your children are, too, but the stress and fear can be magnified because of their vivid imaginations. In addition, children often attribute your suffering to something they did, so they are bearing the burden of guilt for what you are feeling. Some of the ways you and your spouse can help children overcome fears, worry, and stress include the following:

- Take a break from the negative news—turn off or limit time spent listening to the news from television, radio, and other electronic devices.
- Spend time with your children in nature.
- Meditate and de-stress with your children.
- Pray together to the higher power that your family believes in.
- Encourage your children to talk with you and your spouse about their concerns and fears.
- Read joke books (laughter is a great de-stressor).

— EXTRA CREDIT —

If you have a blended family, join a blended family support group and talk about the kinds of stresses your family is going through. Discuss how to help children heal their broken hearts, which can be the result of factors such as the breakup of your or your spouse's previous marriage or the death of a previous spouse, not feeling a sense of belonging in the new family, loss or lack of trust in your new partner, non-bonding with new step-siblings, and the like.

KEEP A SHOPPING
LIST ON THE FRIDGE

The whole industry of human life is employed not in procuring the supply of our three humble necessities, food, clothes, and lodging, but in procuring the conveniences of it according to the nicety and delicacy of our tastes. —Adam Smith, Scottish philosopher and economist

Keep a master shopping list on the fridge that can be pulled off by you or your spouse for a quick dash to the market. Having a list and maintaining it is your best bet for not forgetting foodstuffs and other important staples—like dish detergent, facial tissue, toilet paper, and other household products that often need replenishing. Teach other family members to update the list, adding their favorite items. That way, you have whatever you need always on hand. Think of the master shopping list as the means to avoiding marital and family discord.

— EXTRA CREDIT —

Ask your spouse to help you expand the shopping list idea. Generate a computerized list of the items you most commonly use and need to buy at the store. Or, go to *www.grocerywiz.com* and using the website's free grocery list, customize it to your needs. While there, you can also download coupons from coupon galleries. With your other half, create wish lists, Christmas lists, and other types of shopping lists using the same concept.

KEEP YOUR
BEDDING CLEAN

Sleep faster, we need the pillows. —Jewish proverb

She knows you love her when she gets up to use the shower and comes back to find clean linen on the bed. A spouse who is busy or stressed won't be thinking much about how clean the bed or bedroom is. That's why it is so special for you to pull off the entire bed linen change while she's in the bathroom. Returning to a fresh, clean bed will lift her spirits a little. Tuck her in and then lie down beside her to whisper sweet words of love in her ear. She'll adore that you went to extraordinary lengths for her comfort.

— EXTRA CREDIT —

Buy her an elegant cotton matelassé coverlet for the bed. Cotton, they say, breathes and looks fresh and clean on the bed.

DATE NIGHT

Take her out for a live performance of classical Indian Kathak dance. The nuanced facial expressions, complex footwork, and hand movements, along with the gorgeous costumes, make the Kathak a visual and auditory feast. Like the tempo of lovemaking, the Kathak dance goes from slow to fast, ending in climax.

PUT YOURSELF
IN HIS SHOES

He who incites strife is worse than he who takes part in it. —Aesop, "The Trumpeter Taken Prisoner," Fables

It's a given that you can forcefully argue your side, so try switching sides to debate your partner's viewpoint. Ask your partner to present your side. Call each other by pet names to keep the conversation friendly. Reasoning through both sides of an issue can help the two of you stay on friendly terms at the beginning, middle, and end of the process.

When a married couple discovers that they are fighting more than making love, it's worth the time, effort, and emotional energy to explore why the relationship has become contentious and what can be done to re-establish harmony. He sees the glass half empty and she sees it half full, but both know that whatever the glass held, a portion is gone and a portion is left. That's the place to start—find something you can agree upon.

— EXTRA CREDIT —

Avoid the three worst tactics that husbands and wives sometimes use rather than directly addressing the subject and staying on point: oversimplifying the problem, changing the subject, and circular reasoning (in which an unproven point is used to prove a point).

UNDERSTAND YOUR
OWN AROUSAL MAP

Only the united beat of sex and heart together can create ecstasy. —Anaïs
Nin, French-born American author

Your arousal map is like a unique map of your body where nerve endings, delicate areas that are highly sensitive, and specific erogenous zones are all interconnected in ways that, when stimulated, turn you on. It contains all the fantasies and activities you find sexually arousing. Understanding your own arousal maps makes it possible for you and your spouse to communicate that knowledge to each other. Here are some questions that will help each of you to gain more understanding about your respective unique arousal maps:

- When have you felt the most desire or pleasure?
- What places, times of day, or partners have aroused you the most?
- How is your current sexual life similar to or different from your past sexual life?
- What things currently increase or decrease your desire?
- What is the perfect erotic situation for you?

— EXTRA CREDIT —

Tell your spouse the perfect erotic situation for you and what turns you on. Invite him to help you fulfill that erotic fantasy. Then do the same for his perfect erotic situation. Know you both have superior knowledge about each other's turn-ons can lift your lovemaking to new heights.

PUT OUT AN EXTRA
BLANKET ON A COLD NIGHT

Sleep to the sick is half health. —German proverb

When cold winter nights roll around and your spouse is reading on the couch, show him you care by fetching a warm blanket to keep him warm. Get your best Italian-made washable cashmere blanket out of the hope chest, or find the sports-themed fleece he loves. This is, after all the man you love more than any other in the world, and he deserves the best.

—— EXTRA CREDIT ——

Strip naked, crawl under the covers, and press up against your spouse. Body-to-body contact gets the temperature rising. . . .and sometimes the tent pole, too, if you know what I mean! But, hey, it is an important survival technique!

RUB HER ALL OVER WITH
SCENTED BODY BUTTER

He who enjoys good health is rich, though he knows it not. —Italian proverb

Offer to give her a full-body butter rub. Body butters are used to moisturize skin and come unscented as well as in a variety of scents that include rose, lemon-sage, citrus-lime, cocoa butter, papaya, lemon-sugar, orchid, and lotus nut, to name a few.

To start, ask her lie on her stomach. Apply a dollop of body butter just below her neck, between her shoulder blades. Begin massaging the butter over her shoulders and down her arms and hands, then back to the point where you started. From there, work your way down her back, along her side, and over each buttock. Next, focus on working the butter into her thigh, leg, and foot. Complete one leg and then the other.

If possible, keep one hand on her body at all times (a tip from a massage therapist). It keeps you connected.

— EXTRA CREDIT —

Read her poetry composed by her favorite poet, or essays by an essayist she respects, or take her on a languidly romantic journey through a narrative by her favorite travel writer.

CALL YOUR SPOUSE
OFTEN FROM WORK

Time is/ Too slow for those who wait,/ Too swift for those who fear,/ Too long for those who grieve,/ Too short for those who rejoice; /But for those who love,/ Time is . —Henry van Dyke, "For Katrina's Sun-Dial"

If you've used up all your paid time off and you've got an important meeting scheduled with your boss, team members, and an out-of-town delegation, you simply can't bail. But your spouse is getting a root canal. Just because you are knee-deep in strategizing with your coworkers doesn't mean you can't step away for a minute every so often to place a phone call or send a text message to your poor partner. He'll appreciate those one-minute pick-me-ups from you. It lets him know that although your mind is on business, he's in your thoughts, too.

—— EXTRA CREDIT ——

Send a get-well message from your cell or Blackberry. Or, on your computer, select a musical card to send to your spouse.

BUY HIM A NEW TOOTHBRUSH

The first thing I do in the morning is brush my teeth and sharpen my tongue.
—Dorothy Parker, American short story writer and poet

Have you ever stopped to consider the millions of bacteria that your toothbrushes harbor? Keep your mouths fresh and healthy for a lifetime of kisses by maintaining good dental hygiene and taking care of your toothbrushes. It's not glamorous, but it's important! Doctors and dentists warn that bacteria from unhealthy gums can get into your bloodstream and show up elsewhere in your body and make you ill. Luckily, you can effectively kill those bacteria if you soak the toothbrush in Listerine or other antibacterial solution for about twenty minutes. Alternatively, you could just buy him a packet of new toothbrushes to use on his pearly whites and toss his old brush. Think of your oral health as reflecting your overall body's health. The changes in one often impacts the other.

—— EXTRA CREDIT ——

Give him the gift of a toothbrush sanitizer. Several popular products available at Target, Wal-Mart, Amazon, Macy's, Brookstone, and Walgreens use germ-killing ultraviolet light for three to ten minutes. One product in particular, the Violight, claims to eliminate up to 99.9 percent of the germs on a toothbrush. Although most are countertop models, some are designed for travel and even come with a travel case for business trips and vacations. Tell him your dental-care gift comes with a kissing option. Then brush your teeth, apply a little lipgloss, and pucker up.

DATE NIGHT

Spend the evening making "dream boards" from sheets of poster paper. Give your heart and mind free rein to create a big dream for yourself or for each other, or for your marriage and your life together. Use words or phrases that you cut from magazines that have potent meanings or relevancy to your dream. Write inspiring quotes. Cut photos, pictures, or other graphic images and use glue sticks to paste them onto your board. Put the board in a home office or someplace where you will see it often.

SLOW DANCE WITH
HER IN PAJAMAS

There's just something about dance, . . . It's like a primal thing in all of us.
—Patrick Swayze, American actor and dancer

There's nothing like a spontaneous slow dance to put you both in the mood. Pull her into your arms as you leave the bed in the morning or prepare to crawl in for the night. Slow dance to a tune you both love and can hum, or take the time to switch on the iPod. Let the music lead you around the room, barefoot or in socks. Caress her hair, hold her firmly, kiss her forehead and move together in any direction that calls to you. Let her feel the strength of your devotion. Since the beginning of time, humans have danced as a means to ease away stiffness, sadness, troubles, tension, suffering, and pain—and to draw closer in an ancient, primal way.

DAY 176

—— EXTRA CREDIT ——
Many cultures, including Native American peoples, experience dance as a way to pray and also gain strength, power, and blessings. Just as dancing feet drum a healing rhythm into the earth, so the dancer draws healing energies from the earth.

MAKE FRESH-SQUEEZED
ORANGE JUICE

An orange on the table, your dress on the rug, and you in my bed, sweet present of the present, cool of the night, warmth of my life. —Jacques Prévert, French poet and screenwriter

On a boring weekend morning when you have some extra time, add something fresh to the breakfast table. Nothing is as good for breakfast as a glass of freshly squeezed O.J.

Buy oranges at the local farmer's market or grocery store. Run them through a juicer or simply cut in half, squeeze out the juice, and strain it into a glass. Serve it at room temperature or chilled.

Orange juice contains naturally occurring beta carotene (a clue is its orange color) and is rich in vitamin C but contains none of the additives juice makers might use—for example, preservatives, sweeteners, and citric acid.

—— EXTRA CREDIT ——

Give her the gift of a juicer so that the two of you can make and have an ample supply of fresh juice, whenever you want it, from fruits and vegetables that you grow yourselves or purchase. Many fruits and veggies are high in antioxidants, those compounds that prevent free radicals (highly reactive molecules) from damaging cells.

SHAKE UP YOUR
DAILY ROUTINE

Boredom: the desire for desires. —Leo Tolstoy, *Anna Karenina*

Married couples necessarily slip into daily routines because of the shared context of their lives. The repetitive patterns of living can become so easy and familiar that they provide a welcome sense of belonging and comfort. But when marital routines trigger boredom in one or both spouses, the couple's relationship might suffer. That's a good sign that it is time to shake things up a little. If you do, there's a good chance that a new dynamic will begin to emerge. Excitement, interest, and intrigue can rapidly improve your relationship.

It only takes one of you to shift boredom into a bodacious roller coaster of romantic fun. For example, try giving him coffee and caresses. Engage in foreplay behind the morning newspaper. Have a kiss-a-thon in the coat closet. Turn the eating of fruit into a suggestive, erotic experience.

— EXTRA CREDIT —

Make your own version of the ancient Eastern-cultures pillow book, not as a sex manual but as an erotic stimulant. Create exotic names for sexual positions that you and your spouse enjoy. Draw artful images (stick figures if that's all you can manage) for lovers' positions that you like. Add erotic pictures from other sources along with sexually charged sayings and any other visuals that stimulate your fantasies. When you and your mate look at your pillow book, it should ignite in you the desire for erotic kissing and touching.

TRY A FORM OF
ANCIENT KISSING

"Sex" is as important as eating or drinking and we ought to allow the one
appetite to be satisfied with as little restraint or false modesty as the other.
—Marquis de Sade, French author of erotic novels

The *Ananda Ranga*, an ancient Indian manual of lovemaking (translated in 1885 by the Englishman Sir Richard F. Burton, two years after
he translated the *Kama Sutra*) is divided into many different sections
that focus on types of embraces, erotic arousal activities such as scratching and biting, and positions for lovemaking or congress. Ten types of
kisses are listed, including one that presumably was meant to defuse and
deflect tension between a husband and his wife so that they could get on
with making love. Since an angry wife won't kiss the face of her husband,
the ancient text says, the husband should fix his lips upon her and keep
their mouths touching until her anger is gone. Surely, there is no reason
a modern wife couldn't try that, too.

The male/female power balance is clearly evident in the writing of the
Ananda Ranga. However, the authors of the *Ananda Ranga* and similar
texts write with seemingly genuine concern that both sexes enjoy expressions of love and sexual pleasure. Whether bored, irritated, annoyed, or
just plain angry, why not try a prolonged kiss to move past the issue?

DAY 179

--- EXTRA CREDIT ---

Advance to a type of kissing known as "oblique kissing" in the *Ananda Ranga*. The
husband (presumably taller than his wife) positions himself beside or directly behind
his spouse. He cups his hand under her chin and pulls upward until she faces the
ceiling or sky. He begins to gently bite or nibble on her lower lip.

SEEK PROFESSIONAL HELP TO
PROTECT FINANCIAL ASSETS

Distress, n. A disease incurred by exposure to the prosperity of a friend.
—Ambrose Bierce, *The Devil's Dictionary*

You and your mate undoubtedly want to prosper—who doesn't?—but navigating the world of financial investment can mean having to learn and comprehend many financial terms that can seem a little overwhelming unless you've studied accounting or economics.

If neither you nor your spouse has the time and energy to begin to navigate the world of financial investing, consider hiring a financial adviser or investment counselor to guide you on how to best protect the assets that you already have or are working to gain. For your joint holdings, choose an investment adviser that you both like and trust. Go together to meet him or sit together to teleconference or videoconference with him. Remember to get together and stay together when it involves your finances.

— EXTRA CREDIT —

Share with your spouse the work of learning about living trusts, which can ensure that your estate passes to your heirs without the necessity of going through the time-consuming and expensive process of probate. Discuss with your financial adviser whether or not a trust might be the right choice for you and your partner.

TRY SOME *KAMA SUTRA* POSITIONS TOGETHER

Remember, sex is like a Chinese dinner. It ain't over 'til you both get your cookie. —Alec Baldwin, film and television actor

The *Kama Sutra* is perhaps the best known of all the love manuals, due to its variety of exotic sexual positions. The word *Kama* means "pleasure" or "sensual desire." *Sutra* means "short books" or "aphorisms." To attain *Kama*, one had to pursue the desire for erotic pleasure. Created in the oral tradition by many scholars over thousands of years, the *Kama Sutra* gained newfound attention in modern times when an Englishman named Sir Richard Francis Burton collaborated on a translation of the ancient Sanskrit text and brought it to the West.

The culture that studied, taught, and created the *Kama Sutra* texts honored the sciences, religious duty, and family. It also honored the science of sex, which was seen as a high art form. This society knew that every young couple would need help if they were ever to get to a place where sexuality became a high art form for them.

Invite your spouse to read the *Kama Sutra* with you and try positions. *Kama* is the enjoyment of appropriate objects by the five senses of hearing, feeling, seeing, tasting, and smelling, assisted by the mind together with the soul.

--- EXTRA CREDIT ---

Introduce him to the ancient *Kama Sutra* Clasping Kiss. Take both of his lips between yours and then, just as you would gently suck the tender flesh of a ripe mango, let your kiss slowly evolve until he is smoldering hot and ready for a feverish romp.

DATE NIGHT

Find a local restaurant that has great food, ambiance, and is in a neighborhood you like. Invite your spouse to dinner. If you like everything about the meal and the establishment, relay that information to the owner(s). Patronize that business by eating there often. The restaurant will gain financially, but you and your spouse also will be enjoying some great meals, prepared by a chef or cook that you trust, in a local establishment owned by people who could become friends. Think of them as part of your social network—a necessary element of a longer and more satisfying life.

BUY TICKETS TO A
FEMALE WRESTLING EVENT

A man can stand anything except a succession of ordinary days. —Johann Wolfgang von Goethe, German dramatist, novelist, poet, and scientist

Want to escape the doldrums of television reruns, hanging out with friends, and the usual entertainment event and venues? What could you do that would be interesting and offer a different experience? You could treat your husband to a sporting event, maybe one with his favorite team. He wouldn't expect that, would he? Probably not, but he goes to those with his buddies, doesn't he? Choose something entirely different: female wrestling. The point is to do something out of the ordinary to shift the paradigm. Ask him if he knows what the body scissor/strangle combo is and if he'd like to see it demonstrated.

—— EXTRA CREDIT ——
Shake off the boredom even more. Treat your spouse to another sport-themed entertainment featuring a woman—boxing, for example. Watch the DVD of *Million Dollar Baby*, with Hilary Swank, Clint Eastwood, and Morgan Freeman. The film earned four Academy Awards, including the best actress award for Swank.

TEST-DRIVE A CAR HE'S
ALWAYS WANTED

Drive on. We'll sweep up the blood later! —Katharine Hepburn, American actress

You don't have to buy him the car; just take him down to the dealership to test-drive the car that he'd love to have. Maybe it's a new hybrid or a hot new roadster. It has an astronomical price tag and your budget can't accommodate that kind of strain, but don't let that stop you. As long as you show interest and are polite, the dealer won't mind.

No one really knows what the future holds. You could come into vast sums of money . . . or not. It's irrelevant, since the test drive costs nothing. And your hubby will be having the time of his life.

DAY 184

— EXTRA CREDIT —

Get dressed up for your test drive. Imagine that you are the CEO of a successful business and that your world is one of affluence. For the afternoon of the test drive, imagine that you have all the money you need for that car and more. Lavish attention on the man you love. Tell him how positively *GQ* he looks driving that car and that you will be with him on the highways and byways of America or the autobahn in Germany whenever he feels like taking off to a romantic destination.

RELY UPON EACH OTHER
FOR SAFE HARBOR

I am not afraid of storms, for I am learning to sail my ship. —Louisa May
Alcott, American novelist

Learn to be cooperative partners who know they can rely upon each
other at all times. The course of life is not always smooth. The same is
true for marriage. When you go out sailing, or navigate the rapids while
white-water rafting, or climb a mountain peak, or go camping into a
remote wilderness, you must rely on the people with you to do their part
to ensure the safety and well-being of everyone. Similarly, the more that
you and your spouse learn to rely upon each other, the more you will
trust the process of interweaving and integrating your lives into one life
together. Your marriage serves as your safe haven for the uncertainties of
life that arise from time to time.

--- EXTRA CREDIT ---

Ask your partner to share his ideas on the best way to deal with sudden crisis the
next time one occurs. Discussing all the elements of the situation gives you both a
better understanding of what steps need to be taken right away and those that can
be done later.

BOOK A CRUISE FOR
THE TWO OF YOU

I'm not a smart man, but I know what love is. —Tom Hanks as Forrest
Gump

The world is full of romantic ports of call. If you've never cruised before,
consider that every creature comfort you might need or want has been
anticipated and arranged. Imagine the two of you, arm in arm, walking
around one of the ship's many decks under the shelter of a glorious sky
upon a sparkling blue sea. You take dip in the pool, tackle a climbing
wall, see a musical, eat some the greatest cuisine you've ever tasted, dance
under the stars to Caribbean rhythms played by a steel-drum band, or
listen to a live chamber orchestra. The two of you can tantalize your taste
buds with opulent offerings at every meal and virtually any delicacy you
could desire. Then there are those long, sultry nights between the sheets
with the person you most love in the world.

Why not book a cruise for your next honeymoon, birthday, or summer vacation? Ever consider spending the Christmas and New Year's
holidays on the high seas? It just might be the one trip together that
you'll never forget.

--- EXTRA CREDIT ---

For a more personal experience, explore your options for renting a yacht and sailing
for a week or two in a specific part of the world in the company of one or two other
couples and a small, accomplished crew.

SPLURGE FOR A CLASS THAT
HE IS LONGING TO TAKE

It's been so long since I made love, I can't even remember who gets tied up.
—Joan Rivers, American comedienne

Whether the class your husband wants to take is computer forensics, automotive design, nature photography, fly fishing, or something else, help him get enrolled. Perhaps you've noticed how his eyes shine when he's thinking about it; how animated his voice becomes talking about it. Clearly, your hubby is turned on by the topic.

Stop saying "we can't afford it" and start considering how you can help him get into that class as soon as possible. Don't let worry or negative thinking about lack of money or other obstacles get in the way. Brainstorm through them. For example, he might offer to work a seminar as a volunteer in exchange for attending at a reduced rate or free. You could go through your belongings for things you don't need, want, or use and sell them on Craigslist or e-Bay to fund the class. If you have the desire, intention, and will, it is possible to manifest almost anything. And you've got love as your driving force.

--- EXTRA CREDIT ---

Help your spouse put into practice what he's learned. Set out for a sparkling mountain lake to do a little fly fishing together. Enjoy the fresh, pine-scented air, the dazzling way the sunlight sparkles on the water, the honking of Canada geese in formation, and the happy smile turning up the corners of your spouse's lips.

FIND LOOSE CHANGE
AND SPEND IT TOGETHER

A nickel ain't worth a dime anymore. —Yogi Berra, American baseball player

Talk with your partner about doing some good in the world with that loose change you find in the sofa, on the dresser, or in the washing machine. Of course, you could spend the found money on each other. But what great karma you would be generating together if you decided to donate it to a good cause. If you are living on a tight budget, it might be difficult to make sizable donations to your favorite charitable organization. However, if you set aside a quarter a day for a hunger fund, you can allow the fund to grow until it's big enough for you to take the quarters to the bank for a deposit and then write out a check to your favorite soup kitchen or food bank.

—— EXTRA CREDIT ——

Talk with your spouse about helping out a friend in need. Drop $10 each into an envelope with a cheery card and send it anonymously to a friend or a friend of a friend who is a single mom or dad and struggling to make ends meet.

DATE NIGHT

Attend a lecture by a motivational speaker, then have dinner with your spouse to share any new ideas that might be triggered by hearing the lecture, and then go home and make love in a new and unusual position. After all, Vatsyayana states in the *Kama Sutra* that if a man and woman enjoy their lives and include variations in their lovemaking, they will not fall out of love and may be partnered for a hundred years. Imagine all the dreams you could share.

PICK YOUR
BATTLES

Love is an ideal thing, marriage a real thing. —Johann Wolfgang von Goethe, German dramatist, novelist, poet, and scientist

When marital disagreements erupt, remember the old adage: Don't sweat the small stuff. Many couples—no matter what their age—get all the way to the altar without probing very far into each other's hearts and minds, and without knowing enough about what love is, and isn't. They may have romanticized ideals and unrealistic expectations about marriage. In their first year or so of marriage, it may seem like married life is a chapter in Tolstoy's *War and Peace*. They don't know how to make their marriage happy. Fights erupt over everything—from who left the cap off the toothpaste to whose turn it is to take the dog out, clear the clutter, replace the toilet paper, or pick up the groceries.

To get yourselves through trying periods, evaluate whether or not the toothpaste cap is really an issue worth fighting over. Learn to let go of whatever you can to save your sanity and make your marriage run more smoothly.

—— EXTRA CREDIT ——

Talk with your lover about the expectations you both have. For example, you expect him to put his clothing from work in the laundry basket instead of draping pants and shirts over the bedroom chairs. He expects you to put away your makeup, brushes, and hair products instead of leaving them on the dresser and the bathroom countertop. For a week, try to meet each other's expectations. Figure out which expectations the two of you can release or how you might work out compromises for what still bothers you both.

LEARN TO DANCE A
SIZZLING-HOT TANGO

If you make a mistake, get tangled up, just tango on. —Al Pacino, *Scent of a Woman*

The tango originated either in Spain or Morocco. It was only after Spanish settlers introduced it through their travels to the New World that the tango took on Black and Creole influences and ceased to be a solo woman's dance. Today, who could ever imagine the smoking-hot, steamy dance without a man? The silent screen idol Rudolph Valentino may be responsible for turning the dance into a hit in America, but long before Rudy made his sexy on-screen moves, the Argentinean gauchos or cowboys danced the tango with local ladies in small crowded clubs.

Many local dance studios offer classes in the Argentine tango. You and your hubby can sign up for private lessons or group lessons at all levels. Put a little sizzle back into your life with the dance that's been called risqué, playful, aggressive, passionate, erotic, and even forbidden.

--- EXTRA CREDIT ---

Curl up with your husband on the couch or in the big loveseat or on the sofa and watch the movie *Frida*, about the Mexican artist Frida Kahlo and her muralist husband Diego Rivera. In the movie, Salma Hayek and Ashley Judd dance a sensual, sexy, suggestive tango as Diego and their friends watch. When the movie ends, dance in the dark and whisper "I love you" in Spanish (*Te quiero*, or *Te amo*).

GO ON A
COUPLES RETREAT

If you want to know me, look inside your heart. —Lao-tzu, Chinese Taoist philosopher

Philosopher Lao-tzu, who lived circa 604 to 531 B.C.E., believed that the key to freedom was living in a natural way, with kindness, serenity, and respect. Because of the outside forces acting upon you, your spouse, your relationships, and your life, you may feel that life is beating up on you; that nothing is going the way you wanted, that everything seems convoluted, complicated, and intense. Perhaps you and your spouse no longer use kind, loving words to address each other the way you once did.

How do you break a negative cycle? Try going in a different direction. Sign up for a couples retreat or just make time for the two of you to get away in your community. If you can work on your relationship *and* enjoy some breathtaking scenery in nature, that's a double benefit. During such retreats, there is usually time to reflect and work on yourself as well as your relationship with your partner. Facilitators discuss how couples can repair and restore the bonds of love that they share. Talk with a marriage counselor or member of the clergy to find a couples retreat that will help you reconnect with each other and find the fun in life again.

—— EXTRA CREDIT ——

Lao-tzu wrote in *The Way of Lao-tzu* that the journey of a thousand miles begins with a single step. The wise sage also advocated cultivating love and frugality. Talk with your spouse about the steps you can take to simplify your lives, letting go of lavish consumerism in favor having only what you need. Stretching yourselves too thin financially to purchase things you want, but don't need, can exact a toll on your marriage. Lao-tzu said to have fewer desires. Find your fulfillment in each other.

SEEK HELPFUL
TIPS FROM OTHER PARENTS

It takes a village to raise a child. —African proverb

If you don't always know the ideal way to handle a child-rearing situation, parenting can become stressful. Getting insights from other parents is often helpful. In her book *It Takes a Village*, former First Lady Hillary Rodham Clinton advocates for children to be brought up not only by their parents, but rather by many other people in our interdependent world.

In your "village" (or neighborhood or community), you will meet other parents at the park, in the baby-food aisle at the market, in the pediatrician's office and dentist's waiting room, at your house of worship, on the soccer field, at PTA meetings, and a host of other places. Take the opportunity to form friendships with them. Ask them how they have dealt with particular parenting or family issues that you and your spouse might be facing. Question them about how they intend to raise resilient, well-adjusted children. Gain from their experiential, real-world knowledge. Above all else, be patient, remember that time changes everything, and even if times are tough, better days are ahead.

—— EXTRA CREDIT ——
Read or review *It Takes a Village: And Other Lessons Children Teach Us,* by Hillary Rodham Clinton (Simon & Schuster 1996). Then make it a point to have coffee with another couple who are parenting children about the age of your children. Talk with them about the positives and negatives of parenting in today's American society.

EXPLORE
LIFE GOALS

There are no shortcuts to any place worth going. —Beverly Sills, American opera singer

Marital relationships guided by a shared common vision and life goals are more likely to stay on track and thus be stronger than the relationships without any defined direction. Not knowing where your marriage is headed can be problematic, just as having a shared vision for your lives together can be stabilizing. Any relationship, marital included, can be pushed off track by outside forces and events.

If you haven't already figured out what your life goals are, it's never too late to get started. Some of the areas to consider when thinking about goals for life include health, finances, love, career, physical surroundings/environment, family and friends, personal growth, religious/spiritual, and recreation. Talk with your spouse about how satisfied both of you already are within each of these areas and then brainstorm ways to increase your satisfaction through goal setting. A goal must have a completion date. Without setting a time frame in which to achieve the goal, there is no push, no immediacy, and no sense of willpower for that goal to be reached.

— EXTRA CREDIT —

As a couple, establish one goal in one life area. Make a goal-setting worksheet that includes the following items with space to write after each: "Our goal for the next (number of) weeks is (name the goal). The payoff for us reaching the goal is (reward). The consequence of not reaching our goal is (name the consequence). People who will help us achieve the goal are (list names)." Pledge your support to each other and work together to achieve the goal you've set.

DEFINE
YOUR DREAMS

If one advances confidently in the direction of his dreams, and endeavors to live the life which he has imagined, he will meet with a success unexpected in common hours. —Henry David Thoreau, American author, poet, philosopher

Defining your dream means getting clear in your mind exactly what it is you want to manifest. See your dream in its fullness through the lens of your imagination. Clarify and refine the details of the dream. Law of Attraction proponents have pointed out that as soon as someone begins focusing on the thing he really wants, the universe gets busy arranging or rearranging the necessary elements and circumstances to make manifestation of that thing possible. Myriad opportunities begin to present themselves. It is as if the universe is working with you, putting wind in the sail of your dream ship to take you anywhere you want to go and giving you the experiences, relationships, money, wealth, and things you most desire.

—— EXTRA CREDIT ——

Listen to some beautiful instrumental music such as "Adagio for Strings" by Samuel Barber to further intensify your visualization process as you define and refine your dream. The music can lift the vibration of the spirit. Some spiritual teachers assert that because music is itself a vibration, it shifts mood at a cellular level and helps redirect the mind into a singular, laser-like focus.

DATE NIGHT

Slip on your dancing slippers and your sexy evening wear. Head out to a dance club where couples dance the Argentine tango. When the music starts, step into the first position. Make the evening all about the two of you showing off your skillful and sensuous tango moves. Carry the passion home. Tango into the foyer, through the living room, and all the way into the bedroom. Push that sexy, seductive tango passion to the limit.

ASK YOUR SPOUSE
TO SUPPORT YOUR DREAM

I have spread my dreams beneath your feet; Tread softly because you tread on my dreams. —W.B. Yeats, Irish poet and dramatist

If you've been the one to work while your spouse finished law school, started med school, or launched his start-up company, you may wonder when it's going to be your turn. You have dreams, too.

If the timing finally feels right to you to pursue your own big dream, have a heart-to-heart talk with your spouse. Perhaps you want to start a family, launch a business, return to school to complete a degree, or take a position with an organization that involves a lot of travel. Whatever it is, you are going to need your spouse's support. If your spouse has concerns, don't take it as an automatic rejection or gridlock. Ask him to honor your dream and to patiently listen as you explain why the dream is so important to you. Perhaps the dream is rooted in your childhood feelings or unrealized hopes and aspirations. Resist turning the conversation into a discussion about how he has gained through your sacrifice. Stay focused on the worthiness of your dream.

--- EXTRA CREDIT ---

Give your spouse a role in your dream. He might be more likely to get behind your idea if he feels needed and appreciated and knows that your desire to follow your dream doesn't necessarily mean that he will be somehow displaced.

HELP HER DEVELOP
AN ACTION PLAN

Nothing happens unless first a dream. —Carl Sandburg, American biographer and poet

Let's say that in the course of a conversation about unfulfilled dreams, your wife confides that she's always wanted to own her own business. But she confesses that taking her idea from the realm of possibility to manifestation greatly intimidates her; she can't seem to set aside her feelings of fear to start. Regardless of how difficult or impractical you may think her idea is, acknowledge her passion for it and her courage for sharing the dream with you. Don't undermine her feelings about the dream, but do validate her fears, because for her they are real. They are also the first big barrier she will have to push through if she wants to have that business.

You can help her by pointing out the benefits. Play devil's advocate to illuminate the risks. Find out if she wants to personally work in the business for many years or to build it with the goal of selling it. It isn't likely that she is seeking permission so much as practical and pragmatic advice. Be generous.

—— EXTRA CREDIT ——
Download a template for writing a business plan. Encourage her to start working on specifics. Writing the business plan forces her to clarify her vision and ascertain how much time, energy, and money will be required to launch and sustain it going forward.

PLAY A GAME OF
MINIATURE GOLF

What other people may find in poetry or art museums, I find in the flight of a good drive. —Arnold Palmer, American golfer

Playing a game of miniature golf with your mate allow you to forget the stresses of life for a while and lift your hearts into a lighter mood. A miniature golf course doesn't necessarily have to be relegated to the milieu of childhood. As it turns out, the popularity of those courses apparently increases with economic downturns.

Perhaps it's the nostalgia thing—a kinder, gentler time in America when a family would start the weekend with a round or two of miniature golf with the kids, followed by burgers and fries at the local drive-in. Launched in 1938, the culture craze hit its stride in the mid-1980s, with miniature golf courses seemingly popping up everywhere around the country. In fact, it might be easier now than ever to find a course in your neighborhood.

— EXTRA CREDIT —

Treat your spouse to some spooky fun at a Monster Mini Golf course (*www.monsterminigolf.com*) if there is one near you. You'll feel like kids again as you play eighteen holes through a chills-and-thrills environment that features monster décor and animated props, not to mention creatures with glow-in-the-dark features.

EMPATHIZE WHEN YOUR SPOUSE
SUFFERS A SETBACK

Misfortune, and recited misfortune especially, may be prolonged to the point where it ceases to excite pity and arouses only irritation. —Dorothy Parker, American short story writer and poet

Motivational speakers are fond of pointing to men and women of extraordinary accomplishments who also suffered failures on their way to greatness. What is imparted most often in such inspirational stories are lessons learned as a result of the failures or setbacks.

When your spouse experiences a setback on his way to achieving his dream and shows it through his moodiness or retreat into silence, don't downplay what he's feeling but rather acknowledge the validity of his feelings and empathize with his emotional response to his difficulties.

—— EXTRA CREDIT ——

When he's ready to talk about it, be a good listener and encourage him to talk at length about the setback. Remind him that you have thrown your lot in with him, and that includes sharing his dreams. Sometimes two heads really are better than one in trying to figure out why something failed, what went wrong, why it happened, and how to deal with the consequences. Misfortune's gift will be to figure out how to ensure that same failure will never happen again.

WRITE SPECIFIC
ACTION LISTS

God gives every bird its food, but he does not throw it into the nest. —Josiah Gilbert Holland, American novelist and poet

On Day 194, you and your spouse created some joint goals. Can you feel the excitement at the thought of having your dream show up in your life? That is the most important step to getting it. Thoughts become more powerful when they are magnetized by your emotion. Intent becomes energized through repetitious thinking of the same thoughts and by clarity of focus. It's also important to know your reasons for wanting something. Usually, it will have to do with how it makes you feel.

One way to energize intentional thought is by mapping out an action or to-do list. Think about some of the things you might do to set up a powerful magnetic attraction, drawing to you the object of your desire. Clean the garage, for example, to make the space for that brand-new RV. Write a vision statement for each goal, and then create an action list to help achieve that goal. Don't get too bogged down in detail, but do try to think of major areas that will need attention and action steps.

> — EXTRA CREDIT —
> Read a book on the power of positive thinking. Be ready to receive the person, thing, or situation that you desire. Sometimes that means making space in your life, your business, or your home.

HELP YOUR SPOUSE TRAIN
FOR A SPORTING EVENT

Nothing great was ever achieved without enthusiasm. —Ralph Waldo
Emerson, American essayist, philosopher, and poet

In marriage, as in life, a generosity of spirit is often symbolized by trust, kindness, and respect for others, and mutual aid and support for those whom you love. Yet, supporting your spouse, at times, can be a challenge.

For example, your husband comes home after an evening jog to tell you that he wants to begin triathlon training. Do you greet him with enthusiastic support? Or, do you recoil and remind him that it requires a considerable amount of time to train for a triathlon—time you would prefer he spend with you and your children? Before reacting and asking him to abandon the idea, why not tune into his passion? Connect with his enthusiasm. Before launching into a litany of reasons why it's *not* a good idea, think of why it *is* a good idea. It's his dream for this time in his life; it won't be forever. Discover exactly what triathlon training involves and then have a frank discussion of the consequences of his choice. Discuss what, if any, sacrifices you and your children will have to make. If he still considers it an important goal for his life, then help him create a workable plan and work it . . . together.

—— EXTRA CREDIT ——
Search the Internet for information on training tips, scheduling suggestions, nutrition and diet, injury-avoidance strategies, and bicycle maintenance to share with him. Ask him if he wants to compete in an Iron Man competition next.

RESIST USING
CREDIT CARDS

No man's credit is ever as good as his money. —Edgar Watson Howe,
American novelist and newspaper editor

Do you live off cash and eschew the use of credit cards? Maybe, but
more likely, you use credit cards for at least some purchases. Credit cards
themselves aren't really the problem, per se. The issue is how a couple
uses them.

It's important to recognize and understand each other's financial
temperament if you and your partner desire to keep away marital discord over credit card debt. Sometimes one or both partners will use
their credit cards for "retail therapy," impulse purchases that provide
short-term happiness. Such purchases can play havoc with a family
budget. The high interest rates and hidden fees on credit cards often
undermine a consumer's best intentions to stay out of debt. Resisting
the urge to use them may be your best bet to keep your spouse happy
and your budget intact.

—— EXTRA CREDIT ——

If you have credit cards, read the disclosure information on your monthly statement
or in privacy or other notices sent to you by your credit card companies. Learn about
any new laws that protect consumers who use credit cards. Become informed in
order to more wisely use your available credit.

DATE NIGHT

Head off for an artsy local theater that shows sexy foreign films with English subtitles, or arrange to send the children to their grandparents for the night so the two of you cuddle up to watch one or more super-sexy foreign films like *The Lover* or *Combien Tu M'Aimes?* (How Much Do You Love Me?). Go ahead . . . make it a double or even a triple feature. Sleep late the next morning.

ENCOURAGE YOUR SPOUSE
TO DEVELOP HER TALENTS

You get whatever accomplishment you are willing to declare. —Georgia O'Keeffe, American painter

Your wife has the voice of an angel, but sings only in the shower. She can whip up a meal fit for a royal entourage from what she finds in a nearly empty pantry and dreams of attending a culinary school, if only her day job paid more. Or, she creates beautiful one-of-a-kind purses from silk fabric and embellishments and gives them to her nieces and friends as gifts . . . but can only make those lovely creations when she isn't studying, working, or caring for the baby.

The demands of marriage and family, not to mention a busy career, leave little time and energy left over at the end of the day for many women to fully express or improve their talents. Yet, psychologists say that doing activities that involve our natural talents often boost self-esteem levels and give meaning to our lives. Tell your spouse how talented she is. Ask her how you can help her develop, express, or pursue her talent to wherever it might lead her. Give her the gift of time to work her talents into a hobby or even develop them into a business.

DAY 205

— EXTRA CREDIT —

Offer to find a way to pay for a coach, classes, or a conference. Show that you really mean what you say and that you will support her. Encourage her to reach the full potential of her life, including claiming and developing all her talents.

INVOLVE YOUR FAMILY
IN MAINTAINING YOUR HOME

_____

Many hands make light work. —John Heywood, English dramatist

Cohabitation with your spouse and children (and possibly even other family members) can quickly transform that comfortable, lived-in appearance in your home into a chaotic, cyclone-just-hit-it look. There's really no reason not to involve everyone over the age of three in caring for your shared living quarters. Even little children can be taught to pick up toys and put them in storage bins, retrieve clothing and toss it in a laundry basket, or stack their storybooks on a shelf or into a container.

Grownups need to do their part as well. Shoes go to the bedroom closet the same day or evening that they've been kicked off. Clothing goes into hampers or back onto hangers. Mailers promptly go into the paper recycle bin as soon as you've gone through them. Dishes are rinsed and placed in the dishwasher every evening, not at the end of the week (however, wait until there is a full load before running the dishwasher). Each family member can be responsible for certain areas or specific chores.

When everyone pulls together, the nest remains more appealing and everyone can live more harmoniously.

—— EXTRA CREDIT ——
Have fun involving the entire family in creating a master chores list. Extended family members such as grandparents, parents, nieces, nephews, and cousins ought to be included too.

GO INTO BUSINESS
WITH YOUR SPOUSE

Money . . . will take you wherever you wish, but it will not replace you as the driver. —Ayn Rand, *Atlas Shrugged*

Every successful business or nonprofit organization started as someone's great idea, a seed that visionaries brought into being through steadfast dedication and hard work. Sometimes those visionaries are married to each other and are working together in partnership—merging business with marriage. The name newly coined for that arrangement is "co-preneurship."

Whether it is a film you want to make, a franchise you want to buy, an innovative start-up company you desire to launch, an orphanage or school you are eager to establish, or some other type of venture, funding it will be a major consideration. After you and your spouse develop the business plan, you will have to research your funding options and decide whether to get financial backing through traditional or innovative funding sources. The following list represents six common ways a new venture might be funded.

1. Bank loans
2. Credit cards
3. Angel investors

4. Family and friends
5. Equity financing
6. Venture capital

— EXTRA CREDIT —

Have a Plan B ready to implement. Keep a positive attitude that the funding will go through, but know that often there are unexpected snafus. The fallout for a funding failure can be psychologically and emotionally devastating. Be courageous, allow yourselves time to process what happened, and then get right back on track.

ENJOY WORKING TOGETHER
BUT KNOW THE RISKS

When work is a pleasure, life is a joy! —Maxim Gorky, *The Lower Depths*

Working with your spouse in a business partnership can be fun, but it isn't without some inherent risks. Just make sure you understand the risks before you sign the rental agreement on commercial space.

Spouses who work together—whether as young entrepreneurs just starting out, midlifers shifting direction, or retirees starting over—will face a variety of challenges to their marital and business partnership. For example, you might think it's the right thing to do to invest all your money into your venture, withholding little or nothing for savings, health insurance, retirement investment, or life insurance. You might also underestimate the time your business will require of you and your spouse, and overestimate the amount of time you and your spouse will have to spend with each other. Another problem is automatically dividing the workload along traditional gender lines, with the husband in charge and the wife as the worker, instead of according to skills, ability, knowledge, interest, and talent.

When you know the kinds of challenges, threats, and risks that are inherent in jointly operating a family business, you empower and embolden yourselves to deal with the problems by utilizing the best of what each of you brings to the venture. The result: enjoying the partnership in every sense of the word.

--- EXTRA CREDIT ---

Establish firm boundaries to ensure that your "couple time" doesn't always surrender to "business time." Acknowledge each other's value to the business and how your specific strengths and skills are helping the business become successful. Check in with each other to ensure that both marriage and business are working for each of you.

FIGHT FAIR:
GIVE NOTICE

A majority is always the best repartee. —Benjamin Disraeli, *Tancred*

When you and your partner disagree, don't necessarily discuss it right then and there, and don't spring a difficult conversation on your spouse out of the blue. Many people will have a defensive reaction if they don't receive warning of a potentially difficult discussion. (That's not right or wrong; defensiveness is just a possible reaction you may as well try to avoid.) Instead, ask for a specific time and place to talk about an issue. Requesting an appropriate time for dealing with a disagreement is respectful and supports the resolution of the problem. With advance notice, your partner can prepare his thoughts and sort out his emotions.

Other ways to prepare for a difficult discussion include:

- Know how you'll articulate what you want using "I" statements.
- Be open to what unfolds and don't come with a preconceived notion of what the resolution or compromise is going to be.
- Be prepared to share your emotional baggage if necessary.
- Think about what might you be willing to compromise on.

Offer your potential compromises as suggestions—not ultimatums. With just a little practice, this type of problem-solving discussion becomes a habit. The result: more harmony in your marriage.

--- EXTRA CREDIT ---

If you are experiencing a lot of emotion around an issue and need to release your own frustration or anger before continuing the conversation, try shouting into pillows or taking a walk around the block to cool down.

DATE NIGHT

Snuggle up together to watch *A Flash of Genius*, the 2008 movie about Robert Kearns, a mechanical engineering professor at Wayne State University, who invented the intermittent windshield wiper. He attributed his invention to a champagne cork hitting his eye as he tried to open the bottle on his wedding night. That experience was the incident that propelled him on a landmark journey.

READ TO EACH
OTHER IN BED

The pleasure of all reading is doubled when one lives with another who shares the same books. —Katherine Mansfield, New Zealand–born modernist writer

Reading a little to each other after crawling into bed for the night can settle you down and draw you close as you approach that sleepy state. Recent developments in science suggest that while you sleep, your brains are taking experiences and information from daily activities and processing them in order to learn from them.

Leave the industry trade journals and work-required reading matter for another time. You want to quiet your mind before sleep. Choose a book of devotional poems, a collection of letters written by historical lovers, a spiritual book, a text of erotica, or a relationship guidebook. Read aloud, sharing passages, until you feel sleepy.

―― EXTRA CREDIT ――

Make like bookworms. Together, make a list of books you would love to read and rank them in the order you would like to devour them. Form a book club for two to discuss your respective books.

MAINTAIN A BALANCE
BETWEEN MARRIAGE AND WORK

O far glimmering worlds and wings/Mystic smiles and beckonings/Lead us through the shadowy aisles/Out into the afterwhiles. —James Whitcomb Riley, American writer and poet

American couples are working harder, and working longer hours, to get ahead. It's no wonder that many married couples are left feeling both financial and marital strain. Some couples even choose to have commuter marriages—taking jobs in different cities, or even different countries, to survive. Time spent together is mostly virtual (thanks to Skype and other modern innovations). The separation puts added stress on the relationship. If you have children, you already know that day-care costs and school costs are high, further straining your financial situation.

No matter what your situation, if too much work and too little couple time have created an imbalance in your marriage, try these six tips:

- Find time to nurture yourself (to de-stress, find peace, and show joy to your family).
- Connect with your spouse at the start of your day (even before checking e-mail!).
- Adjust your daily routine to make those small changes that take only a few minutes every day; the moments add up.
- See weekends as your retreat time with husband and family.
- Regard your marriage and children as your number one priority.

— EXTRA CREDIT —

Perfect the art of saying "no" to business colleagues, coworkers, friends, and extended family members when necessary. Don't be rude, but do be resolute.

KNOW WHEN
TO HIRE HELPERS

I hire people brighter than me and then I get out of their way. —Lee
Iacocca, American businessman

According to the U.S. Department of Labor statistics (*www.bls.gov/cps/wlftable7.htm*), there were 24,637,000 women with children under the age of 18 employed in the U.S. work force in 2008. If you were one of them, you probably already understand the challenges and fatigue of juggling family and career. When workers are overburdened with work on the job, there's a chance that your boss will hire more workers.

Think of your work at home in a similar way. Assign a dollar amount to what you think your time doing housework is worth. If it costs you more to do it than it would to hire someone, it might make sense to hire a nanny, housekeeper, babysitter, or cook and put your life back in balance. Consider these ideas if you want to hire someone:

1. Write a job description for each position.
2. Conduct interviews and background and reference checks.
3. Know your legal and financial obligations such as labor laws, immigration, and tax rules.
4. Train your worker(s), communicating clearly do's and don'ts.
5. Review, evaluate, and redirect workers' performance as necessary.
6. Don't be afraid to terminate the worker if necessary.

— EXTRA CREDIT —

Listen to books or podcasts on your iPod or MP3 player about how to embrace the notion that you can delegate work to others, including spouse, children, family members, and hired help.

INVITE YOUR SPOUSE
ON YOUR BUSINESS TRIP

Monkey business isn't just for monkeys. —Anonymous

Even though your spouse's expenses on your business trips generally are not deductible, the perks of having him along can more than make up for any write-off on your taxes. Of course, you also will have to check with your company to ensure that there's no restriction on spouses accompanying their partners on business travel or attending certain functions, like cocktail parties or welcoming/closing events.

Make the trip an awesome twosome holiday by booking a day before and after your out-of-town board meeting, trade show, or convention in a major city in an exciting part of the world. On the days that belong to the two of you, order breakfast in bed, exercise together, take in the sights, explore the area, indulge in great food and wine, and make love until there's not an ounce of tension in your body when you must show up for that business meeting.

When one spouse is a road warrior and the other is left at home to cope with the finances, kids, pets, and everything else, chances are that their intimacy will need more attention than if constant travel wasn't a factor—giving you all the more reason to make the most of travel together.

--- EXTRA CREDIT ---

Save the best until last. Try a little monkey business role-playing after meeting each other in the hotel lobby or bar. Use your imagination. You can be anybody you want. Pretend you don't know each other. Work on your negotiation and seduction simultaneously. After all, they both utilize the skill of persuasion. Have fun.

BRING OUT THE
BEST IN EACH OTHER

You make me want to be a better man. —Jack Nicholson as Melvin, *As Good as It Gets*

Healthy relationships are about bringing out the best in each other. You've probably heard that for years, and the idea sounds so simple, but the truth is that it is one of the most important aspects of healthy marriages. At its deepest, it means that every time you are around the other person, you are bringing the best of you, the total sum of you, to that moment.

This *does not* mean that you have to be happy and joyful around that person all the time. What it does mean is that whether you are in complete bliss or complete pain, you bring that emotion in total to your spouse so that he or she can bask in your joy or help you through your pain. It means that you are willing to bring your total self into your marital relationship and help your spouse do the same.

—— EXTRA CREDIT ——

If your mate is having self-esteem issues over an ongoing tiff with a manager or boss, help him see everything in a clearer perspective. Discuss what makes him unique, what you personally value in him, and what you know his gifts to be. Recount past accomplishments, recognition, and awards associated with his career or job. Remind him of who he is at his core. That's what counts.

MAKE MONEY FROM
YOUR COMBINED SKILLS

Two heads are better than one. —Idiomatic English phrase

"Two heads" means the minds of two people thinking together to solve some problem or to figure out some great strategy for accomplishing a task.

For example, let's say your husband works with computer-aided design (CAD) programs and mechanical CAD software. You are proficient in using Microsoft Office and several financial software programs. Together, your combined knowledge and skills are formidable. Perhaps you already help each other on projects related to your careers. But consider how to combine what you know to work together. With companies going global, you might think of combining your knowledge and talent to form a web-based company or offer to consult. First figure out what you have to offer and whether what you have to offer fills a need in the current marketplace. Then think about how you might function as a team to create income streams from what you know.

— EXTRA CREDIT —

Engage in empire building by figuring out how many ways you can generate income from what you and your husband know and the skills the two of you possess. For example, one or both of you could consult, teach, write books, create short articles for magazines and newspapers, and even become professional speakers on topics related to your areas of expertise. The point is to find ways to exploit what you know in ways that generate income streams.

DATE NIGHT

Go for a tandem bike ride. Pack your bike basket with gourmet foods, a bottle of bubbly or your favorite brew, and something sweet like chocolate truffles for dessert. If there's room, tuck in your portable CD player and a blanket. Strap on your helmets and head out to explore a local scenic route where you can catch the sunset and listen to some sultry, sexy music whenever you decide that you've arrived.

SET A GOOD EXAMPLE
FOR YOUR CHILDREN

———

Children have never been very good at listening to their elders, but they have never failed to imitate them. —James Baldwin, *Fifth Avenue, Uptown,* "Nobody Knows My Name"

As parents, you and your spouse are exemplars for your children. From your behaviors, they learn to show restraint, be respectful, and engage in moral reasoning, from early childhood through their teenage years into young adulthood. Not only are you teaching through example, but also teaching them how to think and reason through moral dilemmas they may face in their relationships with others at home, in school, and in all other activities. Through the way you and your spouse deal with family members, friends, business associates, strangers, and everyone with whom you interact, you demonstrate for your children what patience, kindness, understanding, empathy, self-discipline, self-restraint, and self-reliance look like.

Dr. Deepak Chopra noted in *The Seven Spiritual Laws for Parents: Guiding Your Children to Success and Fulfillment,* spirituality is a skill in living and, as the parent, you are the teacher of spirit for your child. Your work starts from the day your child is born.

— EXTRA CREDIT —

Start a journal that documents your child's developing spiritual and moral character. Write about moments when your child had said something or done something you consider profound or just shows his unique way of being or view of the world. Review your child's progress over time to see if you and your spouse need to reinforce any particular values or beliefs through your own behaviors and counsel.

TACKLE DIFFICULT TASKS
WITH TEAMWORK

It [teamwork] is the fuel that allows common people to attain uncommon results. —Andrew Carnegie, Scottish-American businessman

When you and your spouse must face a difficult task, talk about it, figure out the best- and worst-case scenarios, then work with the Law of Attraction to draw into your life whatever it is you need or desire to complete the task. If, for example, your task involves dealing with an impending layoff, a job transfer, a pay cut, or even a forced leveraged buyout of your company, knowing that your spouse understands the situation and will do everything possible to help shoulder the load provides comforts and offers hope. When you know what the worst-case scenario is, you can formulate a plan to deal with it, if that happens.

However, expecting the *best* outcome is what you will focus on. The secret to working with the Law of Attraction to manifest your desired outcome is to create a powerful, compelling mental video that excites you every time you play it forward in your mind. Feel all the positive emotions associated with having the difficult task completed. See yourselves already on the road to resolution and grand possibilities for your future.

----- EXTRA CREDIT -----

Write an affirmation to help you and your spouse achieve a goal or manifest something you want. Try the following affirmation for finding the perfect new job. "I am elated to know that the Law of Attraction is in the process of guiding me to a new job where I can best express my skills and talents and where my salary increases and my coworkers and bosses appreciate my contributions." Now you write your own affirmation by filling in the blanks. "I feel (name a positive emotion) to know that the job of (name the job) is in the process of manifesting in my life right now."

KNOW THE WARNING SIGNS
OF A WORKAHOLIC

All work and no play makes Jack a dull boy. —English proverb

You love your job. You work hard . . . okay, maybe too hard. One of the many signs of being a workaholic is working more than forty hours a week. However, it is possible that you simply have a strong work ethic and are not a workaholic. The difference is what the workaholic views as a priority. The workaholic cannot seem to differentiate priority—she cannot see certain tasks as less important and some as more important and, instead, sees all tasks as important all the time.

Having a workaholic spouse can take its toll on a marriage. A workaholic cannot seem to live a life in balance, prioritizing activities and leaving work at work. Workaholics often stay at their desks during meals in order to continue working, think about work when they should be focusing on driving or changing the baby, believe working long hours is justified if they love the work, hate being interrupted in their work by family and others who want them to do something else, permit personal relationships to suffer because of work, and often worry about being laid off or fired even when their present job is secure.

—— EXTRA CREDIT ——

If either of you is a workaholic, take corrective action before it harms your marriage. Pull your lives back into balance by modifying your schedule so as not to devote a lot of time to things that are not a priority. Seek professional counseling if old patterns of allowing work to fill all your time begin to re-emerge.

CLIP COUPONS
FOR DESIRED ITEMS

Desire is the very essence of man. —Benedict Spinoza, Dutch philosopher

Coupons help the average couple stretch hard-earned dollars, perhaps even freeing up some cash for some "extras"—vacations, dinners out, tickets to events, etc.—to help you enjoy your marriage even more. Clip coupons from magazines, newspapers, trade journals, and freebie mailers. Specific product manufacturer coupons are often available in coupon dispensers along grocery store aisles where the product is sold. Coupons for all types of goods and services also can found on the Internet, downloaded, and printed at home. Find great deals, hot picks, printable coupons, and more at the following websites:

- *www.ableshoppers.com*
- *www.dealsofamerica.com*
- *www.pricegrabber.com*
- *www.slickdeals.net*
- *www.dealtaker.com*

- *www.shopping.com*
- *www.shopzilla.com*
- *www.couponcabin.com*
- *www.couponcraze.com*
- *www.keycode.com*

—— EXTRA CREDIT ——

Trade coupons with friends or even another couple who share your interest in finding the products at the best possible price. Perhaps you have a coupon for something they are ready to buy. Or, they might have coupons for items that you want. Make the coupon swapping part of a fun get-together.

LISTEN AS YOUR
SPOUSE VENTS

---

*The reason you don't understand me, Edith, is because I'm talkin' to you
in English and you're listenin' to me in dingbat!* —Archie Bunker, *All in the
Family*

Edith and Archie's marriage had many challenges and issues, not the least
of which was communication. Archie's impatient, intolerant, and judg-
mental view of his wife's communication typifies the average listener—
the one who takes only bits of information from the speaker because his
thoughts are darting around or are focused elsewhere. When you are truly
listening to your spouse, you are giving him all your attention. Your mind
can't be engaged elsewhere.

If you thought listening is a passive activity, you'd be wrong. Actively
listening requires focused attention, and it raises your pulse and blood
pressure. When your spouse needs to vent, give him your full attention.
You may think you already know what he's going to say, but interrupting
just shortchanges him. Acknowledge the emotion he's projecting. If he's
angry, for example, you might say, "I can hear the anger and frustration
in your voice. You must feel terribly upset over this turn of events." As
he talks through his emotion, his brain is reviewing all that transpired
to make him angry. By listening attentively, you are helping him process
the events.

— EXTRA CREDIT —

If you don't listen well, consider studying up on effective communication. There
exists a substantial gap in the speed between your hearing and comprehension and
what's being said. That gap means that your thoughts have a tendency to race on,
instead of trying to focus on what's being communicated.

MAKE YOUR
SPOUSE HERB TEA

My hour for tea is half-past five, and my buttered toast waits for nobody.
—Wilkie Collins, English novelist, *The Woman in White*

If your spouse is feeling under the weather, make a cup of hot tea to help soothe what ails her. Echinacea tea made into a tisane, or infusion, is just the type of herb tea that is favored for soothing a sore throat, an achy body, or a pounding head. Alternatively, you might make a pleasing beverage from fresh gingerroot or lotus root or honey and lemon steeped in hot water.

Or, whisk some green powdered matcha into a cup or bowl of hot water until it is frothy. Whole matcha leaves are used to make a healthy green tea. It contains almost no calories and yet provides numerous healthful benefits, including compounds associated with high antioxidant activity—good for the immune system. In addition, matcha green tea reduces bad cholesterol and high blood pressure, evens out blood sugar levels, and delivers several vitamins and trace minerals. If you can't find matcha, try other types of green and white teas, as virtually all contain antioxidants in the form of polyphenols or flavonoids, so you'll still get the health benefits. While the herb tea works its magic, you could remind her that the beverage she's drinking has not only soothing but also medicinal value and that her positive thinking about healing might be equally beneficial.

--- EXTRA CREDIT ---

Make some slices of buttered toast (if she has a sore throat, cut the crusts off the toast) or a plate of scones to go with the tea. Serve with a small dollop of jelly or her favorite jam or fruit butter.

DATE NIGHT

Tear a photo from an adult magazine that graphically illustrates exactly what you want to do with your partner—perhaps with a sticky note saying, "Can't wait to try this with you tonight!" Then throughout the day, call your partner at random times, just to say "Hi, looking forward to our date, which will begin with dinner on the patio, followed by dessert in the bedroom."

ENCOURAGE YOUR SPOUSE TO
PATENT HER INNOVATIVE IDEA

A posse ad esse. —Latin phrase meaning "from possibility to actuality."

Imagine for a moment that your wife has hit upon a great idea for a product that uses very little energy but could have a positive impact on the environment. Although her green invention may take a while to push through the patent process (the U.S. Patent and Trademark Office is currently backlogged on processing patents), it is still worthwhile to pursue it. Not only is there a need for great new ideas to benefit the planet; her innovative idea also could be a big moneymaker if a larger company is either already working on the same type of concept or would want to purchase hers. It has certainly happened to other inventors throughout the history of the patent office.

--- EXTRA CREDIT ---

Help her do a check through the U.S. Patent and Trademark Office (*www.uspto.gov*) to see if her idea would infringe upon another patent or if someone else has already patented her concept or a similar project. If not, encourage her to reach for the stars.

DISCUSS HOW TO FULLY DEVELOP
HER ENTREPRENEURIAL IDEA

Nothing succeeds like success. —English idiomatic expression

If she has a great idea for an entrepreneurial venture, give her positive feedback, emotional support, and your honest view about the project she has in mind, both positive and negative. She's counting on you for that. In addition, discuss the various ways she could take her idea into the world and how to generate revenue from each variation of the same basic idea. Use the following items as discussion points:

- Determine how to mine the basic concept into multiple other ventures.
- Do a SWOT analysis of her idea to evaluate its strengths, weaknesses, opportunities, and threats.
- Project the costs versus income and the length of time before she starts to see a return on her investment.
- Choose a mentor or board of advisers.
- Network with diverse industry groups to expose her entrepreneurial idea, whether it's for a company, service, or product.
- Learn more efficient and cost-effective ways of marketing/promoting/publicizing her idea.
- Examine ways to position her idea in the current marketplace.

—— EXTRA CREDIT ——

Play devil's advocate. When everyone else is telling her how brilliant her idea is, help her to stay grounded and see potential pitfalls. That is not to say you should be negative, but rather point out the risks and help her discover ways to overcome them.

BUILD HOUSES
FOR THE HOMELESS

We make a living by what we do, but we make a life by what we give...
—Winston Churchill, British statesman

If you and your spouse are moved by causes such as homelessness, tackle the problem together. Do something as a couple that addresses your passion and idealism and at the same time deepens your commitment to making the world a better place for the less fortunate of your community. Working together can deepen your commitment to each other as well. In April 2009, a graduate student at the University of California, Los Angeles, presented a great idea: build 1,000 houses for the homeless. With roughly 80,000 homeless people in Los Angeles county, the idea was both timely and ambitious. Teams of students would work with various cities to create a fully developed plan tailored to each city's need. It's a perfect example of what Margaret Mead meant when she uttered her famous quote (Day 43).

Habitat for Humanity, spearheaded by former President Jimmy Carter, is an organization that provides homes for low-income families. Husbands and wives are welcome to help; no experience necessary. There are even all-female building crews for women who like the experience of bonding with other women. This and similar organizations build houses to shelter humankind in order to rid the world of poverty housing and homelessness.

—— EXTRA CREDIT ——

Volunteer with your spouse to build a house with Habitat for Humanity in its Global Village Program. You'll travel to another country, experience another culture, and have fun serving the people of that country. You'll pay for your own airfare and stay in hotels, dormitories, or retreat centers. Find more information at *www.habitat.org*.

CONTROL DEMANDING
SCHEDULES

I confess to Thee, O Lord, that I am as yet ignorant as to what time is.
—St. Augustine, Confessions, Book 11

Sometimes it seems that there just aren't enough hours in the day to accomplish everything that needs doing. You and your spouse have little or no time together and have compared yourselves to trains on different tracks. Demanding schedules involving work, children, and community obligations can deflate even the most buoyant of marriages. Regaining control means giving up something to free up blocks of time to be with your partner—something that's stressed by marriage and family therapists as something a couple needs to do to build and strengthen their marriage, but many couples resist. When both spouses have jobs requiring long hours or extended periods away from home, it is difficult to find even a small chunk of time to be together. It seems that you are trying to do the impossible.

Although there is no substitute for quality time together, commiserating over the situation is one way spouses can convey their sense of longing for the other. Talking to your mate forms a bridge that allows you to reconnect with each other. Try one or more of the following four strategies to free up time for each other: (1) Establish small marital rituals, such as sharing morning coffee, an evening walk, kisses before bed. (2) Communicate often, sharing your feelings of love. (3) Do volunteer activities together when possible. (4) Eliminate time wasters.

— EXTRA CREDIT —

Make a master schedule of a month of activities for the whole family and pencil in appointments with your spouse for a half-hour coffee, a lunch, a lovemaking session, or a time to talk about how you can get a better handle on your schedules in the future.

BE SMART ABOUT
COMMINGLING MONEY

. . . and now we're down to our last $37,000. —Tammy Faye Bakker, American singer and television personality

Many couples decide to take the hybrid approach of "yours," "mine," and "ours" to establish separate checking and savings accounts. Other married couples choose to have a joint account, in which a husband's money is commingled with his wife's. In addition to the benefit of paying household bills out of one account, if one partner becomes incapacitated, ill, or dies, the joint account holder has immediate access to the money. However, a married couple may also opt to keep individual accounts out of which personal expenses such as manicures and haircuts are paid.

Some couples believe commingling their money is an important aspect of their commitment to each other, while others believe it is important to keep their accounts completely separate. The most important thing is to be smart about choosing the approach that you and your spouse believe is the best financial model for the two of you and your marriage.

— EXTRA CREDIT —

Talk with your spouse about keeping cash in the house for small emergencies or for situations where quick access to cash is needed (when the toilet is broken or you need pizza delivery on Saturday night, for example). Establish a specific location in your home where the money will be kept and make sure your spouse is aware of the location. Decide on how much cash is appropriate and how often you will replenish the reserve.

HELP EACH
OTHER DE-STRESS

I hold this to be the highest task of a bond between two people: that each should stand guard over the solitude of the other. —Rainer Maria Rilke, Bohemian-Austrian poet, *Letters to a Young Poet*

Find a place of peace and solitude where you and your partner can relax and de-stress. Simultaneously give each other foot massages. Sit opposite one another with legs outstretched so as not to block the flow of the energy as it is released during the massage. Foot massage has long been used as a way to invoke deep relaxation. In fact, reflexology, an Eastern modality that focuses on the zones or meridians on the body through which vital energies circulate, involves deep tissue massage of the hands and feet, where some of the meridians are located.

You could also combine several relaxation techniques. For example, before or after the foot massages, drink cups of fragrant herb tea, listen to soft relaxation music, dim the lighting, warm the room (if it's chilly) or cool it (if it's uncomfortably hot). Do deep breathing. Focus on eliminating chronic muscle tension that can decrease mental acuity and agility.

--- EXTRA CREDIT ---

Use quiet, gentle speech with each other. Talk to each other as lovers do—that is, when lovers talk they don't have a list of talking points, don't stick to an agenda, and don't have an ulterior motive. They enjoy every moment of the other's company and are reluctant to have such moments together end.

DATE NIGHT

Go out for a casino night. If you each like different methods of gambling—he likes playing cards and you love the slots—the casino offers all sorts of gambling options. Take only the amount of money you can afford to lose. Think of it as your entertainment allowance. Enjoy dinner together (many casinos have restaurants), then set a time and place to meet for a drink and to talk about winning, losing, and how you played your games.

ASK, HOW CAN
WE GET AHEAD?

In union there is strength. —Aesop, Greek storyteller

Sticking together and holding the course is fine, even admirable, especially during tough economic times. However, if you both want to get ahead, you'll need to unite on a plan for leveraging your combined untapped resources.

For example, sell those unused items that are stored in your garage, attic, or basement. If you're still storing your old surfboards, the antique bed, or the butter churn that belonged to your great-grandma, now might be the right time to turn those items into cash. If you have a box of costume jewelry, old family recipes, a collection of stamps or records, or an original World War II medical officer's case of first-aid instruments that belonged a distant relative, sell them on eBay or Craigslist for money that you can leverage into savings or investments. Collectors keep watch on eBay for items they particularly want, maybe those Snoopy & Friends dolls from the heyday of Charles Schulz's comic strip, or the magnificent iris-patterned flow blue dishes that belonged to your spouse's grandmother. Some of the platters could be worth several hundred dollars apiece. Think of them as putting food on the table rather than holding the food.

Or perhaps you have a box of foreign money from your parents' travels around the world. Ask at your bank if it can be exchanged for U.S. money and, if so, where and how.

— EXTRA CREDIT —
Work together to brainstorm other ways to cash in on your resources and to wisely invest the nickels, dimes, and dollars you find to help you build a financial cushion.

FIND WIN-WIN SOLUTIONS
TO PERSISTENT PROBLEMS

Let us not remember our troubles past, since they so happily have ended.
—Shakespeare, *The Tempest*

When you find that everyday stresses are disrupting your marital harmony, start looking for coping strategies and positive solutions to deal with the stress. For example, if the stress is work-related, recognize that fact and resist starting an argument with your spouse instead of showing your happiness at seeing him at the end of the day. What's really got you going is the deadline at work, the difficult supervisor, or the coworker who isn't shouldering her fair share of the load.

The solution may be to set aside time to decompress, unwind, and let go. Another strategy might be to actually schedule a gripe-and-whine session where you could both let it all out, commiserate, and move on.

— EXTRA CREDIT —

Know what makes you and your spouse feel loved and appreciated and make sure you both get plenty of those things in your marriage. For example, perhaps he travels a lot and has to eat out. You work part-time at a job, but also care for the kids when he's away on business, pay the bills, and keep the household running. You enjoy going out for a weekend meal but he prefers the two of you cook rather than eat out again. When you understand the need that underlies the choices you both are making, it's easier to find a compromise.

FOCUS ON WHAT FIRST
ATTRACTED THE TWO OF YOU

Upon the City Ramparts, lit up by sunset gleam,/The Blue eyes that conquer, meet the Darker eyes that dream. —Laurence Hope, India's Love Lyrics, "On the City Wall"

Biological wiring, in part, explains the attraction between you and your spouse that was there even before you dated or became engaged. Although some evolutionary theorists say that men respond to visual cues, such as women with hourglass figures, whose hips are wider than the waist (a possible evolutionary cue for a birthing advantage), women respond to masculine good looks (large open eyes, proportionate facial features) and also to cultural and economic factors such as a man's earning power, intelligence, and personality.

But setting these factors aside, consider what specific qualities or traits initially attracted you to each other. For you, was it his infectious laugh or big heart? Was it his intelligence, tactful diplomacy, or dry wit? When you feel that your differences are separating you and pulling you apart, that is precisely the time to celebrate the magnetism factor that brought you together; the qualities and traits that spelled "attraction."

— EXTRA CREDIT —

Arrange to have sex by appointment. Make the effort to spend time together solely for the purpose of sexual intimacy every week. Make it an unbreakable appointment, and make sure you will have real privacy.

LET YOUR PARTNER
BE WHO HE OR SHE IS

God grant me the serenity to accept the things I cannot change; courage to change the things I can; and wisdom to know the difference. —abbreviated, popularized version of "The Serenity Prayer" by Reinhold Niebuhr, American theologian

Your mate is who he is, just as you are who you are. Getting frustrated, annoyed, or angry with your spouse will not make him change. Pleading or artful persuasion also are unlikely to work. Think about how you feel when someone tries to change you: you resist.

For example, your spouse might complain that you are not meeting his emotional needs. You might accuse him of bad behavior; of not fulfilling his obligations or commitment to you, at least the way you think he should. The focus in the relationship stops being about building romantic love and starts being about lack, disrespect, and dissatisfaction. Sensitive communication can clear the air, but it won't fix the underlying problem. Many marriage therapists and psychologists assert that happiness can only come from within you—it cannot come from another person. That suggests accepting your spouse for the person he is, including the imperfections.

Change, if it comes at all, must come from within. There are no easy fixes, but when two people love each other, they usually find ways to overcome seemingly insurmountable obstacles.

--- EXTRA CREDIT ---

Take the professional approach, just as if you had to deal with a hot-button issue in the business world. If conflict-resolution tactics and respectful dialogue don't move you beyond the impasse to a solution, bring in a third party to arbitrate (a clergy member you both trust to be fair, or a marriage counselor).

BRING YOUR TOTAL SELF
TO THE RELATIONSHIP

Here's to your roof/May it be well thatched/And here's to all under it/
May they be well matched. —Irish toast

A relationship is about moving from "I" to "we." It is about choosing to share yourself with another person on levels that acquaintances and strangers never know. Truly healthy relationships are about bringing out the best in each other. Whether you are in complete bliss or complete pain, you bring that emotion in total to the other person so that he or she can bask in your joy or help you through your pain. You are willing to bring your total self into that relationship and help the other person do the same. To have a dynamic, healthy, loving relationship, consider the following tips:

- Be clear and direct in your communication.
- Be forgiving and understanding.
- Work hard to create a positive, constructive place for both of you.
- Be willing to admit your mistakes and shortcomings.
- Be constructive and supportive.
- Have the courage to be warm and sensitive.
- Don't be afraid to talk about your differences.
- Never be afraid or too strong to be held.

--- EXTRA CREDIT ---

Ask your lover to join you in a two-minute writing exercise. Ask him to jot down on a piece of paper something you do that he can't stand, and something else you do that he adores. Follow the same criteria to write two notes about him. Trade the notes. Use the likes and dislikes to discuss your differences.

VISIT A VINEYARD
AND TASTE SOME WINE

There can be no profit without wine. —Latin proverb

If you want to feel punch-drunk in love again, banish boredom, and get your love buzz going, head out to a vineyard and taste some great wine. Just the word "vineyard" conjures up the image of luscious vines, heavy with fruit, sprawled over hillsides in France, Tuscany, and other beautiful locations where grapes are cultivated. Making wine from grapes dates to the Neolithic period (8500 to 4000 B.C.), as evidenced by resinated wine (wine mixed with tree sap) in jars discovered by archeologists. Since there are wineries and vineyards in virtually every state in the United States and many more in Europe, South America, and elsewhere, it should be relatively easy to find one that you and your spouse will want to visit. You may even find one in your local community.

— EXTRA CREDIT —

Join a wine club to learn more about wine. Many offer different levels of membership, and most offer bottles of wine at a discounted price to members. Many wine clubs produce newsletters and host events. So whether you both like the offerings of boutique wineries or a particular varietal grown by one of the older and better-known wineries (which probably already has its own wine club), consider the various ways that such a club might enhance your enjoyment of fine food and wine for years to come.

DATE NIGHT

Let go of family responsibility for a while to focus on each other. With your children in the hands of a sitter you trust, relax and enjoy your date. Lie on a hammock with your heads together, facing the same direction, and talk about the firsts in your life: your first crush in grade school, the first time you held hands, the first kiss, your first date, and so on. Go on to talk about the effect you had on each other when you first met, your silly fears and anxieties, your joyful discoveries, and your most exhilarating romantic moments with each other.

FIND PURPOSE AND MEANING
IN YOUR LIFE AND MARRIAGE

Vive la différence! —French saying, meaning "long live the difference (between the sexes)"

Differences between you and your spouse can enrich and enliven your marriage. Without differences of opinions, for example, how could you have spirited debates? Or see an alternate view of religion, politics, or history, if not by viewing it through his eyes? Likewise, your different life purposes can impel you and your spouse to look for meaning in your marriage and beyond. Countless people stake their purpose or meaning in life on jobs, material belongings, or accomplishments.

Yet purpose is deeper than a job. It is stronger than another person and more resilient than possessions. You may leave your purpose, but it does not leave you. Purpose is as necessary as a vital organ but as elusive as the soul. Perhaps this is why so few people spend time discovering their purpose, listening to it, or answering its call.

One way to begin your journey toward purpose in life is to take stock of what is happening in your life and marriage. Are you happy? Do your efforts give you the outcomes you desire? Are you constantly asking yourself, *When are things going to get better?* Do you try harder and harder, yet success remains elusive? If so, you may not be living purposefully.

--- EXTRA CREDIT ---

The acclaimed minister Dr. Robert H. Schuller asked: "What would you attempt to do if you knew you could not fail?" List at least ten things that you would do if you knew you could not fail. Choose one item from the list. Why are you not doing it now? How important would doing it be for you to feel a sense of purpose in your life or your marriage?

RUB YOUR
SPOUSE'S TEMPLES

Find a place inside where there's joy, and the joy will burn out the pain.
—Joseph Campbell, American mythologist, writer, lecturer

Headaches are a common symptom of many maladies, such as tension, stress, eyestrain, sinus inflammation, food allergies, the common cold, flu, depression, anxiety, meningitis, diabetes, and a host of other illnesses too numerous to list.

It's little wonder that our fingers go right to our temples when we have a headache. We all need the human touch to feel safe, secure, happy, and loved. Offer to gently massage your spouse's temples if he is suffering discomfort. Crawl up behind him on the sofa or in bed. Cradle his head in your lap, and gently massage his temples in a slow circular motion, using the third finger of each hand. Try using white flower oil—ingredients are wintergreen, menthol, eucalyptus, peppermint, lavender, and camphor—as an analgesic balm to soothe away his discomfort.

—— EXTRA CREDIT ——
Offer to also massage the midpoint between the eyebrows. Use your index finger to apply a little pressure and massage in a circular motion. Then push gently into the forehead for twenty to thirty seconds and release. This same technique can be used on the sinuses.

REACH OUT TO
YOUR MOTHER-IN-LAW

If you're going to have fried chicken, have fried chicken. —Marian Robinson,
President Barack Obama's mother-in-law, on why she doesn't go for organic
foods or making dishes healthier

The news that Michelle Obama's mother, Marian Robinson, would live at the White House to care for the First Family's children was grist for the comedy mill as soon as President Obama was elected to office. Fortunately, it appears as though the relationship between the president and his wife's mother is cordial and respectful.

If you and your spouse don't have such warm and loving relationships with your respective mothers-in-law, it's never too late to extend a welcome. If you are newly married, make your overture, but give your mothers-in-law the gift of time to adjust to you and your spouse, the newest members of their families. Be protective of your love of your mate and your private time together, but open your lives to sharing some time with your families, and especially with each other's mothers. Remember them on Mother's Day, their birthdays, and the religious holidays that they celebrate. It doesn't require much to show them that you consider them important to your lives and to those of your children (even if those babies are not yet in the world).

Resist any impulse to be boastful, rude, or jealous. Having a good relationship with your mother-in-law can be a great benefit and blessing.

— EXTRA CREDIT —

Make the celebration of Mother-in-Law Day a family tradition. Instituted in 2002 as a special day to honor the mothers of your spouses, Mother-in-Law Day falls on the fourth Sunday in October.

SIGN UP FOR
BELLY DANCING

The essence of all art is to have pleasure in giving pleasure. —Mikhail
Baryshnikov, Russian-American dancer and actor

Silk dance veils. Coin hip scarves. Finger cymbals. Just dressing as a
belly dancer can make you feel delightfully sensuous and beautiful. You
can't help but be more aware of your body as you begin to learn how to
pivot your hips and abdomen and gyrate to the strains of Middle Eastern
music. It's good for your body, too, as it gets the heart rate up and tones
and tightens flabby muscle.

   If you have no idea where to start, find a belly-dancing class in the
catalogue of your local park and recreation department. Sign up for a class
at your local community college. Or, find a local dance company that
offers belly-dancing classes for beginners. Develop your own natural sense
of rhythm and control over your body's movements. If you are like many
women, you will feel sexier when dancing. You husband could become
aroused watching you dance, especially if you are uninhibited and obvi-
ously enjoying yourself. Receiving positive attention from your mate can
give you a burst of self-confidence that will translate into more assertive-
ness during lovemaking.

--- EXTRA CREDIT ---

Dancing can be a delightfully erotic and arousing act. Use it as foreplay. Surprise your
partner with a show for his eyes only. The eroticism of your body and its suggestive
power will fire your husband's imagination more than if you take all your clothes off
at once and leave nothing to his imagination. Do your own version of the biblical
Salome's dance of the seven veils that so titillated and inflamed her stepfather Herod
Antipas.

SEE MARITAL DISCORD
AS A GROWTH OPPORTUNITY

A soft answer turneth away wrath; but grievous words stir up anger.
—Proverbs 15:1

Marital discord arises over a variety of issues that stress the marriage. For example, it can develop from unmet needs due to a change of circumstance that then causes a shift in the behavior of one or both spouses (for example, the arrival of a new baby); spouses spending less time together; a relative moving into the house; a job loss; sudden illness; or health and financial worries.

Contrary to popular belief, marital discord doesn't happen as a flash of lightning but rather slowly builds within the relationship until an inciting incident intensifies the feelings of one or both spouses and an argument erupts. Your relationship won't necessarily suffer irreparable damage. You can use your dissatisfaction to finally air grievances, figure out what you can do to restore/repair the relationship harmony, and discuss ways to implement change that will help you both feel better.

— EXTRA CREDIT —

Repair your failures—that is, when you have ongoing discord and you know you've screwed up, reach out and do your part to start to repair the relationship. Your effort could take the form of a goofy grin, some self-deprecating humor, an apology, a spontaneous peck on the cheek, a playful push or hug—in short, anything that shows your spouse that you are trying to move forward with him or her.

TAP THE POWER OF
OPPOSING POINTS OF VIEW

Opposition is true friendship. —William Blake, English poet and painter

You voted for the Democrats and your loving husband voted Republican; you like indigenous ethnic music of the world and he prefers classical compositions; your clothing screams your love of wild colors and patterns but he likes the tailored, traditional look of black and white. Your friends wonder how you make your marriage work when your points of view seem to be polar opposites. But friends might not understand that you and your life partner love expanding your perceptions and widening your worldview to embrace new ideas, experiences, choices, and opportunities.

When you and your mate put your heads together to figure out a solution to a problem, you both bring different insights to the process, thereby widening the arena of possible solutions. In the realm of music, for example, tapping the power of opposing points of view takes you into local clubs, street fairs, and dance halls but also into the opera houses and symphony halls of the world. In short, a marriage that uses opposing points of view to create a larger context and worldview can be enriching and stimulating.

—— EXTRA CREDIT ——

Enjoy an evening of lively discourse with your husband and assorted friends on some obscure or current hot-button topic. You can find discussion groups on the Internet for subjects ranging from medieval Old Norse history to modern Marxist theory or even the changes in the public food supply brought about by giant agribusiness. Check out interesting topics, choose one with your spouse, invite friends over, and let the conversation take you wherever you want to go.

DATE NIGHT

Go camping, toast marshmallows, count the stars, and sleep in a tent. Make it as titillating and erotic as you want. You can pretend you are other people, do some other type of role playing, reverse the roles, or do whatever else you want. The point is to take a break from playing with the kids for a night to play with each other.

DOCUMENT YOUR
JOURNEY TOGETHER IN WRITING

———

There is a fullness of all things, even of sleep and love. —Homer, *The Iliad*

Start a scrapbook, keep a journal, write a blog, or make notes about your progress toward realizing your dream. If you choose, post the notes on social networking sites like Facebook, MySpace, Ning Networks, and others that you like. Keep a record of how you and your partner are working to actualize a life goal or dream that you share. Capture all the significant moments, starting from the first time you sat down together to discuss the possibility of realizing your dream to all the steps you will be taking in the direction of your dream.

In so doing, you set up a powerful attraction for the dream's manifestation and trigger events that can help you on your way. You can also hold each other accountable for making the dream happen when you're chronicling its progress.

—— EXTRA CREDIT ——

If you are not a writer, try using a video camera to capture the important moments on your dream's journey to reality. In short, make your own documentary. Alternatively, when you have accomplished what you dreamed of doing, then you can share the process with others through your documentation of the events.

ACCEPT EACH OTHER'S
ANNOYING HABITS

The fixity of habit is generally in direct proportion to its absurdity. —Marcel
Proust, French novelist, critic, and essayist

You can't stand to see him chewing his thumbnail, but you know he does
it when he feels stressed out and overwhelmed. He tolerates your endless
stirring of sugar in your coffee and says nothing because he knows you
aren't even aware you are doing it, much less that he finds it extremely
annoying.

While nail biting and coffee-stirring habits can be irritating, are they
really worth fighting over? You've heard the old adage about not sweat-
ing the small stuff. Such advice is appropriate when it comes to irritating
little habits. If you can't resist the urge to react, try to do it with empathy,
humor, or negotiation—"Let's make a pact to break our habits. I'll stop
stirring my coffee if you stop chewing your nails." Another tactic might
be to put his habit into larger perspective—think of all the wonderful
things about him, the totality of the package. Now, wouldn't you still fall
in love and marry him despite his annoying little habit? Of course you
would, and he would still marry you, too.

— EXTRA CREDIT —
Put out an empty coffee can. Choose a habit you both want to break—for example,
cursing. You and your mate first decide what constitutes use of foul language in your
home. Then, every time one of you swears, you have to drop a quarter into the can.
Remember, it takes about three weeks to form or break a habit. You'll either stop
cursing or you will have a can full of quarters that you to can use to buy some books
for extra help in breaking the cursing habit.

AVOID CONFLICTS AND
CONFRONTATIONS BEFORE BED

Good battle is healthy and constructive, and brings to a marriage the principle of equal partnership. —Ann Landers, American newspaper columnist

Conflicts at bedtime can come about if one or both of you has not had time to decompress after work or if you have unresolved marital conflict. But when couples argue right before bed, it becomes virtually impossible to relax into restful sleep. Bedtime is the time to exchange the cares of the physical world for the peace and restorative benefits of rest. It's a time to allow your body and mind to recuperate from the assaults of the day and to allow the magical imagery of the dream world to emerge in the depths of your consciousness.

Arguing before bed is unlikely to resolve the issue because you are both tired and not thinking as clearly as you will be after you've had a good night's sleep. Find a more appropriate time to have a healthy and constructive conversation about what's bugging you. Save bedtime as the time for love and rest.

— EXTRA CREDIT —

Make bedtime a special time, perhaps even a favorite part of your day, when you unwind, de-stress, and do those routines that nourish your spirit, restore emotional balance, and nurture your marriage. For example, take a hot shower, share a cup of tea with your spouse, do some couples yoga, give each other a back massage, or read together.

FORM A DREAM SUPPORT
GROUP WITH OTHERS

When we are dreaming alone, it is only a dream. When we dream with others, it is the beginning of reality. —Dom Hélder Câmara, Brazilian Roman Catholic Archbishop of Olinda and Recife

Knowing that your spouse believes in your dream and your ability to manifest it means a lot to you. But there are times when you both might need the emotional support of others to achieve a dream. You and your spouse are not living in a vacuum, but rather in a world of people who may harbor the same or similar dreams that you hold dear. People who share common interests often form groups with other like-minded individuals. Internet sites listing organizations of individuals sharing common interests in everything from astrology, metaphysics, and esoteric topics to New Age healing practices, music, art, literature, the environment, politics, ecology, green jobs, and other topics are proliferating. You can also find Usenet groups for virtually any subject in which you are interested and read or post information or participate in discussions with people the world over.

If, for example, you are interested in ways that vineyards could go green in methods of controlling pests that attack the vines that produce the fruit, you could find information on like-minded vintners and wine aficionados on the Internet or by visiting vineyards in California, Europe, and elsewhere.

—— EXTRA CREDIT ——

Find and read books on the topics that relate to the dream you and your spouse desire to manifest. Visit websites that relate to some aspect of your dream. Write e-mails, make phone calls, and send text messages. Utilize blogs, RSS feeds, Usenet groups, and social networking sites to find others who share your passion.

ESTABLISH GROUND RULES FOR
HEATED DEBATE OF FAVORITE TOPICS

I love argument, I love debate. I don't expect anyone to just sit there and agree with me, that's not their job. —Margaret Thatcher, former British prime minister

You probably love a heated exchange with your partner about certain topics, such as the ones traditionally forbidden to bring up in polite company: sex, politics, and religion. It reminds you of an earlier stage in your romance when you conversed for hours. It's still a good idea to establish some rules that can be applied to your lively discussion so things don't get too confrontational. You can even use these rules for situations in which you and your spouse must resolve a conflict. The following list can help you keep it friendly and focused and avoid the pitfalls, such as bruising egos or inflicting emotional pain.

- No negative name-calling, not even silly names. Loving pet names that you usually call each other, however, is okay.
- Allowing your passions for the topic to escalate is okay, but attacking your spouse's character is not.
- Stay on point.
- Avoid interrupting the speaker.
- Focus on specifics, not sweeping generalizations.
- Keep it respectful at all times.
- Take a break if the discussion becomes too hot.

— EXTRA CREDIT —
Hone your debating skills. Buy a handbook or learn techniques and strategies for oratory debate on websites. Let it help you enjoy even more those lively discussions with the one you love.

REMEMBER THAT SOME
EVENTS RESULT IN JEWELRY

Opportunity knocks for every man, but you have to give a woman a ring.
—Mae West, American sex symbol and movie star

Even in the most loving and solid of marriages, a spouse occasionally will screw up. Not just a little oversight, but a great big mess-up. If a sincere apology and your offer to do better have not worked, it might be time to think jewelry. That's not to say that you are trivializing what has happened, or painting your spouse as some kind of gold digger. But presenting your beloved with a heartfelt gift could have a softening effect. Own up when you screw up and do whatever you have to in order to get your marriage back on track.

— EXTRA CREDIT —
Invite her on a shopping trip for something special just for her. You might be surprised to discover that she's less into choosing carats than choosing to be with you. She knows you are reaching out to her and trying to make things right. Take her to a picturesque street with small shops, jewelry stores, and cafes. Walk, talk, shop, and have lunch. Hold her hand. Kiss her only if she's ready for that.

DATE NIGHT

Visit the racetrack and place modest bets. Find the best seats for viewing the race and cheer your horses to victory. Afterward, whether you won or lost, you can still enjoy a mint julep or a mojito together.

CONSIDER
SEPARATE CLOSETS

I like my money where I can see it . . . hanging in my closet. —Sarah Jessica Parker, American actress, *Sex and the City*

You've looked and looked but can't locate those expensive Italian leather shoes that you want to wear to your law school benefit on Saturday night. Now your wife is mad because in her endeavor to help you, she found your boots caked with dry mud in the corner of the closet floor, crushing up against her favorite black dress. Never mind that she hasn't worn it for two years because of the weight she gained during her pregnancy. Still, you've been sniping at each other ever since the discovery, and it's only Wednesday.

The molehill has become a mountain. This is a perfect example of what it means to not "sweat the small stuff." Separate closets are an easy fix if sharing the closet is causing problems. Divide the closet into his and her sections or find another closet in the house so your stuff doesn't get lost or commingled, and get on with the business of having a loving, happy, meaningful relationship.

—— EXTRA CREDIT ——

If money isn't an issue, contract with a local carpenter to do a closet makeover in the master bedroom to give you both the storage space you need. The makeover doesn't have to be a custom high-end closet if it's hidden behind the closet doors; just functional.

DO WORKOUTS FOR
YOURSELF AND YOUR MARRIAGE

To exercise at or near capacity is the best way I know of reaching a true introspective state. If you do it right, it can open all kinds of inner doors.
—Al Oerter, four-time Olympic gold medalist in discus

Maybe you and your spouse have continued working out in different gyms because that's what you did before you married and you have different routines that you follow. But lately you have been searching for less expensive ways to stay fit. Working out at home is one alternative. Working out at home together benefits your marriage because it keeps you both healthy, reduces your expenses, and provides quality couple time.

Even if you have different routines, exercising at the same time, and in the same room, can be effective and fun despite the fact that it doesn't afford the options of a professional gym. Start by doing stretches and bends such as yoga poses to warm your muscles. If you have a treadmill, rowing machine, stationery bike, or a weightlifting machine, you could work out on the machine while your spouse does resistance exercises with stretch tubing that can be knotted and hung over a door that is then closed (holding the knot in place behind the door).

—— EXTRA CREDIT ——

Arrange for a masseuse to come to your house once a month to give you and your spouse massages after your workouts. It still will be cheaper than gym memberships.

MAKE A LIST OF PLACES
TO SEE BEFORE YOU DIE

All journeys have secret destinations of which the traveler is unaware.
—Martin Buber, Jewish philosopher

Okay, so you are too young to be thinking about kicking the bucket. Aren't we all, but, hey, you don't want to put things off too long. Invite your spouse to join you in visiting websites that list someone else's top ten sites to see before he or she dies to give you some ideas. Download pictures of places within and beyond your community's borders. Widen your cyberspace journey to also see images of the Taj Majal, the Great Sphinx, Machu Picchu, Jerusalem's Old City, Beijing's Forbidden City, the Greek Acropolis, and others.

Let the pictures stir your imaginations and awaken the wanderlust in you both. Consider timing your adventure to an exotic place to see it under a full moon, during a sunrise, or after a tropical storm clears the air and the steam is rising. Those are the kinds of memories that you will always hold dear.

— EXTRA CREDIT —
Spend a quiet evening at home watching *The Bucket List,* a 2007 movie starring Morgan Freeman and Jack Nicholson. It's about two men meeting at a crossroads in their lives and deciding to make up for lost time, doing everything they've wanted to do before kicking the bucket. Consider where you and your spouse might want to go, or what you would want to see or experience, if you knew you had only a limited amount of time to do it.

DON'T DISPARAGE YOUR
PREVIOUS PARTNERS

Your allegiance is with your spouse; you cannot break that by showing allegiance to your ex-spouse. —Connie Selleca, American actress and former model

Your new marriage is vitally important to you, and you want to convey that to your current spouse. However, make sure you avoid making out your ex-mate as being your adversary. Ridiculing or disparaging your ex says more about you than him or her. At best, it demonstrates ill will, resentment, intolerance, and even vindictiveness. If you and your ex have had children together, also watch what you say around them. Hearing one parent disparaging the other is distressing for a child and can even inflict emotional and psychological damage.

It's much better for all if you and your ex can find a way to not harbor resentment and instead become friends. Such a relationship takes nothing from your current marriage but could ease tensions for all concerned, especially your children.

> ### —— EXTRA CREDIT ——
> Sit with your current spouse and have a heart-to-heart chat about your ex or your spouse's ex to discuss ways to warm the relationships you both have with your ex-spouses. This is even more important if you share custody of children or if you have a blended family. Keep the past in the past and focus instead on what you can do to make the present relationships more harmonious and helpful.

DAY 256

ENROLL IN
COUPLES TENNIS

The serve was invented so that the net could play. —Bill Cosby, American
comedian

If you and your spouse find watching coed tennis exciting, why not
become players instead of spectators? Maybe you've both watched the
healthy, toned bodies of players of the opposite sex competing on the
court and find it more than a little, ahem, invigorating. Perhaps you've
developed your own refined system of ranking players by looks and
physique.

If you are a die-hard tennis fan, enroll in a class to work on your own
serves, volleys, forehand and backhand strokes, and returns. Surely there
is a tennis club or court near you!

Tennis requires a partner. You have one who shares your love for
the game. Imagine kicking your game up a notch or shifting it into a
competitive high gear.

—— EXTRA CREDIT ——

Hire a private tennis coach to work on your strokes. Or, sign up for a tennis fantasy
camp with your spouse. Imagine heading off to a resort in Jamaica, Florida, the
Arizona desert, or elsewhere. You and your spouse can immerse yourselves in every
aspect of the game, possibly playing with pros. That should put a little excitement
back into your marriage.

REDUCE THE MOUNTAIN
TO A MOLEHILL

Inner peace begins with a relaxed body. —Norman Vincent Peale, Protestant preacher and author

Take a huge step forward in divorce-proofing your marriage by nipping any marital discord over small issues early on. Avoid using words that trigger emotional responses and instead find words or new ways to talk about marital issues. Falling out of love is often given as the reason when a breakdown occurs within the first five years of a marriage. However, if you have a bond of friendship with your spouse and take the time to learn more about human behavior and why most people take counterproductive actions when stress occurs in intimate relationships, there is hope.

Both men and women are susceptible to disappointment when the initial romance of marriage wears thin, or when their original expectations fail to materialize. Even the smallest issues seem to get blown out of proportion, resulting in anger, frustration, and marital dissatisfaction. Both sexes express marital disaffection similarly—by blaming the other partner and withdrawing emotionally from the relationship. These patterns are what create the violent mood swings in a dying relationship just when the opposite behaviors are needed to save it.

— EXTRA CREDIT —

Make a list of all the things that your spouse is doing that upsets, annoys, frustrates, or angers you. Ask your spouse to do the same. Each of you can then cross through those items that you can live with, but the items that remain need your joint attention. Make the effort to be honest with each other, increase the level and quality of your communication, negotiate your differences, and not take your partner's words and actions personally.

DATE NIGHT

Have a coffee in the café of your local bookstore and then make your way
over to the architectural and interior design section. Spend a blissful hour
or two looking at images of houses—indoor and outdoor spaces—that
inspire you to create new structures for the two of you to enjoy.

KNOW THE STRESSES
OF BLENDED FAMILIES

Being married is like having somebody permanently in your corner, it feels limitless, not limited. —Gloria Steinem, married for the first time at age sixty-six

If your marriage created a blended family, chances are you already know how stressful certain situations can be and how much patience it takes to work things out. Today in America, roughly three out of five families are blended. In some, parents are raising adopted children; in others, the parents have divorced and remarried and are raising children from those previous marriages. Some are also having children of their own.

Life in the home of a blended family can feel at times like being caught up in the vortex of a whirlwind. Blended families face many stresses from outside forces as well as struggles from within their parents' or stepparents' marriages. Children in blended families often act out as a result of the stresses they feel, and it will be up to you and your spouse to establish the rules (and consequences for breaking them). You must also train your children to make good choices and guide, inform, and supervise them. It takes diligence, perseverance, and patience as well as a commitment to each other to coparent your young charges, united in your values, beliefs, and parenting philosophies.

— EXTRA CREDIT —

Develop a joint policy agreement in which you and your spouse enthusiastically agree (no ambivalence) on rules for the children, methods to enforce the rules, and discipline and consequences for those who break the rules. Having an agreement encourages both spouses to be fair and to negotiate changes to the rules with the other spouse instead of arbitrarily allowing a rule change.

MODEL
SELFLESSNESS

Any good therefore that I can do or any kindness that I can show to any human being, let me do it now. —Mahatma Gandhi

As a couple, you and your spouse have opportunities every day to lift up another person—a child, a homeless veteran, a friend, a struggling single mother, and countless others in your community. You and your mate can stand as exemplars of selflessness to others when you help them out in some way, and you generate good karma.

Acts such as helping a sick child get medical treatment when her parents have no financial resources to pay for it, engaging in a campaign to let a victim of torture know the world has not forgotten him and is working to secure his release from prison, or cleaning out your pantry to feed the homeless generate good karma as well. When you and your spouse listen to your hearts and honor your instincts to take action, you will be guided into making the right choices. You don't have to save the whole world by yourselves. If each of you tries to do good deeds every day, your acts will make the world a better place.

— EXTRA CREDIT —
Teach selflessness to your children by being exemplars to them. Husbands and wives are their children's first teachers and thus are in a better position than anyone to demonstrate acts of altruism. Teach your preschoolers to share with other children and to donate their unwanted toys to organizations that serve needy families.

BUY ASSETS TO
GROW YOUR WEALTH

It is not the creation of wealth that is wrong, but the love of money for its own sake. —Margaret Thatcher, former British prime minister

It's never too late to think about ways to put your money to work earning a higher interest rate in an online savings account, a conventional savings account, money market account, or a certificate of deposit (commonly known as a CD). If you have inherited money, there's a good chance that you are looking for places to invest it, perhaps for your retirement.

You and your partner can make smart choices about where to put your money by reading information posted on financial websites and in investment books and periodicals, by taking financial planning and strategy classes, or even by starting your own investment discussion group with other couples who want to learn more about preserving and growing their wealth.

--- EXTRA CREDIT ---

Join or start a small investment club. Learn about investing in stocks and other assets. Invite financial planners to speak before your group. Host regularly scheduled meetings to discuss individual and group investments. Track investment performances. Share information with your group and your spouse.

GET RID OF
ARCHAIC ATTITUDES

Attitude is a little thing that makes a big difference. —Winston Churchill, former British prime minister

In the comfort and security of a marriage, spouses can let down their guard and are not always on their best behavior. Because negative thinking and archaic attitudes can emerge in any marriage and adversely impact the spousal relationship, it is worth the effort to replace such intolerant attitudes with empathy and respect.

Whether or not you realize it, your attitudes, dictated by your beliefs and feelings, drive your behavior to do certain things; for example, to align with some groups but partition yourself from others, or to insist that gender dictates certain marital responsibilities. Similarly, showing a bias toward people because of their race, color, religion, gender, sex, age, disability, and country of origin is no longer acceptable in our society, even though it was widely accepted during other eras of history. However, just because the mainstream of modern society doesn't accept bias, bigotry, and intolerance of diversity does not mean that such attitudes are eradicated. When they crop up in your marriage, do your best to reverse them.

— EXTRA CREDIT —

Register for a sensitivity training class to make yourself and your partner more aware of any prejudices or biases you may hold toward others whom you perceive as different. To make substantive, rather than symbolic changes, you'll likely learn specific strategies, tips, and techniques.

TALK IT OUT TO REDUCE
STRESS ON YOUR NEW MARRIAGE

I would be willing to bet that if one day a woman walked barefoot to the moon and back and a man cleaned out his desk, when the two of them sat down to dinner that night he would say, "Boy was that desk a mess." —Margo Kaufman, humorist, writer, and radio commentator

Married couples might not think too much about the stress levels and how they pertain to health issues when they have so many other considerations. However, stress and its relationship to health shouldn't be ignored, either. Talking together is an easy way to de-stress and decompress after you both get home from work.

Scientific research has shown that stress levels drop in women who come home to a loving husband after a stressful day on the job. For men, the stress levels became lower when they returned home at the end of the workday, whether or not they were returning to a loving spouse and a happy marriage. Scientists from the University of California, Los Angeles, determined the stress levels by the amount of cortisol (a hormone released when the body experiences stress) in their subjects—thirty couples, married, working full-time, and parenting. It's worth noting that long-term high levels of cortisol are associated with relationship issues, burnout, chronic fatigue, and depression.

--- EXTRA CREDIT ---

Make a pact between you that the first spouse home prepares a beverage for the other—a tall, cold glass of a favorite drink like lemonade or iced tea for hot days and a warm, steaming cup of tea, cocoa, or broth when the temperature outside is chilly.

HELP CHILDREN ADJUST

Even when freshly washed and relieved of all obvious confections, children tend to be sticky. —Fran Lebowitz, American comedienne, essayist, and book author

Some children whose living arrangements and life circumstances are far from ideal overcome the odds and succeed, thanks to their own innate resilience and the caring and compassion of at least one person who serves as a positive role model. Children want to succeed in life and will live up to high expectations, provided they are given the necessary support and guidance. You and your spouse can impart messages to your children and stepchildren that they are worthy of success and that they have everything they need to succeed in life.

Help them adjust to your new spouse or blended family by promoting resiliency in your children in the following ways:

- Demonstrate and promote caring relationships.
- Express expectations that are high, positive, and attainable.
- Establish and promote opportunities for meaningful participation at home, at school, and in the community.
- Let them know that they can count on you to be a powerful advocate for them.
- Earn their trust, and let them know you value that trust.

—— EXTRA CREDIT ——

Teach children a simple life- and success-affirming saying such as, "I am and I can." Remind them to repeat the affirmation whenever they have doubts or feel fearful. Promote the idea of self-empowerment.

DATE NIGHT

Invite your lover to celebrate Oktoberfest, even if it isn't October. Create a shared outdoor space on the patio of your apartment, condo, or house. Set out some blooming petunias or begonias, throw a white tablecloth over a small table (cover it with transparent plastic to protect it from spills if you wish), buy a variety of different beers, or apple cider, and snacks, put on the polka music, and tell each other "I love you" in German (Ich liebe dich).

EXPLORE EACH OTHER'S
EROGENOUS ZONES

The mind can also be an erogenous zone. —Raquel Welch, American film actress

Your erogenous zones are areas on the body that elicit sexual feelings or sensations. While it is possible for your entire body to be an erogenous zone, most people respond to a few specific areas of their bodies that, when touched, bring sexual arousal. Aside from the obvious erogenous zones—the penis, the testicles, the clitoris, the labia, and the vagina—here is a list of other common erogenous zones:

- ears
- feet and toes
- groin
- hands and fingers
- inside of the thighs
- lips, tongue, and mouth
- neck
- perineum
- pubic mound

- sacrum
- scalp
- shoulders and spine
- small of the back
- stomach
- underarms
- underside of the elbows, forearms, and wrists

--- EXTRA CREDIT ---

Ask your partner to outline your body while you lie on a large piece of paper (like a roll of butcher paper). Do the same for him. Use colored pens and mark the erogenous zones on your body chart where you feel an erotic sensation when that area is stimulated in some way. Use purple to mark your nipples as highly erotic zones, or write in red that having your neck gently kissed really turns you on. Then use a different color to mark more subtle erogenous zones and the kinds of stimulation they like.

CONNECT
THE ZONES

The more connections you and your lover make, not just between your bodies, but between your minds, your hearts, and your souls, the more you will strengthen the fabric of your relationship, and the more real moments you will experience together. —Barbara de Angelis, American relationship consultant and personal growth teacher

Your brain is capable of making connections between erogenous zones, and you can enhance this potential with a little practice. Making erogenous zone connections is a concept championed by erotic pioneers Steve and Vera Bodansky, authors of *Instant Orgasm*. They train people to connect the arousal in their genitals to different parts of their bodies.

Start by focusing on the arousal in your genitals. Then shift your attention to another part of your body. You can do this cognitively or with the help of touch. Your brain then begins to make associations between the new parts and your overall sexual arousal. You begin to open the channels and enhance the arousal potential of your more subtle erogenous zones. With enough practice, touching the various nongenital parts will signal arousal to your genitals, spreading the potential for pleasure throughout your body.

—— EXTRA CREDIT ——

Turn the lights down or off. Get naked and lie on the bed with your mate. Put a layer of pillows between your bodies. Individually explore your erogenous zones by connecting genital arousal to different parts of your body. When you are both ready to take the arousal to the next level, slide your hand under the pillow to touch each other. Remove the pillows and allow the sensual pleasure that you have initiated lead you to enjoyment of each other.

SELF-PLEASURE
TOGETHER

Joy is never in our power and pleasure often is. —C.S. Lewis, British scholar and novelist

Self-pleasuring has the potential to be much more than just "getting off." Yes, there is a time and place for the simple and quick release of sexual tension. Sometimes, however, you might choose to go for more than that. Why not give both you and your partner the gift of an erotic ride that will nourish you, inspire you, and make you feel more alive? Try having your spouse self-pleasure alongside you. The following suggestions may give you a whole new experience:

- Move Your Body—Movements such as standing or leaning against a wall, bending over a desk or table, or down on all fours can involve your whole body and contribute to arousal.
- Make Noise—Sighing, squealing, or screaming can instigate a positive feedback loop and may arouse you even more.
- Involve All Your Senses—Create a beautiful space that stimulates your sense of sight, smell, touch, and hearing in order to intensify your pleasuring experience. Light candles, throw a soft blanket or pretty tapestry where the two of you will pleasure yourselves, and burn incense to scent the air.

— EXTRA CREDIT —

Continue the erotic pleasuring in the shower. Use a scented soap or shower gel. Let the pleasurable sensation of water flow over your body. Allow your head, neck, shoulders, and back to release any tension. Caress each other.

DEAL WITH PAST
UNFINISHED BUSINESS

We must be willing to let go of the life we have planned, so as to accept the life that is waiting for us. —Joseph Campbell, American mythologist, writer, lecturer

If one or both of you were previously married, you're especially likely to enter your current marriage with a very strong desire to make things work out—so as not to face a second divorce. But if your new marriage has created a blended family, and if you've never been part of a blended family before, much of what you're about to do is new, and requires a fresh approach. It also requires higher-level relationship skills than have been necessary in the past.

For all these reasons, it's important to let go of any anger or regrets you may be carrying from a previous marriage or prior relationship. You can't get the past back, not yours or his. Still, there are spouses who hold on to jealousy, insecurity, or anger about a current partner's past marriage, ex-spouse, or children with that ex—well into a new marriage.

There's a general rule of thumb that an adult requires a minimum of three years following a divorce in order to emotionally recover; that is, before he's ready to detach from the last relationship and fully engage with a new partner. However, if you and your ex have children together, you will never be completely disconnected from each other. Each child-centered interaction following your marital breakup is an occasion to stir up whatever's unresolved between you—or lay it to rest.

— EXTRA CREDIT —

It only takes one person to shift a relationship paradigm. Make it you. Change your stance, your attitude, your expectation, or your tendency to avoid or close off to a former spouse and see how your ex-mate changes in response.

USE HUMOR
TO DEFUSE TENSION

Sexiness wears thin after a while and beauty fades, but to be married to a man who makes you laugh every day, ah, now that's a real treat. —Joanne Woodward, American actress and wife of actor Paul Newman

A corny joke, a silly saying, and a little fun poked lovingly at each other and at life's predicaments can go a long way toward lifting or deflecting tension. Laughter is contagious, and cajoling or joking around is a tool that can be used effectively against rising tension.

Handling marital differences requires not only tolerance for individual differences and the ability to forgive in order to move beyond pain, but also a sense of humor to laugh at absurdity. Marriages have to handle the speed bumps of life. It is how you two handle the difficult experiences that determines the success or failure of marriage—not how well you handle your best days together. Relationships are not a contest; they are a support system. Unlike sports, when competition enters a marriage, the relationship sours. All successful relationships actively practice the art of forgiveness and humor, so whenever the going gets tough they can more easily find the way to laughter instead of fighting. Successful couples surrender into harmony, love, and the joy of becoming one.

--- EXTRA CREDIT ---

Tell your spouse a really funny joke and laugh at the punch line together. If you don't know any jokes, do a search on the Internet using the keyword "funny jokes" or "marriage jokes." Lighten up. Start joking around.

CREATE A PLEASANT
HOME ENVIRONMENT

But if each man could have his own house, a large garden to cultivate
and healthy surroundings; then, I thought, there will be for them a better
opportunity of a happy family life. —George Cadbury, British businessman
and social reformer

When your home is tidy and smelling clean, your mood becomes more positive, doesn't it? Undoubtedly, you feel differently when it looks cluttered or reeks of odors from the kitty litter box, dirty laundry, or stale food.

The home environment is the heart of family life; it is the place where the family regularly reconnects. Just as it affects you, it also triggers negative and positive feelings in your spouse and other family members. But just cleaning it might not be enough. Utilize the ancient Chinese principles of feng shui (pronounced *fung shway*, meaning "wind-water"). Feng shui is the art of placement in the home or business. Proper placement of objects can create a family environment that is aesthetically pleasing and inspires feelings of joy and harmony. Go beyond basic cleaning; take time to de-clutter, rearrange the furniture, hang a wind chime, put in plants (no spiky leaves), bring in natural or soft lighting, add a fountain, and set out some scented candles.

--- EXTRA CREDIT ---

Hire a feng shui consultant to examine your landscape and interior spaces. You may not be aware of problem areas or simple ways to fix them, but a feng shui expert will spot them right away. With his or her help, you and your spouse can execute a tune-up on your home environment, ensuring it will always be pleasant and uplifting.

DATE NIGHT

Make a time capsule and bury it in your backyard to be opened ten or twelve years from the burial date. Plan a fun and festive party for its retrieval and opening.

STICK TO YOUR
SHOPPING LIST

Wal-Mart . . . do they, like, make walls there? —Paris Hilton, American
socialite and media personality

Curb your spending to avoid marital friction over finances. Sticking to a
budget and resisting the urge to spend impulsively will help you to maintain harmony with your mate over money issues. A simple way to avoid
the tendency to buy things on impulse (typically items positioned at
the front of the store, on end caps, display tables, or along the checkout
aisle) is to make a shopping list before heading out to the store. Buy only
those items that you've included on the list. (Take your reusable store bag
with you!) Working with a finite list of things to buy and a grocery bag
that will hold only so many items will curb any tendency to buy extrane-
ous stuff. If shopping for groceries, you might even have a master list that
you keep on your refrigerator. Add food items to the list as necessary.

--- EXTRA CREDIT ---

Walk to the store if it's within a mile or two from your home. The walk will be good
for your health and you will only be able to carry what you can fit into a couple of
shopping bags.

ENCOURAGE HIM TO DO
A LITTLE DREAM DABBLING

Now join hands, and with your hands your hearts. —Shakespeare, *King Henry VI*

Some dreams seem to emerge fully formed and complete in concept, while others need a lot of incubation time. When your spouse talks for months about some great idea that came to him and he believes it has merit, encourage him to get involved with it, but on a limited basis at first.

If, for example, he wanted to someday be governor of your state, or a senator, encourage him to dabble in local politics. Suggest that he join a political action group or run for city council. That way, before he's invested a huge chunk of his life (and yours, too), he can get involved for a while to see if he likes politics enough to stay in for the long haul.

— EXTRA CREDIT —

Once your spouse has begun dabbling a bit in his dream, suggest that he try dream incubation as a way of exploring his dream more fully. Planting a seed (a thought that deals with what you want to dream about) before you fall asleep can sometimes trigger a dream on that topic. Of course, the language used by the dreaming mind is the language of symbols, so having a good dream symbol dictionary will more than likely be a help in deciphering the dream.

CREATE A LOVER'S
RITUAL TOGETHER

The personal life deeply lived always expands into truths beyond itself.
—Anaïs Nin, French-born American author

Bring more meaning into your marriage by establishing a ritual or two. For example, designate a small table with a couple of chairs as a fitting sanctuary for the two of you to pray or to meditate together, if only for a few minutes each day. Turn the table into an altar with a vase of flowers, an incense burner, a candle, and perhaps even a piece of art, such as an icon, prayer beads, or a picture.

Having a ritual such as prayer can be a great way to start your day with grace and beauty and serenity. Or, how about creating a love ritual to do once each year, perhaps during the summer or winter solstice?

—— EXTRA CREDIT ——

The ancient Celts marked the beginning of the pastoral season during the month of May with the celebration of Bealtaine. For the pagans, it coincided with the springtime season of fertility. Plan a pre-summer holiday in May or enjoy a staycation (stay-at-home vacation) with your spouse. If the two of you are ready to start a family, create a sensual, seductive, frisky ritual that could be your own fertility rite. For example, go tuck a blanket in your picnic basket. When you find a secluded hollow, roll out the blanket and make love to the sound of bird song under the canopy of trees and the shelter of the sky.

BE STAUNCH ALLIES IN
SPITE OF DIFFERENCES

Two imperfect people got married and it was the promise that made the marriage. And when our children were growing up, it wasn't a house that protected them; and it wasn't our love that protected them—it was that promise. —Thornton Wilder, *The Skin of Our Teeth*

Your spouse is your marriage partner, your best friend, and confidant. You may not see eye-to-eye on everything, but your marriage is about your partnership in life, sealed by the promise to love, honor, and cherish each other to the end. Make yours a spectacular marriage by remembering that promise, not once in a while, but daily.

Serve as each other's staunchest allies in the face of adversity, even when you have completely different ideas about the best way out of the situation. Be ready to defend the marriage when tough choices have to be made and you and your spouse can't seem to agree about what the right choice is. Consider the life of Elizabeth Barrett, who married Robert Browning and remained with him though her father disowned her and refused to see her or read her letters. Still, she upheld her marriage promises to Robert, and their love produced some of most romantic poems and letters in modern literature.

— EXTRA CREDIT —

Write a page about a time when your spouse defended you, and put it into a book of love that you create. Plan on reading it on special occasions, such as anniversaries or birthdays, as you grow old together. Remember that poetic invitation of Robert Browning to Elizabeth to grow old with him: "The best is yet to be, The last of life, for which the first was made."

TURN DOWN
THE VOLUME

You don't have to be noisy to be effective. —Philip Crosby, American businessman and author

A simple way to improve the ambient sound in a room where you and your spouse (and possibly your children) have gathered for the evening is to encourage everyone to use soft "inside" voices. In addition, the television volume can be lowered or turned off. If others are listening to a YouTube video or music, or playing a computer game, suggest they plug in their headphones.

It's well known that noise interferes with sleep, but it can also trigger antisocial behavior, cause a higher incidence of errors when you are engaged in doing cognitive tasks, and has even been associated with increased levels of stress, high blood pressure, and learning disabilities in children. With the noise volume lowered, you might be able to whisper "I love you" to your mate and have him actually hear it.

—— EXTRA CREDIT ——

Ask your spouse (and children) to join you in a daily half-hour noise break, during which you do all activities in silence. While you and your spouse are observing silence, you might catch up on reading magazines, newspapers, or even a chapter of your favorite book. Such quiet time is also conducive for doing homework, and is especially important for the mental concentration kids need.

REMOVE CLUTTER AND
CREATE A CALMING SPACE

The consumption society has made us feel that happiness lies in having things, and has failed to teach us the happiness of not having things. —Elise Boulding, American sociologist, peace activist, and author

If you and your spouse have ever talked with a real estate agent or home stager, you might have learned that in houses staged for sale, the owners or stagers usually remove excess furniture and position the pieces left in such a way as to allow potential buyers to see 70 percent of walls and floors. That's because potential buyers want to see the home's walls, ceilings, floors, and windows—not furniture, art, and rugs, regardless of how beautiful or tasteful. Likewise, according to feng shui belief, floors and walls should be somewhat open to allow the free flow of life-affirming chi.

Invite your spouse to help you remove clutter, especially if it blocks easy navigation through the entry and any other area of the house. Remember the adage "less is more." Share ideas about colors to paint your interior, to freshen and update it in order to create a warm welcome or suggest serenity, calmness, and peace.

— EXTRA CREDIT —

Designate a corner, room, or other area of your home as sanctuary. Use a shelf to display sacred art or something else that makes you feel peaceful. The space can be personalized according to the spiritual beliefs you share with your mate. For example, you could hang a cross, an Egyptian ankh, or Native American medicine wheel, an icon, or other symbol or piece of art.

DATE NIGHT

Feel young again together. Return to your old high school to attend a high school musical. If you've moved, find a school in your neighborhood. Enjoy exuberant performances by young aspiring actors and actresses, see creative sets, and support the high school's drama department while enjoying your night out together.

CELEBRATE YOUR SPOUSE'S
GOAL ACHIEVEMENTS

But they, while their companions slept / Were toiling upward in the night.
—Henry Wadsworth Longfellow, American poet, "The Ladder of Saint Augustine"

Whether it's a major or minor goal that your spouse has accomplished, think of some appropriate way to mark that special achievement. We all need encouragement—it helps us to stay on course, reinforces our belief in our abilities, and enables us see that our goals and dreams are within reach. The following is a small sampling of ways to express your admiration and offer enthusiastic encouragement.

- Get out champagne flutes, fill them with bubbly, and toast him.
- Write him a heartfelt congratulatory note or card.
- Display a brightly colored "congratulations" helium balloon.
- Create a congratulatory banner and get family, friends, and neighbors to sign it.
- Prepare his favorite dessert.
- Give him flowers. While flowers are traditionally thought of as gifts that men give to women, some men adore flowers and plants; if your guy is among them, give him his favorite flowers.
- Put on red lipstick, smother his face with your kisses, and take a picture of him to document the celebratory moment.

—— EXTRA CREDIT ——

Put together a scrapbook to detail each step of his journey. Include motivational quotes and snapshots showing him deep in thought, expressing despair or elation, or toiling away on his project. Include images and notes about how you celebrated all the milestones he achieved along the way to realizing his dream.

CREATE CHEERFUL
KID SPACES

Maybe we should develop a Crayola bomb as our next secret weapon. A happiness weapon . . . And every time a crisis developed, we would launch one. It would explode high in the air—explode softly—and send thousands, millions, of little parachutes into the air. Floating down to earth—boxes of Crayolas. . . . silver and gold and copper, magenta and peach and lime, amber and umber and all the rest. And people would smile and get a little funny look on their faces and cover the world with imagination. —Robert Fulghum, American preacher and author

Whether your children are toddlers, grade-schoolers, tweens, or teens, involve them in decorating their rooms. Help them choose basic wall colors in a neutral shade, and then add borders, decals, sayings, or wall prints in primary colors to enliven the space. Incorporate color and theme into the soft furnishings (curtains, cushions, bed linens, and rugs) along with hard surfaces (furniture, floors, walls, ceilings, fans, and so on) to personalize the space according to your children's interests. Your husband might enjoy remembering his own boyhood bedroom to give the boys some ideas for their rooms.

— EXTRA CREDIT —

Take your children with you to visit new housing developments. Spend the afternoon walking through the model homes with your camera (ask permission first from the salesperson). You and your spouse will come away with lots of ideas, and you'll know exactly what they like and don't like about each room.

COMPARISON SHOP BEFORE
MAKING BIG PURCHASES

Anyone who believes the competitive spirit in America is dead has never been in a supermarket when the cashier opens another checkout line. —Ann Landers, advice columnist

Get together with your other half to find the best value and price for purchases of big-ticket items for your home. That way, you'll avoid any potential misunderstanding over how the money was spent. The Internet has made comparison shopping exciting, helpful, and downright easy to do for almost any item you might desire. You can also look online for:

- Competitive prices on inventories that have been marked down through companies like Overstock.com.
- Discounted (and sometimes free) shipping.
- The site Bizrate.com, where you can search for a specific item to find out which stores carry it, and the price they charge for it.
- The site Bing.com, which lists cash-back deals.
- Amazon.com's wide array of products, especially books.

If Internet shopping isn't for you, call or visit stores and outlets for big-ticket items. Enlist your partner's help in doing the research to find the best price, and then make that big purchase together.

EXTRA CREDIT

Choose a big-ticket item—for example, electronics, appliances, or a car—that you and your spouse need to purchase. Surf around the Internet for competitive pricing for that item. You might be surprised to discover deeply discounted pricing in several places. Take your time to find the lowest price.

HAVE A PLACE IN YOUR
HOME TO UNWIND

When you learn to love and let yourself be loved, you come home to the hearth of your own spirit. You are warm and sheltered. —John O'Donohue, Irish philosopher, poet, and scholar, *Anam Cara: A Book of Celtic Wisdom*

You and your spouse may have different ways of unwinding at the end of a busy workday or a stressful week. For example, you may like to have a cup of tea, whereas he needs a nap. It's important for the two of you to have a place conducive to unwinding.

Create a space in your home that draws you to it the minute you enter the house. Let it be an area that beckons you to kick off your shoes, stretch out, and unwind. Maybe you and your spouse are ready for such a room, but don't know how to carve it out of your existing home. If so, talk with friends who have done it, or watch Home and Garden Television for shows about garden and outdoor rooms. Let your fingers do the searching for you on the Internet. Talk with contractors to get their input if necessary. Then take the steps necessary to create a place in your house that nurtures your spirit by inviting you to unwind, either alone or together.

— EXTRA CREDIT —

Take a walk in your neighborhood and chat with neighbors who live in a condo, apartment, or house with a floor plan or layout similar to yours. If they have a favorite place in the home to unwind, ask to see it in order to get ideas for your place.

SIT CLOSE TOGETHER
IN A BIG CHAIR

When two people come together, an ancient circle closes between them.
. . . When you really love someone, you shine the light of your soul on
the soul on the beloved. —John O'Donohue, Irish philosopher, poet, and
scholar, *Anam Cara*

Do you own a chair big enough for the two of you to sit in at the same time? Or, a loveseat where you can snuggle together to watch an hour of *American Idol, Monday Night Football, PBS Mystery!,* or *NCIS*?

If you've got that piece of furniture, use it; if you don't, make do with the couch. The point is to not just watch television, but to enjoy a program together as inseparable lovebirds. When you first fell in love, you probably hated having to sit apart from each other, even if it was just across the table. Recapture those old feelings again whenever you have the chance.

— EXTRA CREDIT —

Grab your hubby and go shopping for a lovebird chair. Find one that has a large hassock so you both can put your feet up. Alternatively, look for an extra-wide recliner that has a leg lift. No reason why you can't be as comfortable as possible for that hour.

SOOTHE YOUR SPOUSE'S
FEVERISH BROW

Feed a cold; starve a fever. —American proverb

When you caress your lover's feverish brow with cool fingertips, the sensation can calm and soothe him. Think of how refreshing it feels to sip a frosty glass of lemonade or a mint julep on a sweltering summer afternoon, occasionally touching your neck or cheek with the cool glass. It's the same kind of momentarily sweet relief your spouse will feel when your cool fingertips trace soft lines across his warm skin.

Wash your hands in cool water and dry them. Stroke your fingers across the top of his brows, with extra circular stroking at the temples and between his eyebrows. Then dip a washcloth into a bowl of cool water scented with lavender or citrus. Add some crushed fresh mint leaves. Wring the water from the cloth. Gently dab his hot cheeks and temples before folding the cloth and placing it across his forehead. The subtle aroma of the mint and lavender or citrus, coupled with the coolness of the fabric, creates a pleasantly soothing sensation and calms his senses.

—— EXTRA CREDIT ——

Ayurveda is an ancient Indian healing system that uses different modalities to treat illness, including herbs, diet, yoga, acupuncture, breath work, and massage. Suggest to your spouse that he should try to meditate, visualizing himself relaxing in a lush, quiet garden where he receives healing energy through your touch. Then as his breathing becomes regular and slow, indicating a state of relaxation, begin to stroke his forehead very slowly, from side to side. He's bound to feel better, if for no other reason than from your reassuring, loving touch.

DATE NIGHT

Go window-shopping together. No purchase necessary. Stroll arm in arm around your city or town and check out the window displays. Pop inside a shop for a closer peek at items that appeal to you or your spouse. Work up an appetite walking around and then stop for a slice of pizza or coffee and a pastry. Date nights don't have to cost a lot; they just have to be about the two of you rediscovering the "us" in your otherwise busy lives.

DON'T THROW OUT HIS
THINGS WITHOUT ASKING

So long as the great majority of men are not deprived of either property or honor, they are satisfied. —Niccolo Machiavelli, Italian dramatist, essayist, and historian

When you and your husband married, each of you likely brought items that you had in former homes, some possibly acquired from previous relationships—his painting of horses and polo riders, for example. It's not your thing. Or that model of an old ship he built in high school that consumes space in the living room where a perfectly good chair could go. The ship is a dust collector, for sure, but while getting rid of it would make you happy, you'd better check with hubby before tossing it.

Remember that you are now players on one team. You might not have the same tastes in décor, but work it out. You wouldn't want him throwing away something that had personal meaning for you, say your Aunt Anne's handmade ceramic bowl, which sits on the dining room table and serves no purpose other than as a gathering place for the daily mail. Instead of grumbling about wanting to remove those ugly and dust-collecting items (that just happen to be his), invite your spouse to propose possible alternatives. Perhaps he would permit his items to be wrapped and stored in the attic, basement, garage, or storage facility. Seeking his input shows that you respect his property and care about his feelings.

——— EXTRA CREDIT ———
Purchase a few boxes, bubble wrap, and tape. Use them to safely pack items that you and your spouse have decided you can live without, and put those items in storage. Discuss whether or not you want to bring in something more aesthetically pleasing or functional.

PUT THINGS BACK
WHERE THEY BELONG

There is nothing nobler or more admirable than when two people who
see eye-to-eye keep house as man and wife, confounding their enemies and
delighting their friends. —Homer, Greek poet

After using an item, such as a hammer, screwdriver, knife, pen, scissors,
tape, or glue, do you and your spouse return the items to the toolbox or
drawer where you found them? Having to track down a borrowed item
can be exasperating and a source of marital conflict. If such items must
be shared by the entire family, it's even more important to put things
back where they belong.

Talk with your mate about the message you are sending your children by not returning borrowed items. When you and your spouse
make a special point of respecting each other's property and putting
things back where they belong, you demonstrate organizational and
time-management skills to your children, as well as respect for other
people and their property. Remember that saying of Ben Franklin's: "A
place for everything, everything in its place."

— EXTRA CREDIT —

Find a good organizer system to store like items, and involve your spouse in the
process. Colorful plastic crates are great for kids to store toys, for example, and see-
through containers with lids are excellent for storing craft or home office items. Tools
can be stored in toolboxes, bags, or tool chests. Also consider a small utility box for
the kitchen to hold screwdrivers, pliers, and a hammer.

FIX BROKEN APPLIANCES
IMMEDIATELY

Now, Bart, since you broke Grandpa's teeth, he gets to break yours. —Dan Castellaneta, American comedian and actor

Not only are broken appliances dangerous (bad wiring could shock you or spark a fire) but if they aren't reliable, why keep them around? Recycle, repair, remove, or replace. Keeping broken things around the home establishes an intention of attracting more broken things into your life—that's the opposite of what you and your spouse really want, isn't it? Most couples want to attract more goodness, harmony, prosperity, and love, and you can do that by fixing in a timely manner whatever is broken.

If you have broken his favorite piece of furniture or tool, or he's damaged your krumkake iron or electric skillet, get the broken item fixed or out of the house if a repair is not possible. Additionally, if you and your spouse are using appliances that intermittently don't work very well, and if they are under warranty, send them back to the manufacturer or the retail outlet where you purchased them and get them properly repaired. Or, if the appliances are old, a local repair shop may be able to fix them for you.

--- EXTRA CREDIT ---

Examine your home for anything that represents disrepair, for example, cracks, leaks, broken drains, chipped paint or countertops, burned-out light bulbs, broken lamps, and pillows and furniture with holes or broken seams. Repair everything you can and get rid of things you can't. In feng shui belief, repairing what's broken in your home is a metaphor for repairing what's broken in your life.

PLAN AHEAD FOR
FAMILY VACATIONS

No matter what happens, travel gives you a story to tell. —Jewish proverb

If your family is comprised of just the two of you, consider a cooking class in Tuscany, a week at a spa resort, or even a romantic hotel in Hawaii, New York, Paris, or the Caribbean. If you have children to consider, figure out what they might enjoy doing.

Then you and your partner sit down together and work out a family vacation budget that includes destination, type of travel to and from, accommodations, dining and entertainment, and travel insurance. Estimate as closely as possible the costs associated with each. Whether your family camping trip is to Colorado, with mountain biking and horseback riding, a weeklong stay at Disneyland, or an educational eco-friendly vacation, knowing the costs upfront allows you and your mate to focus on spending quality time with your children and each other.

—— EXTRA CREDIT ——

Visit the botanical gardens in your community or region. Discover species of plants indigenous to your area of the country. Take along your digital camera and photograph each other. Ask other visitors to take pictures of you and your spouse embracing amid the beautiful plants. That way, you'll have beautiful images to remember that special time together.

SEEK YOUR SPOUSE'S
INPUT ON GOING GREEN

Thank God men cannot as yet fly, and lay waste to the sky as well as the earth. —Henry David Thoreau, *Journal 3*

You likely already know where your spouse stands on important issues, including the environment. Possibly you have already talked about eating healthier (perhaps buying organic or growing your own food), the energy saved by changing out the incandescent light bulbs for fluorescents, and the importance of recycling. Take the green discussion to the next level. Talk about what else you could implement to reduce your part of the collective carbon footprint. Could installing solar panels be in your future? What about purchasing a hybrid or electric vehicle? Selecting more energy-efficient appliances? Recycling more diligently? Involving your respective companies, if they haven't already gone green?

Share ideas with each other about how you can make a difference in your lifetime on the planet just by the choices you can make every day.

— EXTRA CREDIT —

Join one or more organizations, such as Greenpeace and the Sierra Club, that are fighting climate change. Take eco-tourism trips that focus on protecting the environment of the trip destinations. Talk about raising eco-conscious, green-friendly children. As a Native American proverb goes: We do not inherit the earth from our ancestors, we borrow it from our children.

ESTABLISH A PLAN FOR
RELIEF IN TOUGH TIMES

It is not the size of the dog in the fight; it is the size of the fight in the dog!
—African tribal saying

For many Americans, life is a dogfight every day as the burden of hardship on their backs becomes greater, requiring more resiliency, stamina, and motivation than ever to keep fighting for survival. It is not possible to go backward and figure out a plan for surviving tough times, but you can certainly do it for the future. As a couple, ask each other what-if questions and then brainstorm answers that are viable and make sense for dealing with worst-case scenarios.

It's no longer possible to rely simply on a fat savings account based on stocks. That's a good thing for you to have, but it might not be enough to solve other problems. Your savings account can be depleted quite readily if you and your spouse lose your jobs. Your problems are exacerbated if your credit cards become maxed out, you can't get new credit, and your home goes into foreclosure. That's when you resort to that all-important Relief Plan for Tough Times.

--- EXTRA CREDIT ---

Create a binder that includes the plans you and your spouse have devised for dealing with disaster, much like the kind of binder (or book) that a hospital or business might create for dealing with various aspects of a natural disaster or catastrophe.

DATE NIGHT

Make X's and O's from sugar-cookie dough, bake them, and frost them. Put on your tight jeans and your black leather jacket, grab your spouse, and head out to a local coffeehouse for open-mike poetry readings. Just slip some of those hugs-and-kisses cookies into a bag and take them along to savor with mugs of steaming hot cappuccino or espresso.

BE FORWARD THINKING
ABOUT FUTURE HEALTH CARE

Take care of your body with steadfast fidelity. The soul must see through these eyes alone, and if they are dim, the whole world is clouded. —Johann Wolfgang von Goethe, German dramatist, novelist, poet, and scientist

Talk with your spouse about basic health care, and then take the discussion into the area of health directives. Will you appoint each other to make health-care decisions for you in the event you cannot? Does your spouse know whether or not you wish to be resuscitated? If you choose to be resuscitated, under what circumstances would you not want to be? These questions are worth answering in writing and then kept with your and your spouse's wills and other important legal papers.

—— EXTRA CREDIT ——

Initiate a discussion with your spouse about marriage in the context of what the German philosopher Hegel meant in his comment about how the familiar—because it is familiar—is not known. When two people settle into a marriage and the years pass, they may think they know each other well—or well enough—but do they? Explore this topic in the context of your health, your lives, and your end-of-life wishes.

MAKE A PLAN
FOR WHEN TO RETIRE

When you retire, you switch bosses—from the one who hired you to the one who married you. —Gene Perret, television comedy writer and producer

Most people start thinking about retiring when they reach late midlife or around ages sixty-five to seventy. It's a time of life that many people anticipate with great excitement—more time for family, hobbies, travel, and personal development. Some people never retire, while others are so successful (for example, a successful entrepreneur or individual who wins the lottery) that they are able to retire earlier.

It might surprise you to learn that retirement sounds great but can actually be hard on a marriage. When a spouse retires too early, it can lead to feelings of resentment in the other spouse, who must keep working. Studies have shown that couples who retire roughly at the same time have the smoothest transition. In addition, couples who plan the timing and share the same retirement goals (for example, traveling around the United States in an RV) have less conflict than those who don't have a plan for retirement.

--- EXTRA CREDIT ---

See your respective retirements as a new life stage. Read books about marriage and retirement. Get on the same page with your spouse through a discussion of how you want to spend retirement with each other. Talk frankly about the stresses and pitfalls as well as how to avoid them. Plan for the psychological and financial impacts that retirement will have on your marriage in order to keep your marriage strong and secure.

HELP YOUR SPOUSE BRAINSTORM
THROUGH JOB JUNCTURES

Confidence can get you where you want to go, and getting there is a daily process. —Donald Trump, American business magnate, author, and television personality

Your spouse feels like he's in a dead-end job. He was told by his immediate supervisor that he was being considered for promotion, but was passed over while others with less seniority were advanced. He's definitely at a juncture in his career or job life and has turned to you to help him brainstorm about where to go next. Take this opportunity to offer your loving support, suggestions, and opinions.

This is an excellent exercise, since brainstorming through a problem together can produce innovative ideas that your spouse might not readily see in his "stuck" place. You might talk about the pros and cons of a lateral move—for example, if he's a law officer, he could join another department in a different community but at his same job level. The tradeoffs might mean having to move and perhaps suffering a pay cut, but on a positive note, it would be a new start with better potential for career advancement. Alternatively, he could apply for work at a completely different agency. For example, if he's a city police officer, he might seek positions with the FBI, the Justice Department, or Homeland Security.

— EXTRA CREDIT —

Be his research assistant. After you and your spouse have brainstormed options, support those options by doing the initial research. For example, you could scan law enforcement magazines for job openings in local departments. Or you could do an Internet search, downloading those position descriptions and applications you think would be most appropriate for what he seeks in his career.

USE MUSIC TO
FEEL EROTIC

Music is the mediator between the spiritual and the sensual life. —Ludwig van Beethoven, German composer

You have probably experienced the essence of an erotic song or dance in your lifetime. Can you remember being swept away by the rhythm, the beat, and the words? You can feel when something is erotic in your body. There will be "movement" of a sort that is hard to describe but is definitely there. Paintings from the *Kama Sutra* era often depicted dancers and musicians; frequently, the woman was the musician and she may even have been playing the lute while she was making love. Playing music and singing songs are grand forms of communication that have changed little in thousands of years.

Use music that makes you feel erotic to get into the mood. Talk with your spouse about what genres of music or specific tunes put him in the mood. For example, does he like to feel the rhythm of hot Latin music or the quiet, expressive sounds of Sade? Perhaps the sexy music of Stéphane Pompougnac, the smooth acoustic sound of Bebel Gilberto, or the ambient sounds of Zero 7 is more to his liking.

—— EXTRA CREDIT ——

Expand your musical horizons. Invite your spouse to join you in listening to some new music, perhaps, for example, drumming. Tune in and turn on to the sounds that draw the two of you into erotic embrace. Share your thoughts with your mate about the way music makes you feel sexy.

HIRE A LAWYER TO
DRAFT YOUR WILL

The only thing you take with you when you're gone is what you leave behind. —John Allston, American civil engineer

You and your mate can draw up basic holographic (handwritten) wills yourself, downloading forms online, provided you are eighteen years of age or older. However, if you and your spouse want to ensure that your wishes are recorded in proper legal format compliant with the laws of your state, are signed and witnessed in order to be properly executed, and are set down precisely as you desire along with instructions for carrying them out, you might feel more comfortable hiring a lawyer to guide you through the process.

Many financial advisers recommend their clients create wills, even if they are young adults who do not yet think about end-of-life issues. If you do not have a will, your heirs will have to figure out your assets and liabilities, and be responsible for sorting through your financial issues. People sometimes write their wills and forget where they put them, so this, too, is a reason to have a lawyer help you draft yours. Once your will is written, be sure you have a copy for safekeeping. You could also give a copy of your will to the person whom you've chosen to be the executor of your estate.

— EXTRA CREDIT —

Talk with your spouse about whom you would want to carry out the wishes you have put forth in your will. This person will be the executor of your estate, so it is important that you choose someone whom you trust and whom you believe to be fiscally responsible and clear-headed to make decisions over your estate.

HIT A LOCAL
HIKING TRAIL

Do not go where the path may lead; go instead where there is no path
and leave a trail. —Ralph Waldo Emerson, American essayist and poet

If you and your mate enjoy working up a sweat together, especially in
nature, go for a hike. If your workday is just too long and there's no way
you could do a hike in the evening before dinner, arrange to hike on
the weekend. Get out early when the air is still cool and enjoy the fresh
beginning of a new day. Plan to hike an hour or two along a local, scenic
trail. Take along water. If you and your spouse love to take pictures or
make notes about what you see, also slip your camera and a journal into
your backpacks. That way, if you see some breathtaking scenery or head
off the path to explore the woods, you can document special discoveries
along the way.

—— EXTRA CREDIT ——

Participate in a hike organized by the Sierra Club or other local organization.
Such hikes often have guides who can share insights as well as show you new
trails. In addition, you can meet other trailblazers who share your interests in the
rugged outdoors.

DATE NIGHT

Make the world's largest banana split and devour it together. Split a ripe banana down the middle and place it lengthwise in a banana-split dish. Add scoops of ice cream in different flavors, or vanilla ice cream with a variety of toppings such as chocolate, strawberry, pineapple, or caramel. Add a dollop of whipped cream on top of each mound of ice cream, sprinkle with chopped nuts, and place a maraschino cherry on top. The pleasure of licking your lips can only be topped by a playful licking of your partner's luscious sweet lips.

ESTABLISH COLLEGE FUNDS
FOR YOUR CHILDREN

College is a place to keep warm between high school and an early marriage. —George Gobel, American comedian

When your children are babies and you and your husband are elbow deep in laundry and diapers, it is hard to imagine eighteen years down the road when you'll be helping your teenager pack suitcases as she heads off to college. Financial consultants say, however, that the best time to start saving for your little Einstein's college education is in her infancy.

When you and your spouse have a block of time, check out the state-sponsored tuition programs known as 529 plans, which offer terrific tax breaks. Consider other investment options too, since college tuition is outpacing inflation. Mutual funds are also good bets, and the fund manager keeps focused on stocks so you don't have to. If the college fund for your child isn't growing as quickly as you had hoped, take heart; you don't necessarily have to have the entire four years of college costs covered. Private, state, and federal loans and grants can make up the difference between college costs and what you've saved. It is also easier to obtain a loan for college than for other reasons. Grants and scholarships are also marvelous resources because they are usually tax-free.

--- EXTRA CREDIT ---

Look into federally funded need-based loans such as Stafford and Perkins. Students must start repaying the Perkins loan nine months after they graduate, with ten years to repay the loan. A Stafford loan is also a needs-based loan, and no interest accrues until six months after graduation.

SET SHORT-TERM GOALS
TO REACH THE DISTANT ONES

Give yourself something to work toward—constantly. —Mary Kay Ash, American businesswoman and founder of Mary Kay Cosmetics, Inc.

For couples who want to reach a big goal in life or even a distant goal, like retirement at age forty or making your millions by the time the two of you reach midlife, it's a good idea to start with smaller, more easily accomplished goals: daily, weekly, monthly, or yearly, for example. Reward yourselves for attaining those short-term goals and feel good that you are right on track.

You can continue looking forward, even when you experience small setbacks, which are bound to happen. But when they do, you won't be knocked back for long because you know you have goals to meet each day, week, month, or year, and you are supporting each other in the effort. Setting the goals without the intention to achieve them, or without commitment, is really just wishing, not even dreaming. You both must be willing to make the commitment, learn from the failures, stay focused, and believe in yourselves and your abilities to reach the distant goals that you've set. It's just a matter of keeping your eyes on the finish line.

——— EXTRA CREDIT ———

Talk about your long-term, distant goals with your spouse and friends or family—other people who will also support you in reaching your goals. Then get the tools you need to help you get to where you want to go; for example, financial books, CDs, classes, and professional guidance to help you make your millions.

DISCUSS WHERE YOU WANT TO BE AT AGE FORTY AND BEYOND

In the end, it's not the years in your life that count. It's the life in your years.
—Abraham Lincoln, U.S. president

Couples in America have an 80 percent chance of marrying before the age of forty, according to findings of the 2002 National Survey of Family Growth. February 2010 poll findings released by CBS News revealed 90 percent of married couples in America would indeed marry their spouses again, and those polled ranked several factors in order of importance: "respect," "trust," "sense of humor," and "sex."

While those factors remain important for couples who would choose each other again, future financial stability is not to be overlooked. When you and your spouse are age forty, you are still young enough to be aggressive in your investments. Depending on economic conditions, your adviser may suggest that you revisit your portfolios to rebalance them. At age forty, you and your spouse may be still raising a family, and you'll want to ensure that you still have purchasing power, can borrow if you need to, and understand how to minimize personal risk factors (financial and also health).

—— EXTRA CREDIT ——
Schedule regular visits with your portfolio manager and also with your primary care physician. Regular checkups in both areas to age forty and beyond can ensure that you catch and deal with any problems along the way.

SHIFT THE
FANTASY FOCUS

The gift of fantasy has meant more to me than my talent for absorbing positive knowledge. —Albert Einstein, German-born American physicist

There are limitless ways to become aroused, and if one isn't working for you, you may be able to shift your focus to find another. Bringing your attention to physical sensations might help. Or you might actively create a fantasy that is more comfortable for you.

If you find that you cannot get comfortable with certain fantasies that turn you on, you may benefit from exploring your uneasiness with a sex therapist. Such exploration may help you get to the root of your discomfort. This might enable you to more easily enjoy the eroticism your fantasies can provide for you. Alternatively, you may discover something in your self-exploration that changes the troubling fantasy or its power to turn you on. If you are afraid of acting on a sexual thought or feeling, fearing it would get you into trouble, you should seek professional help. It is important to recognize when you do not have control over your behavior with regard to certain sexual thoughts and feelings.

--- EXTRA CREDIT ---

Ask your partner to help you explore touch intensity. Have him touch you in various spots on your body with different qualities of touch. What you both learn may make your sex play more enjoyable.

LEARN TO BE POSITIVE ABOUT
THE CHALLENGES OF AGING

———

Age is not a particularly interesting subject. Anyone can get old. All you have to do is live long enough. —Groucho Marx, American comedian

As a couple, the two of you will go through the aging process together and deal with the challenges and joys of getting older. For some couples, aging brings burdens to one or both spouses, burdens such as a chronic illness, memory loss, sexual inactivity, possibly the loss of ability to drive, and even trouble with paying bills.

Yet, the benefits of growing old—time with family, less stress, more respect, and financial security—are the factors you should focus on. Approach the challenges of aging with a positive outlook, enjoying each other and each moment of your lives. Married couples live longer than singles and also have higher levels of life satisfaction, according to studies on aging and happiness. Neither money nor prescription drugs bring about happiness, but the happiest people have strong friendships. Aging well and experiencing happiness both seem correlated to factors that spouses can control, like having a positive attitude.

—— EXTRA CREDIT ——

Have a conversation with your spouse about aging. Talk about what to do if the two of you can no longer live independently. Who will make medical decisions if neither of you can? Who will you rely on for money if you need it?

SEEK MONETARY LIMITS FOR
EX-SPOUSES AND CHILD SUPPORT

You can make a lot of money in this game. Just ask my ex-wives. Both
of them are so rich that neither of their husbands work. —Lee Trevino,
professional golfer, Mexican-American icon

A lot of people are paying alimony and/or child support to an ex-spouse.
If you have remarried and are paying alimony and child support, money
gets tight, right? And what if you lose your job? What happens to your
financial obligations to the ex-spouse if you have a loss of income and
haven't yet found another job?

If that happens, consider modifying your judgment of divorce or
settlement agreement with your ex. You can do it one of two ways—a
consensual agreement with your ex or a nonconsensual application for
modification that must go through a court application. The consensual
route can be done through your attorney, informing the ex-spouse of
your change in financial circumstances. The lawyers can exchange the
financial documents—proof to support your claim of wage loss.

If you are the custodial spouse and are going through a similar scenario and need a temporary increase in alimony or child support, the
same rules apply. Both spouses will have to agree to new terms and have
a judge sign a legal document or consent order.

—— EXTRA CREDIT ——

Check in with your accountant, lawyer, and banker to make sure your beneficiary
forms on your retirement accounts and pension plans have been updated. If you
don't make the change in beneficiaries after a divorce, your ex gets whatever his
or her name is on when you are no longer around, regardless of when you were
divorced or to whom you've chosen to bequeath your estate.

DATE NIGHT

Play paintball together. It's a great way to release the tensions that you might not have gotten rid of during the week. Chasing each other with a paintball gun and taking aim and firing can release more than a paintball; it can dissipate pent-up aggression. You can kiss and make up afterward.

WHY WAIT TO MOVE
INTO A SMALLER PLACE?

Where thou art, that is home. —Emily Dickinson, American poet

Perhaps you and your wife have talked about downsizing into a smaller home once the children are grown. Maybe now the last one has left the nest, but you and your spouse are still in that beautiful, four-bedroom house in the highest-priced and academically highest-rated school district in your area. You might want step up the timeline for your move and put that house on a fast track to sell.

According to some polls, more than 60 percent of boomers plan to move when they retire. Why wait? Hanging on to the big house long after the kids are gone might not make the best fiscal sense. Consider selling and finding a new, smaller one in a neighborhood that you both love, perhaps closer to shops, cafés, the theater, and art galleries. You have myriad options to buy foreclosed homes, short sales, and real-estate owned (REOs), as well as conventional homes on the market. Moving now might mean you could live for less and invest the rest of the money from the sale of your house in growth funds. That will give you more money to live on when you do retire.

--- EXTRA CREDIT ---

Go on the Internet together and surf to Trulia.com or any number of other real-estate websites to find houses for sale. Search by Zip code, city, or a neighborhood address to find those where you think you might want to live.

DON'T QUIT YOUR
DAY JOB JUST YET

Employment is nature's physician, and is essential to human happiness. —Galen of Pergamum (modern-day Turkey), Greek physician and philosopher

A dream job with a hefty paycheck might be calling to you, but unless you've already got it locked down, it's probably wiser for you to stay put. Of course, if you and your spouse have plenty in savings and a healthy financial portfolio, then go after that dream job.

However, consider the timing. How will making the switch affect your nest egg? Will you be able to continue saving when you switch to the new job? If you are not saving, one of the ways to lift the pressure off of you and your spouse is to plan on both of you working longer. A 2005 survey conducted by Merrill Lynch revealed that you would have to save approximately $12,500 each year (if you are fifty years old with an income of $62,500 and also have $60,000 saved) in order to retire comfortably at age sixty-two. If you remain working full-time for two more years past sixty-two and go part-time until age seventy-five, you could reduce that $12,500 annual savings amount to between $3,750 and $7,500, according to CNNMoney.com. Working longer at a job you love is also an important benefit.

— EXTRA CREDIT —

Subscribe to a money-management magazine to learn more about how to prepare financially for your future, starting where you are right now. If you are already in your forties or fifties, there are things you can do to play catch-up.

ENJOY YOUR
SEXUAL FULFILLMENT

When you really feel understood, you feel free to release yourself into the trust and shelter of the other person's soul. —John O'Donohue, philosopher, poet, and scholar

A sexually fulfilled woman beams her happiness to anyone she encounters. A sexually fulfilled man greets his day with unrivaled enthusiasm. Sexual pleasure is one of the primary joys of being human, but it is much more than a pleasurable physical experience. In addition to the possibility of creating new life, sexuality represents the joining of two people on the most essential level of their being.

The direct experience of many people over the millennia suggests that the coming together of powerful energies in sexual intercourse makes it a sacred, creative act—with or without procreation as the couple's intent. By joining your most vulnerable self with the one you love in sacred sexuality, you have the potential to give and receive human love at its most profound and productive level. As a result of this deep emotional and spiritual connection, you become a more loving, more giving, and more fulfilled person—alone and together. Using the scientific method and plain common sense, it's plain to see that sexually satisfied people are healthier and happier.

— EXTRA CREDIT —

Surf the Internet for articles in bona fide medical and psychology journals about the health benefits of sex. Discover how you can keep sexual interest alive and derive the benefits of a healthy sex life throughout your marriage.

SCHEDULE DAY
TRIPS FOR TWO

Chains do not hold a marriage together. It is threads, hundreds of tiny threads which sew people together through the years. —Simone Signoret, French film star

Day trips can provide a much-needed break away from stressful work routines and demands at home and allow you to enjoy the pleasurable company of your spouse. Every region of the country can lay claim to some scenic area. Of course, the more scenic, the more likely it is that you'll also find more tourists. But that's not necessarily all bad. You may make some new friends on a day of sightseeing, wine tasting, antiquing, riding in a hot air balloon, walking through bogs or a wooded area, photographing each other in natural settings, rock climbing, enjoying a theme park, riding the rails, skating around in a new city, biking along mountain trails, people-watching along a boardwalk, or even whiling away the afternoon at a couples day spa.

Day trips needn't take a toll on your budget, and they can provide a welcome shakeup in your daily routine. But the biggest benefit is time alone to enjoy your best friend and traveling companion—your spouse. Make it a point to try to get away at least once a month for a day trip to another city, somewhere in the country, or just down the road. Short breaks give you time for togetherness away from the drudgery of home routines.

— EXTRA CREDIT —

Visit a zoo. While you are walking around, nibbling on a pretzel and taking in the fresh air, you'll likely notice what the birds and bees are doing, not to mention the lions and tigers and bears. You might even discover some new positions to try later, at home alone in your own nest.

UNDERSTAND THE DIFFERENT
WAYS OF EXPRESSING LOVE

A good marriage is one which allows for change and growth in the individuals and in the way they express their love. —Pearl S. Buck, American author, recipient of the Pulitzer and Nobel prizes

If you and your spouse aren't talking much and it's becoming an issue, consider that the problem might be different communication styles. In marriage therapy, the spouse wanting emotional intimacy may complain that her partner does not love her, which is usually false. The wife wants to communicate her feelings of appreciation and love in words. Her husband, however, prefers to express his love through his actions. The action the husband often prefers is sexual expression, while his wife wants communication, emotional connectedness, and then sexual expression.

However, it is not always the female who complains about a partner being emotionally distant. Many men have the same complaint about women. The male usually prefers to express emotional intimacy less through conversation and more through sexuality. The issue married couples face is what to do when their emotional needs are different. The first step is to cease thinking that either of you is to blame for the difference, and stop judging the difference between the two of you as evidence of dysfunction.

—— EXTRA CREDIT ——

Ask for what you need. Encourage your husband to tell you what he needs, and when. Try to communicate clearly and more openly than you ever have. That helps to keep confusion from building up and blocking the easy expression of love between you.

SEE YOUR UNION
AS UNBREAKABLE

I think a man and a woman should choose each other for life, for the simple reason that a long life with all its accidents is barely enough time for a man and a woman to understand each other and . . . to understand—is to love.
—William Butler Yeats, Irish poet and dramatist

The formation of a marriage should not trigger in either of you the anticipation of marital problems and conflicts or the notion that if things don't work out, you'll separate, divorce, and move on. Marriage is more than two lovers deciding to shack up. In the starkest and most sterile terms, marriage is a legally binding contract between two free adults (that is, they are clear of any other contractual obligations or circumstances barring their marriage) who are willing and able and have freely made the choice to form a union as husband and wife, obliging them to live together during their lifetimes until death.

Perhaps one of the reasons that divorce rates are so high is because people actually see the marriage as breakable. Instead, consider the view your marital union as unbreakable. Do everything within your power to keep your contract intact.

—— EXTRA CREDIT ——

Watch movies about marital conflict that can break a marriage—not just infidelity, but tragedy (like cancer), dysfunctional family patterns repeating themselves in a spouse, compulsive lying, and other such stresses and strains. Talk with your partner about the movies afterward and about how you would or wouldn't deal with those issues differently. Here's a sampling of movies to get you started: *Four Christmases*, *War of the Roses*, *Life as a House*, *Stepmom*, *Mrs. Doubtfire*, *The First Wives Club*, *The Way We Were*, and *Liar, Liar*.

DATE NIGHT

Go to your local karaoke bar and pick a duet that you and your spouse can sing together, perhaps even harmonize on. Choose an oldie but goldie, such as "I Got You Babe," by Sonny and Cher, or take turns doing a rap song by Jay-Z followed by a hip-hop or rhythm-and-blues song by Beyoncé Knowles, Jay-Z's wife.

KEEP A POSITIVE
OUTLOOK

Watch your thoughts, for they become words. Choose your words, for
they become actions. Understand your actions, for they become habits.
Study your habits, for they will become your character. Develop your
character, for it becomes your destiny. —Anonymous

Engaging in positive thinking certainly makes life and married life, in
particular, more pleasurable. How can relationships be expected to thrive
and survive when couples engage in negative thoughts and behaviors?
But positive thinking brings you the good things you desire in life. One
positive thought is likely to generate another, creating a cycle. The steady
stream of thoughts will flow, whether you direct it or not. In that way,
habitual positive thinking yields positive results and outcomes.

Positive thinking and goal-setting are now considered scientifically
viable methods for changing a person's life. If you and your spouse are
like many other couples, you have the highest levels of happiness when
you see life as pleasant and when you are engaged with life in a meaningful way. Express what you want using positive language. For example, "I
am excited to be in the process of getting my dream job because I am
skilled at what I do and am passionate about doing it." Give focused
attention and energy to your positive affirmation statements.

--- EXTRA CREDIT ---

Learn more about how to focus positive attention on achieving a happy and meaningful married life. Thoughts repeated daily become the instructions for your subcon-
scious to carry out. Reinforce the instructions by writing down your goals, repeating
affirmations, and spending time in creative visualization.

STAY LOYAL
AND PROTECTIVE

If you are not too long, I will wait here for you all my life. —Oscar Wilde,
Irish playwright and poet, *The Importance of Being Earnest, Act III*

Loyalty and fidelity in marriage as well as your relationships with others is a predictor of happiness. You and your spouse bring to your marriage the friendships that you had before you were married and those that you form after the big event. If you are like most of us, you want to know that you can count on the people in your inner circle. Unreliable and fickle friends often bring more heartache than happiness. As a couple, you want to believe that you can depend on your friends as well as each other.

Marriage partners who are consistently loyal (meaning delivering on the promises made to each other both before and after the trip down the aisle) are happier than those who made promises but didn't keep them. The message about loyalty is that it is more than a marital virtue; it's necessary for marital happiness.

— EXTRA CREDIT —

Stay true to your promises to love, honor, protect, and defend your spouse. And then take it to the next level: keep your promises. Do everything in your power to help your spouse attain his or her dreams. In a Northwestern University study, just having the understanding that your spouse will help you achieve your dream was a substantial contributor to a satisfying marriage.

ENLIST YOUR SPOUSE'S
INPUT ON THE HOME REMODEL

A successful team beats with one heart. —Anonymous

Your home is the place where you both relax and enjoy space you've created together. But if the time has come to make some minor repairs, or the place is looking tired and old and needs a little renovation, invite your spouse into the decision-making process. Perhaps you just bought the house and knew going in that you were going to have to do a substantial remodel. Don't rush out to sign up the architect without spending as much time as necessary with your spouse going over ideas, forming a vision that you hold together, and developing a budget and timeline.

Make the process a fun journey that involves both of you capturing ideas in a journal, including magazine pictures you've clipped that reflect your tastes in colors, furniture, fabric, and styles. Talk about the end result; what you both want to see as the finished project. Do you need to add more storage, run cabling or wire for a speaker system that runs throughout the rooms (it's cheaper to do when the walls are open), add another story, or a playroom for your children, or a garden room? The new home you will create together will reflect a merging of your hearts and minds. The clearer you are about your vision, the easier it will be to communicate with an architect, a general contractor, and others involved.

—— EXTRA CREDIT ——

Put together a three-ring notebook or an accordion file (or both) with tabbed sections to organize the various aspects of your remodel and help you keep track of the thousands of details involved.

ENGAGE IN
IMPROMPTU TRYSTS

I wasn't kissing her, I was whispering in her mouth. —Chico Marx, comedian, film actor

Don't wait for Valentine's Day. Try a chocolate-themed tryst. Book a hotel or bed-and-breakfast someplace where you'd like to spend the weekend with your lover, or take a staycation if you're on a budget. If you're pressed for time, sneak off with your spouse for a lunchtime tryst!

Choose your spouse's favorite chocolate truffles and wrap each in a photocopied image demonstrating an ancient Kama Sutra position. It's pretty much assured that in the time it takes that chocolate to melt on your lover's tongue, and for him to study the image, thoughts of the two of you engaged in that position will have flooded his brain. That, in turn, will trigger all the right responses in his body, ensuring you both will enjoy the tryst.

— EXTRA CREDIT —

Book a flight to some exotic destination for a *really* special tryst. Ask your spouse how golf, buttery scones, and steamy sex in a Scottish castle sound. He's probably not going to reply, "Uh, sorry, no. I am planning to clean out the garage this weekend."

STAY ATTRACTIVE
FOR EACH OTHER

Sex appeal is fifty percent what you've got and fifty percent what people think you've got. —Sophia Loren, Italian actress and sex symbol

Beauty may start on the inside, but it's a pretty safe bet that no one is going to compliment you on your gorgeous gall bladder. While taking care of your body is important (exercise, eating right, reducing stress, getting enough sleep, and being positive) so, too, is keeping up your appearance. Put another way—don't stop looking nice for your spouse once the ink on the marriage certificate has dried. Try a new look from time to time. Keep that sexy, confident attraction going between you.

Wives: Buy a new lipstick. Invest in a facial once in a while. Get your nails done. Color your gray. Buy a bra that pushes your boobs north and wear it with a low-cut blouse.

Husbands: Purchase cologne with a sexy scent that she loves. Get a GQ haircut, grow a mustache (or shave it off), get the hair between your brows waxed, and invest in a new cut of jeans or slacks.

Consider the expenditures as the vitally important cost of "looking good for each other."

—— EXTRA CREDIT ——

Invest a little more in your sex appeal. Book an appointment for yourself and your spouse at your favorite nail salon for his-and-her manicures. Also try his-and-her massages and his-and-her facials.

LET THERE BE SOME MYSTERIES
IN YOUR TOGETHERNESS

Sing and dance together and be joyous, but let each one of you be alone,
Even as the strings of a lute are alone though they quiver with the same
music. —Kahlil Gibran, Lebanese American artist, poet, and writer

Do you really need to share with your spouse the minutiae of intimate details about your sexual liaisons before you met, fell in love, and married him? Probably not. In the spirit of transparency and honest communication, it should be sufficient to let him know that you had other relationships and you moved on. The minutiae would be painful to hear and probably not interest him. Likewise, the use of feminine products and breast pumps probably won't either. Relegate such information to the realm of female mystery.

The truth is that husbands and wives really don't need to know *every* teensy weensy bit of detail about you and your life. Who wants to see a woman shaving her underarms or a man clipping nasal hair? You just want that finished, well-groomed look, right? Also, to get too up-close and personal is to start feeling somewhat suffocated. Although early in your marriage you might desire to cleave to each other as only newlyweds can, later on that same intense closeness pushes you away from each other again to reclaim your individuality and a little self-focus. It happens. Marriage provides a fertile ground for both oneness and separateness and that, like other aspects of marriage, is one of its mysteries.

— EXTRA CREDIT —

Write down three ideals about marriage that you harbored before you were married. Ask your spouse to do the same. Then discuss whether your ideals were too far-fetched.

DATE NIGHT

Spend the evening putting your most dazzling digital images in an online album on Flickr, Facebook, or in a family album on your website, so family and friends, whether in your same town or in other parts of the world, can enjoy the images you choose to share.

GIVE A LOT TO
GET EVEN MORE

In almost every marriage there is a selfish and an unselfish partner. A pattern is set up and soon becomes inflexible, of one person always making the demands and one person always giving way. —Iris Murdoch, Irish-born British philosopher and author

You are crazy in love and you want to keep it that way . . . but how do you do that once you've come off your wedding high? Passionate love—the kind that happens when you first fall in love with another person and spend hours on end gazing at each other, totally enraptured, caressing and kissing—can't stay at such dizzying heights forever. It wears off. You start to see your spouse not through the rose-colored glasses of a passionate high, but rather in the harsher light of reality. And he also sees you differently. Character flaws become apparent.

Despite these changes, your bonding is still taking place in the form of companionate love, as Jonathan Haidt calls it in his book *The Happiness Hypothesis*. Give selflessly to your spouse without thought of what you're going to get back. Love your mate unconditionally. Stick to your promises and uphold your marriage commitment. The love you share can see you through a lifetime.

— EXTRA CREDIT —

Address each other from your hearts about how your love might have changed from its earliest form to the kind of love you each perceive it to be now. Feel gratitude that the two of you have created a close and wonderful and enduring relationship that provides security and comfort for both of you. Renew your promise to each other to always love one another for the rest of your life.

SING TOGETHER
IN THE SHOWER

Every heart sings a song, incomplete, until another heart whispers back.
—Plato, Greek philosopher and mathematician

Who cares if the singing is off-pitch or out of key? You and the other half of your darling duo are in the shower, for goodness' sake, naked, soaped up, and ready to belt out a Puccini aria. Or maybe a little ditty by Fergie and the Black Eyed Peas is perhaps more your style. Go ahead, shake your booty and belt out that number. It will likely endear you to your spouse. You can wash her hair and she can scrub your back to the rhythm of the music.

Heighten the shower singing experience by ensuring that you've got everything you need in the stall before you step in. Set out a basket with scented shower gel, shampoo, conditioner, a back scrubber, and a loofah or two. There is a saying in Spanish, *Dímelo cantando*, that means "Say it singing." So, go ahead. Say it, and sing it: "I love you."

— EXTRA CREDIT —

Put some waterproof adult toys in your shower basket. Make the bathing experience a lot more fun and give it new meaning when you invite your spouse to join you. Warning: Shower singing and hot sex can be habit forming.

SEEK AGREEMENT BEFORE
REPLACING FURNITURE

We had gay burglars the other night. They broke in and rearranged the furniture. —Robin Williams, American comedian and actor

You might remember that episode of *Frasier* where Frasier was reveling in the new upscale look of his bachelor pad and realizing that the only thing that didn't work was his dad's recliner . . . but his dad was not willing to give up that chair, and thus the conflict for that television episode was quickly established. Replacing a piece of furniture without talking to your spouse is a bad idea. Seek agreement with your spouse on blending your styles. Discuss what to remove and what will replace the piece or pieces in terms of style and functionality. The following checklist can get you started:

- Set aside emotional attachment. If you simply can't part with something, stick it in storage.
- Make a furniture list in two columns—essential and nonessential. Each of you must create your own two-column list. Items that you both noted as essential go on an agreed-upon master list of essentials. All other items the two of you listed are negotiable.
- Play give-and-take when shopping. If your spouse insists on a recliner, suggest that you pick the color.

— EXTRA CREDIT —

Talk with the furniture salespeople about pieces you would like to purchase. Take your time and shop around for the best pricing. If you want help on pulling together a look using disparate pieces, seek insights and expertise from store personnel, including designers (if the stores have them). Community colleges also have instructors teaching interior design who possibly could help guide you.

LIE TOGETHER IN THE
AFTERGLOW OF LOVEMAKING

Who could refrain / That had a heart to love, and in that heart / Courage to make love known. —Shakespeare, *Macbeth*

All humans need physical touch to feel safe and connected. In psychology, there is something known as the attachment theory, which postulates that infants and young children need to be held and touched when distressed in order for them to learn how to soothe and calm their own nervous systems. Research in the fields of neuroscience and psychology is finding a significant link between emotional needs being met in the first years of life and the ability to form healthy adult relationships.

The pleasure our bodies can feel is a great gift. Combine that gift with a sense of connection to someone you care about and you can open yourself to even greater satisfaction. Don't shortchange each other by rolling over and falling asleep after sex. To lie together in a loving embrace after sex is to enjoy an important part of the process. Having your lover to play with creates many new options for enjoying your sexuality, But it can also invite more complexity and complications. It helps to attend to your relationship and keep it in harmony, making sure you both get what you need. When you feel relaxed after lovemaking and are wrapped in the warm cocoon of loving arms, you feel contentment and security that you may not experience any other way during your day.

--- EXTRA CREDIT ---

Play soft music on the radio or iPod. Make sure you set a time for it to shut off, then relax after lovemaking and take your time drifting off to sleep. Pray, meditate, or incubate a dream as you sink deeper into the in-between state between wakefulness and sleep.

PUT YOUR SPOUSE
BEFORE OTHERS

Women need a reason to have sex. Men just need a place. —Billy Crystal, American comedian and actor

You are a good parent, friend, sister, and auntie. You rescue and otherwise are quick to be there for those in your life who have needs, but are you giving equal attention to your husband and his needs? Women often see themselves as mothers first and spouses second. Some women prioritize all the juggling they must do, relegating spousal intimacy to just below work/career and children. In fact, in numerous studies, couples who have children find that the quality of their sex life, and its frequency, declines.

Reasons women may not want sex are fatigue, stress, poor body image, and desire discrepancy (being out of sync with their partner's desires). Wives seek tenderness, appreciation, foreplay, and then sex, while husbands generally just want the sex. Problems will develop if you don't talk, don't touch, and don't make love. A recent estimate put the number of U.S. marriages suffering lack of physical intimacy at a whopping 20 million. Don't let your marriage be a statistic—prioritize each other to ensure you both feel loved, respected, and cared for.

--- EXTRA CREDIT ---

Whether you are a wife or a husband, think about all the reasons you might want to put your spouse's needs in top-priority position, ahead of the needs of all the other people in your life who might be clamoring for attention. It may surprise you to learn that it is often the husband who decides to stop being sexual in marriage or committed relationships, rather than the wife. But regardless of which partner loses interest, both spouses need to be full partners in the solution.

OFFER TO MENTOR
YOUNG NEWLYWEDS

Guard well within yourself that treasure, kindness. —George Sand,
French novelist

Marriage is one of the most important commitments a couple ever makes. Every newly married person knows how to enjoy the happy times; it's when they hit the rough patches that they need help, sometimes professional and sometimes just the support of another couple who's been there, done that. All newlyweds are hopeful, at least in the beginning, that their love will enable them to meet any challenge so that theirs will be a long and happy marriage. However, if their expectations are not grounded in practical reality, if they haven't had a good marriage modeled for them, it's entirely conceivable that their marriage will encounter some major challenges.

That's where couples who are no longer newlyweds can help. If you and your spouse have been married for a while and have weathered more than a few marital storms, offer to be sounding boards for newly married young couples. You might volunteer to help through a church-based or social services program. If you are old enough to have your own children walking down the aisle to say "I do," make sure they know you are there to help them when they need suggestions for navigating through the more challenging moments of marriage.

--- EXTRA CREDIT ---

Consider collecting your marriage advice and aphorisms in a booklet and make it available for young newlyweds. Alternatively, you could produce a CD or establish a blog. You might even write an advice column in your church or temple newsletter.

DATE NIGHT

Visit a local carnival or New Age fair for a lighthearted session with a fortuneteller or a psychic. Get your palms read, or have your fortunes told by someone who uses the Tarot or other type of cards. Or visit an astrology booth to learn more about your couple compatibility. Have fun, but remember that you shouldn't necessarily believe everything you hear. You two will determine your own future, what it holds, and where it takes you.

NEVER STOP KISSING
AND TOUCHING

———————

A kiss can be a comma, a question mark, or an exclamation point. That's the basic spelling that every woman ought to know. —Mistinguett (Jeanne Bourgeois), Theatre Arts

Married couples slip into routines that can become ruts, forgoing intimate touching such as kissing. Some become so lapse in expressing affection that they won't even give the most perfunctory of kisses, a peck on the cheek. Your spouse is your partner, best friend, helper, sounding board, confidant, and lover. To keep your marriage exciting, use the sense of touch to express your love, and use it often. It brings a sense of comfort and closeness that both husbands and wives crave. A touch can be electrifying, especially for a spouse who hasn't been suggestively touched in a while. Kissing can be so expressively erotic.

Some wives may think that even spending an hour kissing their husbands would not be enough to get them really turned on. But kissing for any amount of time, if done tenderly, slowly, and sensuously, can really get you going and serve as the prelude to hot and heavy intercourse. This would include oral sex. Using your mouth to kiss and caress your lover's body all over is a very erotic experience. Kissing, licking, blowing warm air, and even light sucking on the neck, face, and other areas add to the sensuous arousal.

——— EXTRA CREDIT ———

Kick the kissing up a notch. Purchase a creamy, flavored lip balm for him, and some sensational lip-plumping, palate-pleasing lip gloss for you. Brush your teeth, floss, and finish with a nice-tasting mouthwash. Set a timer for five minutes. Now lube your lips and let the kissing begin.

CULTIVATE FRIENDSHIPS
THAT INCLUDE YOUR SPOUSE

You are responsible for your life. —Oprah Winfrey, television talk show hostess

You're bound to make new friends as you go through a life together as a married couple. Talk with your spouse about including him or her in those new relationships. Although most couples find it important to retain independent interests and friends after marriage and thus give each other "time off" from being part of a marital duo, the question is degree. Some couples permit each other substantial separate lives, while others are comfortable with much less separateness.

If you didn't talk with your partner before your marriage about how much socializing you'd like to do individually and as a couple, make it a topic of conversation now. Spouses who have trust issues or insecurity issues may feel discomfort with the other spouse socializing with members of the opposite sex. For example, your wife wants to have her usual weekly lunch date with a girlfriend, whom you've met, but suddenly the plan includes two guys, whom you haven't. You trust your spouse, but you don't know the men and you have concerns. The best course of action is to talk over your concerns with your mate and keep asking questions until you are satisfied that neither safety nor impropriety is an issue.

--- EXTRA CREDIT ---

Cultivate friends around interests that you share with your life partner, whether gardening, art, music, sports, cars, remodeling, or food and drink. Plan activities around those interests and involve your spouse. Sharing your passion and knowledge with others and learning new things from them can add layers of meaning and purpose to your life and build a strong social network, an important factor in longevity and life satisfaction.

WALK AWAY FROM
ADVANCES BY OLD FRIENDS

Friend, there's a window that opens heart to heart, and there are ways of closing it completely, not a needle's eye of access. —Rumi, Persian poet and philosopher, *The Illuminated Rumi*, translated by Coleman Barks

Maybe your husband's old girlfriend can't seem to keep her hands off him when you all run into each other at a party. Or, your boyfriend from years ago shows up at the local art and wine festival, where he has had too much to drink, and comes on to you as if nothing had ever changed. He knows you are married and waited to make his move until your husband left to feed coins into the parking meter.

The actions of your previous relationship partner and that of your husband's old girlfriend are totally inappropriate. Like misbehaving children, these adults are not respecting boundaries. You and your spouse need to put up a united front with such people, reminding them that you are married, that the behavior is making you uncomfortable, and that it demonstrates a lack of respect you won't tolerate. Ask the person to leave you alone. Take your spouse's hand or interlock your arms and walk away. As flattering as an advance from another person might be, it's in your best interest to intercept, obstruct, or deflect the advances and leave the situation as quickly as possible.

— EXTRA CREDIT —

Walk away from any situation that puts you in a position of having your personal boundaries violated. Things do not have to get out of hand for you to call the police, especially if you have asked the offending individuals to back off and they haven't. You have the right to protect yourself and your spouse.

PUT TIME AND ENERGY INTO
NEW FRIENDSHIPS AS A COUPLE

What is my life if I am no longer useful to others? —Johann Wolfgang von Goethe, German dramatist, novelist, poet, and scientist

If you and your spouse are young newlyweds, you might find that the people you used to pal around with sort of fall away—that is, they don't call you much anymore and don't seem very interested in putting the time and energy into the friendship that they once did. It's as if they liked doing things with you when you were single, but now that you are married, they don't know how to be with you. It may seem strange, but actually, it's a fairly common occurrence.

All friendships require an investment of time and energy. If you are the only one who ever calls the other couple to set up a date for getting together, you might want to verbalize that you view friendship as a two-way street. What typically happens is that the couple who never calls to initiate a get-together most likely is not interested enough in the relationship with you to keep it going. So you and your spouse must make new friends. It will get much easier after you've had a child, because you will meet other young couples with children at the pediatrician's office, the day-care center, the library, and perhaps even at the grocery store where you buy your diapers and baby food.

--- EXTRA CREDIT ---

Extend the hand of friendship to other young married people whom you meet at church or possibly even when you go out to dinner. For example, if you sometimes eat in a restaurant with limited seating and there is generally a long line of couples waiting for a table, start a conversation with one or two couples. Invite them to share a table with you.

HIRE A PERSONAL TRAINER
FOR BOTH OF YOU

———

A bear, however hard he tries, grows tubby without exercise. —A.A. Milne, English author, "Teddy Bear"

Exhaustion is a common excuse for not exercising. For working parents, it's difficult to find time. The truth is that you probably just want a hot meal and some downtime when you finish your workday. But if you have children or pets, there are chores to be done at home, too. Sometimes those chores seem as endless as a second shift of work, only it's one that requires infinite patience and no financial compensation.

The motivation to exercise must evolve from the desire to stay healthy and physically fit, not only for yourselves but for your family. If you and your spouse could find an extra half hour or more each weekday, you could work out together, reinforcing each other's effort. Consider hiring a personal trainer to psych you up, teach you the right way to trim the weight, work muscle groups, and build up or slim down specific areas of your bodies. You need not buy expensive equipment or set up a home gym. Nor do you have to spend a small fortune to get personalized attention. The trainer can help you develop a complete routine, answer your questions, encourage you to stick with the program, and support your efforts to get in shape.

——— EXTRA CREDIT ———

Put together a cardio routine that can replace an outdoor run or an aggressive workout on the treadmill and stairclimber. Include side steps with knee lifts, squats that evolve into pushups, and then upright jumps with hands to the sky. Finish with a forward lunge, returning with a step back and standing, then the reverse lunge. Add in some high kicks and jumping jacks and your heart soon will be pounding as if you were running the mile in record-breaking time.

DON'T LET DRINKING WITH
FRIENDS BECOME A PROBLEM

Wine lets secrets out. —Chinese proverb

The occasional drink with friends who invite you out for an evening of catching up and talking about the old days can be a lot of fun. But if meeting your friends always means excluding your spouse and if the meeting always involves drinking at a bar or club, you have to be concerned about the impact on your relationship and your marriage. Drinking alcohol can lower inhibitions, and while you may see no harm in having drinks with friends in a setting like a bar or nightclub, situations that aren't healthy can develop.

Your marriage may be strong and loving and you and your mate trust each other. But what if you have let down your guard and possibly aren't thinking quite as clearly as you normally would because of the alcohol you've consumed? It's flattering when someone finds you attractive and flirts with you. Do you flirt back because you think it's harmless, maybe gratifies your ego? Do you leave? Do you tell your spouse? If not, what happens when your spouse finds out the truth? The prudent choice is to exercise caution and restraint; think through your choices before going out with friends for drinks on a regular basis, and ask if your mate is invited, too.

—— EXTRA CREDIT ——

Throw the party at your house. Wives might invite their girlfriends for a tea party or a potluck. Husbands could invite the guys over for a poker night or to watch the game. Or, find an activity everyone can participate in, like a trivia game night. That way, spouses get to know each other's friends and acquaintances, and frequent outings with the focus on alcohol won't be necessary.

DATE NIGHT

Take the elevator to the top of the tallest building in your town or city to watch the sunset and make a wish on the first star you see in the sky. Then enjoy the expansive glittering veil of night as she descends over the sky. Think of how remarkable it is that you and your spouse found each other in all of the earth, seemingly as full of beings as the night sky is full of stars.

COLLABORATE ON PLANS
FOR YOUR DREAM HOUSE

Where is home? Home is where the heart can laugh without shyness. Home is where the heart's tears can dry at their own pace. —Vernon Baker, U.S. Army Medal of Honor recipient

Perhaps you and your mate have reached that stage of life where your nest is now empty, you are in your early midlife, and you have the desire and enough money saved to finally build your dream house. You are in the enviable position of tackling the next big adventure of your married life with gusto, as ready as you'll ever be to collaborate on that beautiful dream home. Perhaps you already have purchased the site and you know the most advantageous view.

Stand with your spouse on the site and gaze out over that view while you envision yourselves naked and enjoying it from the master bedroom. It can be your gift to yourselves if you situate the house and the room properly on that site. Envision your master bed and bath as the most romantic space in the house. Most likely, your new home will have areas for entertaining and spaces to accommodate your children and their families, but be sure to also design spaces in your dream house for just the two of you to enjoy for the rest of your married lives.

—— EXTRA CREDIT ——

Go green. Work with an architect and builder who are savvy about designs that can utilize green materials to create an environmentally sustainable house and environs. Plan carefully so that you can go off the power grid through the use of solar or wind or Bloom Box clean energy power.

MAKE RENEWAL A THEME
OF YOUR MARRIAGE

Do not fear going forward slowly; fear only to stand still. —Chinese proverb

Keep your marriage vibrantly alive and interesting through an ongoing process of renewal. Renewal is one of those cultural buzzwords that you often hear at the beginning of a new year when people are busy making resolutions or during early spring when everyone sees the natural world undergoing a renewal process following winter.

Marriage renewal strategies can be implemented throughout the year by changing the way you handle the relationship or by shifting your perspectives and attitudes. For example, practice flexibility, talk openly, give up control more often, find ways to balance your togetherness with your individuality, work on managing your differences, and put more thoughtfulness and energy into your relationship. Some of the things to give up or at least work on would be the tendency to hold on to resentments, nagging, and forgetting to be respectful.

DAY 338

— EXTRA CREDIT —

Make a Promise Book, a blank journal in which you and your partner can write messages to each other whenever you feel inspired. Use the book to write of renewed hope, trust, belief, and love. Also, you can record new promises in the book, such as "I promise to keep your confidences and earn your trust, putting you first before all others in my life."

GO CAMPING WITH
ANOTHER FAMILY

Rainstorms will travel thousands of miles, against prevailing winds for the opportunity to rain on a tent. —Dave Barry, American humor columnist

Camping can be incredibly fun and can teach you and your spouse about mutual respect, responsibility, resiliency, and survival strengths and weaknesses. Having the right gear and camping know-how can make the experience a lot more enjoyable. Talk with your spouse about where you'd like to camp and for how long. Spending time together in nature can draw you closer to see the wonder of creation and enable you both to renew and recharge body and spirit.

Get together with another couple or family who would enjoy joining you on the camping trip to talk through any concerns. Make safety the number one priority. Make a reservation, especially if your camping trip is to a national park during the summer. Get travel maps and become familiar with park regulations before you head out. Check the weather and take along the appropriate clothing, supplies, and gear, including a GPS or compass as well as a first-aid kit. Plan on taking out of the park whatever you bring in.

—— EXTRA CREDIT ——

Pick up things you find while hiking on your camping trip—feathers, pretty leaves, a colorful wildflower that has separated from its stem, a twig with an unusual shape. Assemble these in a keepsake box or book, which can also include photos that you take of yourself and your spouse on the camping trip. Write captions for each picture, as well as poems or thoughts associated with the items you found.

HELP TEENS ADJUST
TO A BLENDED FAMILY

The music that can deepest reach / And cure all ill, is cordial speech. —Ralph Waldo Emerson, American essayist, philosopher, and poet

Many parents and stepparents trying to blend families find that preteen and teenage children can have a particularly difficult time with the transition. If you're stuck in conflict with or about an adolescent's behavior, and particularly if your marital relationship is suffering, consider family therapy. Here are some guidelines for helping children and stepchildren adjust and thrive in a blended family:

- Put your marital relationship first; without it, the other relationships will fall apart.
- Present a united front with your partner when disciplining.
- Make time for activities involving the whole family.
- Keep solo outings for biological parents and children to reassure each child that he or she still has a special bond with the parent.
- Don't take it personally if your stepchild refuses your conversations or invitations or wishes his biological parents would reunite.
- Encourage positive behavior rather than dwell on the negative.
- Don't yell at or shame a child.
- Let your child or stepchild take the lead in how much togetherness or intimacy he's ready for with his stepparent.

—— EXTRA CREDIT ——
Do not underestimate the difficulties of adjusting, and the time needed by everyone to do so in a blended family. Adjust your expectations based on age and specific developmental levels.

ESTABLISH LIMITS
AND ENFORCE THEM

Any kid will run any errand for you if you ask at bedtime. —Red Skelton,
American comedian and actor

Child psychologists and family therapists will tell you that children need
boundaries to feel safe. Toddlers to teens, children need to know what
the limits are in order to push up against those limits and test them.
Having firm limits (age appropriate, of course) enables children to learn
self-control to regulate their own behavior so that it is acceptable within
the family unit and also in the wider world of school and community.

When there are no consequences for a child pushing past a boundary
or limit that parents have established, power shifts from parents to child.
This is not comforting to the child. By setting limits, saying no, and
enforcing the consequences for rules that are broken, your children learn
they are responsible for their actions. Also, teach your children about
establishing emotional boundaries (so he or she isn't pushed around at
school or in relationships) and for taking ownership of their own emotional feelings of frustration, sadness, or anger.

—— EXTRA CREDIT ——
Talk with your spouse about establishing a basic short list of house rules. Post the
rules where everyone can read them, say in a corner of the kitchen, the mudroom,
the laundry area, or the game room. When everyone knows the rules, a level and fair
playing field is established.

KEEP A COMMUNICATION NOTEBOOK THAT CAN TRAVEL BETWEEN FAMILIES

If our American way of life fails the child, it fails us all. —Pearl S. Buck, American author, recipient of the Pulitzer and Nobel prizes

A communication notebook can be a vital tool when parents share custody of a child and that child has special needs or health issues. The communication notebook can contain a list of medications, special foods or food restrictions, and allergy reminders. The notebook could also contain important phone numbers (pediatrician, dentist), medical plan and coverage info, and eating schedules and bedtimes. The communication notebook can put your mind at ease when sending your children off to their grandparents, allowing them to sleep over at a friend's house, or taking them to the ex-spouse for the weekend. Everyone will be on the same page; for example, knowing the rules in your household about snacks before bedtime and what constitutes a healthy snack, and whom to call in an emergency, besides you.

—— EXTRA CREDIT ——

Get your spouse and children involved in making a communication notebook for each child. Let each kid personalize his or her notebook with a picture, a fingerprint, and anything else that would make it unique.

DATE NIGHT

Visit a chocolate shop and buy one piece of dark chocolate for each other. Chocolate, called the food of the gods by the ancient Mayans, is chock-full of antioxidants and good for you in moderation. Enjoy your sweet treat and each other's chocolate-flavored kisses afterward.

CREATE A PLAN FOR
YOUR FUTURE EMPTY NEST

Always be nice to your children because they are the ones who will choose your rest home. —Phyllis Diller, American comedienne

The years have passed (more quickly perhaps than you anticipated) and those early marriage discussions seem to belong to another lifetime. Now that your nest is empty, or almost, tension rather than excitement and anticipation reigns supreme. It might help you to know that when transitions happen with a marriage, such as a change in employment status, a new baby, or a suddenly empty nest, tensions can arise. Transitional changes put strain on any existing weaknesses in the relationship.

Identifying stresses that tend to produce fighting in your marriage is a vital part of the communication process. Disagreements in times of transition can be a blessing in disguise if they help you address an underlying issue so you can work on resolving it. It's never too late to start planning again just for you and your spouse.

— EXTRA CREDIT —

Crunch some numbers to evaluate whether or not selling or remodeling might make sense now. Imagine having that studio you always wanted, or the kitchen of your dreams. Or, maybe you just want to take a vacation someplace near an ocean, lake, or river to see if you might enjoy a boat and life near the water.

ASK EACH PERSON TO
TAKE RESPONSIBILITY FOR HIS
OR HER WORDS AND ACTIONS

It is easy to dodge our responsibilities, but we cannot dodge the consequences of dodging our responsibilities. —Josiah Charles Stamp, English economist

Before you hold others responsible for their words and actions, you have to practice personal accountability for what you say and do. In business and organizations, leaders outline their expectations and then hold workers accountable for meeting or not meeting the desired expectation or outcome. In the same way, you can advise your mate, other family members, children, and ex-spouses of your expectation that everyone get along, show respect, honor boundaries, and be civil to one another. Further, you can do so in a positive way that gets you the desired results. If you have an expectation of others, you have to monitor progress (this is especially true for children) to determine that they are following through and not reverting back to a habitual pattern of pushing blame onto others. Give positive reinforcement when people in your life take responsibility for their actions. That is the surest way to get responsible behavior repeated.

— EXTRA CREDIT —

Get to the bottom of a recent argument or marital problem. Ask your mate to join you in this exercise: First, each of you writes about a disagreement or an event that has occurred for which you blame the other spouse or someone else. Then, consider how your thoughts, words, deeds, attitude, choices, or actions contributed to the outcome of that specific event. Discuss with your mate how, knowingly or unknowingly, you might have contributed to the outcome. Then talk about how to initiate change.

MAKE CHILDREN
ACCOUNTABLE

There are only two things a child will share willingly—communicable diseases and his mother's age. —Benjamin Spock, *Dr. Spock's Baby and Child Care*

When you and your spouse are parenting your children and/or step-children, remember to teach them accountability. The earlier they get that connection in their brains about linking their actions to the consequences, the better. Let them experience natural consequences. For example, you've told your youngest not to stand on his toy truck because he could fall. Yet he defiantly stands on it, while you continue to tell him to get off as you run over and carefully remove him from it. If he falls off once, he will immediately understand why you did not want him standing on it and repeatedly told him not to.

Child psychologists say that it is often more difficult, but still necessary, to teach accountability to older children who haven't formed that connection in their brain; that there are always consequences to their actions.

--- EXTRA CREDIT ---

When your child does something right, like picks up his room or brushes her teeth before bed without your having to remind or nag, give positive reinforcement. Praise the behavior you want repeated. Or as the late Alex Haley loved to say, "Find the good and praise it."

MAKE CONVERSATIONS
WITH EX-SPOUSES BE ABOUT
THE CHILDREN

Words are, of course, the most powerful drug used by mankind. —Rudyard
Kipling, British author and poet

Perhaps you and your ex are on really good speaking terms. That's great.
Even still, keep the focus of your conversations on the kids you've had
together, and not about each other, your lives with your new partners, or
reminiscences about your shared past history. There's no point in being
best friends with your ex. That's a role reserved for your current spouse.
Establish guidelines for a relationship with your ex and stick to them.

For example, no working out at the same gym at the same time,
no talking about the intimate details of each other's new marriages, no
displays of affection toward each other that exceed the limits you have
established in your ground rules. Conversations with your ex can certainly address such issues as which holidays you each will celebrate with
the children (for example, Christmas Eve with her; Christmas morning
with you), and when you might both have them. Don't gossip, rehash
the loss of that marriage (and perhaps custody of your children), or criti-
cize your ex or your ex's new spouse. It's time to focus on the positives in
your life with your new partner.

> — EXTRA CREDIT —
> Learn to talk straight to the point (men often do this better than women) when you
> have to discuss your child's school report card with your ex. Keep it short, tightly
> focused, civil, and nonemotional.

ENVISION YOUR THIRTY-YEAR ANNIVERSARY

A successful marriage is an edifice that must be rebuilt every day. —Andre Maurois, French author

Imagine bouquets of sweet peas and gifts of pearls (the flower and gift of that notable anniversary) and your friends and family gathered around for the celebration. Imagine the toasts and the usual anniversary jokes. Can you see a soloist singing your song? A chamber orchestra playing romantic classics? Strolling instrumentalists like mariachis or bagpipers? A barbershop ensemble? Or, just a karaoke machine? Can you see your children all grown up, perhaps with children of their own, singing songs you taught them? Can you envision them taking turns to dance with you and your spouse? Let your minds wrap around the idea of everyone paying homage to the two of you, whose wedding bliss has lasted to the thirty-year mark. Have fun dreaming about the future with your spouse. As you talk about what you both envision, you just might feel love's hold growing stronger.

— EXTRA CREDIT —

Why not go further into the future? Use your powers of imagination and visualize your fiftieth anniversary party. Your family can request that the U.S. president, whoever he might be then, call you. The only catch is that you and your spouse must both be U.S. citizens and married for fifty years or more. Then you have bragging rights forever!

LEARN TO ADMIT
YOUR WEAKNESSES

Let him who would move the world, first move himself. —Socrates, classical Greek philosopher

In the movie *Fatal Attraction*, the character played by Michael Douglas has an extramarital affair with the character played by Glenn Close. When she discovers that he is married, she begins to use information she has learned against him, information that will be damaging to his personal and professional life. It is not until he actually tells his wife about the affair that his lover loses the power of negotiation and her tool of destruction.

If you ever tell a lie to someone and another person finds out that you lied, that person has power over you until you admit the lie yourself. In doing this, you take the power away from the person who knows about the lie. You strip that person of his or her negative tool of persuasion. Once you admit the lie, his or her power is gone. Many people will learn your weaknesses, your fears, and your shortcomings, and once discovered will use this knowledge against you at every turn. The *only way* to combat this is to be comfortable in admitting your own shortcomings, thus taking the power away from other people to use this against you.

— EXTRA CREDIT —

Point out a character flaw or a weakness in your spouse, but do so in a loving way. Then ask your spouse to identify yours. Work on those weaknesses in order to develop greater self-esteem, individually and as a couple. Seek professional help if necessary. Sometimes a weakness is so deeply ingrained from early childhood that it is difficult to understand how it has become embedded in your psyche.

DATE NIGHT

Visit a clinic together for a traditional Chinese acupuncture treatment to release tension and to improve the flow of energy zipping along the unseen meridians of your bodies. Acupuncture isn't just for treating illness or disease, but also for the prevention of illness and the promotion of well-being. Afterward, have a light meal, drink green tea, and spend the evening with your spouse playing chess or watching the latest movie Netflix has delivered. Enjoy the wonderful restorative feeling of your bodily tune-up. Later, snuggle together, wrapped in a cocoon of warm, loving feelings that flow from your spouse's heart to yours and from yours to his.

DON'T
PROCRASTINATE

The world is a dangerous place, not because of those who do evil, but because of those who look on and do nothing. —Albert Einstein, German-born American physicist

Stop procrastinating. Couples might gripe and complain to each other about their respective weaknesses, but that won't make their shortcomings go away. Procrastinating will not eliminate the problems. If you really want to work on them, you must be relentless. Fighting your weaknesses will require that you are mentally and emotionally aware at all times. It means that you are going to address your shortcomings until you change them or until they no longer concern you.

Make a dedicated decision to work on your weaknesses every day and ask your spouse to support you in your efforts. Ways to reduce or eliminate your weaknesses include:

- Visualize your life without the perceived weakness.
- Set realistic goals to overcome the weakness.
- Work toward that goal with every action and interaction.
- Talk to others about your attempts to overcome this weakness.
- Catch yourself not doing the "thing," and reward yourself.
- Do not engage in self-defeating habits to eliminate the weakness.

--- EXTRA CREDIT ---

End each day with a short period of self-examination. Celebrate your effort and accomplishments. If you are replacing a bad habit, remember it takes roughly three weeks to form a new habit, so be patient. Be supportive and loving of yourself. Remember, everyone has weaknesses. Admitting that you have it is half the battle in eliminating it.

SET GROUND RULES BEFORE
HOSTING A BLENDED
FAMILY MEETING

If you're walking down the right path and you're willing to keep walking, eventually you'll make progress. —Barack Obama, U.S. president

Stepfamilies benefit from establishing ground rules before calling a joint meeting to air grievances or work through their children's schedules, transportation, visitations, discipline, health, or financial issues. Why? Because the conversation can move from civilized to heated and confrontational at warp speed. Set some ground rules for a meeting with your partner and his ex-spouse and/or yours. Here are a few to consider:

- Avoid complaining about the past; focus on the present issues.
- Make the meeting about finding solutions to problems.
- Have an agenda.
- Keep the conversation positive.
- Communicate issues and problems without blame or accusations.
- Ask everyone to offer their best solutions.
- Acknowledge the fact that everyone has hot-button issues, but ask everyone to set them aside for the sake of accomplishing the goals set forth in the agenda.

—— EXTRA CREDIT ——

Let go of expectations. When you have expectations, whether or not they are realistic, you are setting yourself up for disappointment if they aren't met. Accept your previous spouse or your current husband's previous spouse for who they are. You can't change them, nor should you try. Take responsibility for what you do, say, and feel and, if you can, try not to sweat the small stuff.

AVOID INTERNET RELATIONSHIPS
THAT EXCLUDE YOUR SPOUSE

Bisexuality immediately doubles your chances for a date on Saturday night.
—Woody Allen, American screenwriter

It's one thing to log onto the Internet with your husband or wife to chat with friends through Skype or Paltalk. But it's quite another to slip away from your spouse and log on to surf to friendship and dating sites looking for a little titillation. Some people might not view a cyber-relationship as being unfaithful to their spouses because they are not having sex. But regardless of how it is justified by the cheating spouse, the cyber-relationship can be hazardous to the marriage.

If you feel more fulfilled surfing the Net and looking at all the possible partners you could hook up with rather than being with the partner you married, ask yourself why. The Internet is an easy escape for spouses who want to feel the exhilaration of a cyber-flirtation, sexual attraction, and a pseudo-romantic fling without having to reveal it to their mates or having to make any kind of commitment to their cyber-lover.

However, the pseudo-intimacy you get from a cyber-relationship can lead you away from your true spouse. You may think that you are not being unfaithful because you aren't having an affair in the traditional sense, but your husband or wife might see things differently. Instead of spending time online, invest the time in your spouse, working on building a healthy, intimate relationship. Once you do that, cyber-romance won't be as tempting.

—— EXTRA CREDIT ——

Share your passwords and access questions with your spouse and ask your partner to reciprocate. If your work requires you to remain active in social networking, let your activities be transparent to your spouse.

ESTABLISH FINANCIAL
GOALS FOR DECADES AHEAD

Youth is a wonderful thing. What a crime to waste it on children. —George
Bernard Shaw, Irish playwright

According to findings published in 2009 by Sun Life Financial, Inc.,
only about 28 percent of American workers believe they will have sufficient retirement resources, and 27 percent think they will have to work
five years longer before retiring than they had expected. Clearly, longevity might be an expensive prospect for you and your spouse. But even if
you are already a couple of decades into your marriage, you can still do
some financial planning for the future.

Start today to implement that plan so that you will reach the goals
decades from now. For example, if you aren't already saving, you can
start. You might even take a second job or figure out if it makes sense to
turn a hobby into a moneymaking enterprise. If you both decide to do
that, you'll have four revenue streams to help you meet future financial
goals. As you approach your retirement as a couple, you'll be glad you
gave some thought to the future when there was still time to impact it in
a significant and positive way.

— EXTRA CREDIT —

If you or your spouse own your own company or are self-employed and working
together, honor the cardinal rule of self-employment: pay yourselves first, and try to
save. According to the Employee Benefits Research Institute, more than 54 percent
of baby boomers between the ages of forty-five and fifty-four have saved less than
$50,000 for their retirement. Even supplemented with Social Security and pensions,
that's not a lot.

RENEW YOUR VOWS AND
TAKE THAT SECOND HONEYMOON

For this cause shall a man leave his father and mother, . . . and shall be joined unto his wife, and they two shall be one flesh. —Ephesians 5:31

Your wedding cemented your love for each other. Renewing your vows and rededicating your life to your spouse can deepen your appreciation and love for each other, thereby strengthening your marital bonds. Deciding to embark on a second honeymoon is the proverbial frosting on the cake.

It is important to note, however, that your vow renewal ceremony is not a second wedding. You are already married, so the emphasis is on that loving commitment that holds you two together. Forget the bachelor or bachelorette party, the bridal shower, the wedding dress, and lavish, towering cake. You, not your parents, bear the costs associated with the event. It's orchestrated by you and your spouse with a member of the clergy present to oversee the actual renewing of your vows. A party can follow. Plan a honeymoon that won't break the bank but will still be fun.

— EXTRA CREDIT —

Create a new tradition. For example, ask each person to write a short note to offer advice for a long and happy marriage, share a warm and fuzzy memory of a time spent with you and your spouse, provide a prayer, or share a funny story about you. Read a selection of these at one of your future anniversary celebrations.

PUT THE WEIGHTS
BY THE COUCH

Intention without action is useless. —Caroline Myss, author, mystic, and medical intuitive

Everyone suffers muscle wasting as they age. Weightlifting can help lessen that wasting. Can't get to a gym? Purchase a set of graduated weights that you can keep by the couch. That way, every time you are tempted to drop onto the couch cushions, you'll see those weights and be reminded of your intention to get fit. Weightlifting will not only firm and strengthen your muscles; you'll get leaner and have better posture. All of those benefits are important for everyone, but especially so for baby boomers and seniors.

You can use weights with squats, lunges, over-the-head arm lifts, and other positions. Consider weight training in tandem with your spouse, taking turns exercising various muscle groups. Although an hour a day twice a week is all you need to help keep your muscles in shape, more is better. Weight training aids in fitness by increasing the delivery of nutrient- and hormone-rich blood to your muscles. You might notice you are sleeping better, too. So do your muscles a favor. Instead of sinking into the couch for your favorite television programs, work with the weights while you watch.

--- EXTRA CREDIT ---

Buy a membership at a gym that has a weightlifting room. When you have worked with the weights at home for a while, you might be ready for a more intensive program that involves professional-level equipment, dietary changes including supplements, and possibly advice from a professional weight trainer.

DATE NIGHT

Read some sixteenth-century erotic writing. Go shopping with your spouse to a local bookstore to find a copy of the old Arab treatise *The Perfumed Garden of the Shaykh Nefwazii*. Alternatively, you could plan an evening in and read the text online at *www.sacred-texts.com/sex/garden/index. htm*. The treatise reflects the language and the customs of the Arabian Middle Ages (some are strange and ill-advised), and yet the information titillates and celebrates intimacy in its own amusing way. The English translation by Sir Richard F. Burton makes the content much more accessible.

Open yourself to the flowery language that uses euphemisms such as verge and member for the male sex organ and describes heavy breathing and red lips as proof of the exquisite pleasure man and woman have experienced during their lovemaking.

CONSUME
MORE HERBS

Another parable put He forth unto them, saying, The kingdom of heaven is like to a grain of mustard seed, which a man took, and sowed in his field: Which indeed is the least of all seeds: but when it is grown, it is the greatest among herbs, and becometh a tree, so that the birds of the air come and lodge in the branches thereof. —Matthew 13:31–32

Couples who cook know that herbs can subtly flavor or intensify the flavors of a dish. You can consume herbs as teas, dried and sprinkled into food, freshly picked from your own garden, or mixed into soups and sauces. Since they are often healthful additions to food, you and your spouse would benefit from learning how to consume more of them.

Whether grown in the wild or cultivated, herbs not only add interest to food, but also have health benefits such as lowering blood pressure, calming anxiety, relaxing menstrual cramping, and so on, and for that reason have often been used as medicinal aids for the treatment of common ailments. Feverfew, for example, prepared as a tea, was used in previous centuries for headache and melancholia, whereas sage, comfrey, and horehound were used for respiratory ailments. Today, herbs occupy an important place in alternative medicine modalities. For example, bog bean, white willow, and arnica are herbs useful in relieving muscle pain and inflamed joints associated with acute arthritis.

— EXTRA CREDIT —

Take your spouse to a farmer's market, or to a Fresh Market, Whole Foods, or other grocery that has excellent-quality fresh produce. Buy organic, if possible, or better still, grow your own herbs.

AGE TOGETHER
GRACEFULLY

I want to get old gracefully. I want to have good posture, I want to be healthy and be an example to my children. —Sting, British musician, actor, activist, and philanthropist

Marriage is a work in progress, never static. If it's standing still, that's a danger sign for you and your spouse. Each of you matures by going through crises and happy milestones or life passages that will change you, and by extension the marriage.

You will be very different people at the middle and end points of your marriage than you were at the start. By the time you're many years into your marriage, you most likely will have mastered the art of keeping sexuality alive in whatever ways work for the two of you. Know one thing: as your bodies and minds change, the children come and go, and careers wax and wane, all the ways that work to keep sexuality alive for your relationship will change too.

— EXTRA CREDIT —

Take a good look at what's happening between the two of you the next time you experience a crisis, and then turn your gaze inward. Is this crisis an opportunity to alter your own thinking or behavior, to give more, to let go of an old hurt, or to renew your relationship? More often than not, the answer is yes to at least one of these!

RIDE BICYCLES ON A
SUNDAY AFTERNOON

When the spirits are low, when the day appears dark, when work becomes monotonous, when hope hardly seems worth having, just mount a bicycle and go out for a spin down the road, without thought on anything but the ride you are taking. —Sir Arthur Conan Doyle

Ask your spouse to join you for some exercise on a Sunday afternoon and the reply quite possibly might be no; entice your spouse out of the house on Sunday afternoon with a promise of a cycling excursion, and you might get a different answer. Cycling just conjures a different image than exercising, yet it's an exceedingly effective way to work out. You'll have some together time and enjoy some aerobic exercise, which can reduce the risk of high blood pressure, heart disease, obesity, and diabetes.

It is when you are in the fresh air, breathing heavily but not out of breath, that you will experience optimum results. Some studies show that riding a bike briskly for twenty minutes results in fat burning for twenty more minutes after the ride has ended, because doing a faster exercise is more effective than exercising slowly.

--- EXTRA CREDIT ---

Go bike shopping with your significant other. Select a bike that you can easily navigate over the terrain in your local area, since studies show that most people don't ride more than five miles. Therefore, you need not buy an expensive professional mountain bike, but do invest in a helmet.

SUPPORT YOUR SPOUSE'S
EFFORTS TO LOSE WEIGHT

_____

I've been on a diet for two weeks and all I've lost is fourteen days. —Totie Fields, American comedienne

When you and your spouse nibbled on your wedding cake, you probably didn't know that as a married couple you will gain more weight through the passing years than your unmarried friends, according to studies. Yet helping each other lose weight is not as easy as you might think. All too often, the spouse trying to lose will get annoyed with the repeated reminders of the nondieting spouse.

That's why it's better to back off and instead model good eating habits. Serve smaller portions of healthier foods. Drink water instead of sodas and other sugar-laden beverages. Replace high-calorie sweets and desserts with lower-calorie counterparts such as fresh fruit with a dollop of creamy soy yogurt. Prepare his favorite dishes, only make them healthier by using the lighter, lower-calorie, lower-fat, lower-sugar or -salt versions of ingredients such as cream cheese, mayonnaise, and milk. Encourage your spouse to exercise by asking him to walk with you around the block (to start). Suggest weighing in once a week, not every day. Focus on living a healthier lifestyle. Celebrate the accomplishments, however small. Offer encouragement. Everyone, especially spouses, need that.

—— EXTRA CREDIT ——

Buddy up with another couple who are also trying to lose weight. Share weight-loss ideas, low-fat recipes, and information on how to cut salt in the diet.

LIVE IN TUNE
WITH YOUR PASSION

Catch on fire with enthusiasm and people will come for miles to watch you burn. —John Wesley, English-born Anglican cleric, co-founder of the Methodist movement

What's your passion? Does your spouse share it? When couples share a passion for something—a hobby, a cause, a noble belief—they strengthen their pair bond. It's the sharing of common interests that keep relationships going when that intense sexual attraction and passionate form of love cools a bit. The following list includes some interests couples might share:

- Protecting human rights
- Working to get better labeling of genetically altered food
- Fighting racial, gender, and cultural intolerance
- Finding ways to feed the hungry
- Saving the planet and endangered species

Humans are wired for pair bonding, which means that when you and your mate are in tune with your visions and passions, the altruistic acts of generosity you do together can promote healthy bonding and closeness to each other. That, in turn, suggests positive implications for your life satisfaction and longevity.

--- EXTRA CREDIT ---

Find ways to get involved in what stirs your mind and heart. For example, if you want to help abandoned dogs, join your spouse in volunteer work with your local animal shelter. Become a member of a rescue team. Help find families for abandoned or mistreated animals. Pay for getting some dogs and cats spayed or neutered.

DAY 362

HELP BEAUTIFY
YOUR COMMUNITY

We are the leaves of one branch, the drops of one sea, the flowers of one garden. —Jean Baptiste Henri Lacordaire, French Roman Catholic priest and orator

Take time to beautify your neighborhood with your spouse working alongside you. That conjoined sense of purpose will make you feel better about yourselves individually, strengthen your bonds as a couple, and give you both a deeper sense of belonging to each other and the community. If you and your wife feel strongly that something must be done about graffiti in your neighborhood, let your community leaders know. If a cleanup crew of volunteer workers already exists, join them; if not, get permission to form a group and ask city leaders to provide a fund for paint and brushes to use on the removal of unsightly graffiti on walls, fences, and overpasses.

Alternatively, adopt a section of a highway to keep clean. Start with any service organizations you and your wife belong to and see if members of those groups would like to help. One weekend each month could be used to clean up the trash along that section of the freeway. Do what you have in your power to reclaim your community's natural beauty. All it takes is for one person to feel passionate about the neighborhood to get the ball rolling. When neighbors and small businesses also get involved, a dramatic transformation becomes possible.

— EXTRA CREDIT —

Ask your spouse to get the hedge trimmer, gloves, and pruning shears while you ask the neighbor if he would like for you and your spouse to tackle those hedges and rose bushes he hasn't been able to deal with for a while. You'll be doing a good deed while also improving the look of the neighborhood.

DATE NIGHT

Pack up your gear for a fun adventure in the great outdoors. For example, rent a houseboat and sail around for a month, or pack your tent along with fishing and cooking utensils for a weeklong camping trip in the mountains. Learn to share the chores, deal with the frustrations, and enjoy the solitude with your best friend and lover.

LEARN TO
SKYDIVE

The way is not in the sky. The way is in the heart. —Gautama Buddha

If you are up for a little high-risk enjoyment, try to think of something a tad more exhilarating than holding the hands of the person you most love in the world—your spouse—and leaping out of an airplane together at 10,000 feet. For the first big adventure you take in your life together, what could beat lessons in skydiving, followed by a couples tandem jump? Or, how about using a dive to mark a special anniversary?

Contact the U.S. Parachute Association (*www.uspa.org*) for information about schools and lessons. Then go and jump out of a plane into the sky together. Lots of regional airports around the United States offer skydiving. There might be an outlet for skydiving classes near where you live. Imagine how much easier small talk will become when you have successfully skydived together, are relaxed, perhaps lying in bed, reliving all the exciting, breathtaking moments of your great adventure. It might even lead to . . . ahem . . . other tandem activities.

—— EXTRA CREDIT ——
Book a destination vacation with a focus on skydiving. You and your spouse could see Lake Pontchartrain and the New Orleans skyline, the coastline of Florida, or one of the most beautiful drop zones in the world, above Aruba.

INDEX

Abstinence, 64

Accountability, 345, 346

Achievements, 281, 303, 304

Acupuncture, 286, 350

Aesop, 87, 169, 232

An Affair to Remember, 2

Affirmations, 116, 219, 265, 316

Aging gracefully, 306, 359

Alcohol, drinking, 335

Alcott, Louisa May, 185

Aldrich, Thomas Bailey, 67

Alice's Adventures in Wonderland, 123

Allen, Woody, 150, 353

All in the Family, 222

Allston, John, 299

The Analects, 71

Anam Cara: A Book of Celtic Wisdom, 284, 285

Ananda Ranga, 61, 179

Angelis, Barbara de, 268

Angelou, Maya, 148

Anna Karenina, 177

Anniversaries, 121, 277, 348, 355, 365

Apologies, 118, 142, 243, 251

Appreciation, 1, 96, 233

Aristotle, 44, 79

Aromatherapy, 36

Arousal map, 170. *See also* Lovemaking tips

The Art of Money Getting, 134

Ash, Mary Kay, 303

Attentiveness, 164, 327

Attire, 12, 57, 67

Attitudes, 263, 270

Attraction, 116, 117, 195, 219, 234, 320

Aurelius, Marcus, 50

Baker, Vernon, 337

Bakker, Tammy Faye, 229

Baldwin, Alec, 181

Baldwin, James, 218

Banana splits, 301

Barber, Samuel, 195

Bargain hunting, 136, 141

Barnum, P. T., 134

Barrett, Elizabeth, 277

Barry, Dave, 339

Baryshnikov, Mikhail, 242

Baths, 32, 154

Bayly, Thomas Haynes, 64

Bed linens, 45, 167, 171

Bedroom sanctuary, 23

Bedtime conflicts, 248

Bedtime kiss, 92

Beethoven, Ludwig van, 298

Belly dancing, 242

Bergman, Ingrid, 2

Berra, Yogi, 188

Beverages, 160, 161, 177, 223

The Bhagavad Gita, 146

Bickering, 86, 130. *See also* Disagreements

Bierce, Ambrose, 54, 180

Bike rides, 70, 217, 360

Bill-paying, 134. *See also* Financial issues

Bingen, Hildegard von, 159

Birthdays, 3

Blake, William, 244

Blame, 123, 163, 258, 313, 345

Blended families, 52, 102, 165, 260, 270, 340, 352

Bodansky, Steve, 268

Bodansky, Vera, 268

Bogart, Humphrey, 2

Bombeck, Erma, 136

Bookstores, 91, 259

Bookworms, 211. *See also* Reading together

Boredom, 177, 183

Boulding, Elise, 279

Boundaries, 60, 83, 87, 321, 332, 341

Bourgeois, Jeanne, 330

Bowling, 133

Brainstorming, 297

Breakfast at Tiffany's, 2

Broken items, 290

Brothers, Joyce, 108

Browning, Robert, 277

Buber, Martin, 255

Buck, Pearl S., 93, 128, 313, 342

The Bucket List, 255

Buddha, 29, 128, 365

Budget, 134, 139. *See also* Financial issues

Bunker, Archie, 222

Burbank, Luther, 27

Burns, Ken, 95

Burton, Richard Francis, 61, 179, 181, 357

Bush, George H. W., 113

Business plans, 198, 207, 216

Business trips, 214

Butter rub, 172

Byron, Lord, 6

Cadbury, George, 272
Calling spouse, 173. *See also*
   Text messages
Calming environment, 272,
   279, 284, 318, 337
Câmara, Dom Hélder, 249
Campbell, Joseph, 240, 270
Camping, 245, 339, 364
Car, test-driving, 184
Career options, 297, 310.
   See also Business plans
Carnegie, Andrew, 219
Carnivals, 98
Carroll, Lewis, 123
Carter, Jimmy, 227
Casablanca, 2
Casino night, 231
Castellaneta, Dan, 290
Celebrations, 3, 121,
   266, 281, 348. *See also*
   Anniversaries
Cervantes, Miguel de, 82
Chair-sharing, 285
Chandogya Upanishad, 23
Charitable deeds, 43, 146,
   157, 188, 363
Child, Julia, 25, 137
Children, blended families,
   102, 260, 265, 340, 352
Children, boundaries for,
   60, 341
Children, disciplining, 135.
   See also Parenting skills
Children, examples for, 99,
   100, 108, 120, 218
Children, spaces for, 282
Children, and stress, 165
Child support, 307
Chocolates, 343
Chopra, Deepak, 218
Chores, sharing, 88, 145,
   206
Churchill, Winston, 227,
   263
Classes, 187, 205
Clinton, Hillary Rodham,
   193
Close, Glenn, 349
Clubs, 77, 196
Clutter, removing, 272, 279
Coco, James, 35
College funds, 302
Collins, Wilkie, 223
Combien Tu M'Aimes?, 203
Communication tips, 39,
   75, 83, 85, 89, 94, 107,
   222, 236, 313, 342, 347
Community, 43, 146, 157,
   188, 193, 363
Conflicts, resolving, 73, 83,
   86, 233, 248, 253, 258.
   See also Disagreements
Confucius, 60, 71
Cookies, baking, 28, 294
Cooking together, 25
Cosby, Bill, 106, 257
Couples retreat, 192
Coupon-clipping, 221
Credit cards, 204
Credit score, 144
Crisis, handling, 185, 293
Crosby, Philip, 278
Cruises, 186
Crystal, Billy, 327
Culinary delights, 42, 105
Cultural events, 38, 42
Curtis, Tony, 2
Cyber-relationship, 353

Dancing, 15, 168, 176, 191,
   196, 242
Date nights, 13. *See also spe-
   cific activities*
da Vinci, Leonardo, 124
Dean, James, 59
Debates, 169, 239, 250
Defensiveness, 89, 163
Dental hygiene, 174
The Devil's Dictionary, 54,
   180
DiCaprio, Leonardo, 2
Dickinson, Emily, 309
Differences, 125, 236, 239,
   244, 313
Diller, Phyllis, 344
Dining out, 77, 182
Dinnertime, 57, 109, 132
Diplomacy, 74
Disagreements, 71, 80, 81,
   89, 100, 108, 118, 162,
   190, 209, 345. *See also*
   Conflicts, resolving
Disaster plans, 293
Discipline, 96, 135
Disraeli, Benjamin, 209
Dissatisfaction, 243, 258
Divorce-proofing, 258
Douglas, Michael, 349
Doyle, Arthur Conan, 360
Dreams, sharing, 6, 35, 36,
   82, 104, 116, 175, 195,
   197, 198, 249, 275
*Dr. Spock's Baby and Child
   Care*, 346
Durant, Will, 142
Duras, Marguerite, 118
Durning, Charles, 113
Dyke, Henry van, 173

Eastwood, Clint, 183
Edward, Duke of Windsor,
   102
Einstein, Albert, 86, 305,
   351
Electronics, repairing, 290

Electronics, unplugging, 34
Emergency funds, 229
Emerson, Ralph Waldo, 34,
    40, 145, 202, 300, 340
Emotional baggage, 72
Emotional intimacy, 111,
    313
Empty nest plans, 344
Endearments, 71
Environmental issues, 292
Erogenous zones, 61, 158,
    170, 267, 268
Erotica, 69, 178, 211
Esquivel, Laura, 57
Essays: Second Series, 34
Estate planning, 46
Euripides, 30
Exercise, 33, 254, 334, 356,
    360, 361
Expectations, 155, 190, 352
Ex-spouses, 256, 270, 307,
    347, 352

Families, blended, 52, 102,
    165, 260, 270, 340, 352
Family, planning, 20, 66
Family boundaries, 83
Family meals, 109
Family rules, 120
Fantasies, 111, 155, 158,
    170, 178, 305
Fatal Attraction, 349
Feng shui, 272, 279, 290
Fidelity, 317. *See also* Prom-
    ises, keeping
Fields, Totie, 361
Field trips, 30, 44
Films, 2, 35, 100, 113, 183,
    191, 203, 210, 255, 314,
    349
Financial issues, 54, 66, 134,
    144, 150, 180. *See also*

Investments
Financial planning, 46, 68,
    262, 296, 304, 310, 354
Finger foods, 119
The First Wives Club, 314
Fisher, Helen, 41
A Flash of Genius, 210
Flirting, 149, 353
Flowers, 21, 22, 48
Foreign films, 203
Forgiveness, 73, 118
Forrest Gump, 186
Fortune-telling, 329
Four Christmases, 314
Franklin, Benjamin, 62, 289
Freeman, Morgan, 183, 255
Frida, 191
Friendship, 18, 331, 333
Frost, Robert, 76
Fulghum, Robert, 282
Furniture, replacing, 325

Gable, Clark, 2
Galileo, 125
Games, playing, 29, 49, 108,
    133, 140, 199, 308
Gandhi, Mahatma, 261
Gardening, 27, 48
Garr, Teri, 113
Gautama, Siddhartha, 29,
    128, 365
Gender roles, 113
Ghost, 2
Gibran, Kahlil, 321
Gifts, 251. *See also*
    Celebrations
Goals, achieving, 281, 303,
    304
Goals, sharing, 59, 116,
    194, 198, 201. *See also*
    Visualization
Gobel, George, 302

Goethe, Johann Wolfgang
    von, 9, 45, 183, 190,
    295, 333
Gone with the Wind, 2
As Good as It Gets, 215
Gorky, Maxim, 208
Gossip, 164
Grant, Carey, 2
Gratitude, 1, 96
Green issues, 292

Habitat for Humanity, 227
Habits, 247, 316
Haidt, Jonathan, 323
Haley, Alex, 346
Hammock-sharing, 84, 238
Hanks, Tom, 186
The Happiness Hypothesis,
    323
"Happy hug," 50
Hayek, Salma, 191
Healthy choices, 137, 295,
    304, 361
Hegel, Georg, 295
Helpers, hiring, 213
Hepburn, Audrey, 2
Hepburn, Katharine, 183
Heywood, John, 206
High school date, 280
Hiking, 300, 339
Hilton, Paris, 274
Hoffman, Dustin, 113
Holland, Josiah Gilbert, 201
Holmes, Oliver Wendell, Jr.,
    24, 160
Home-buying, 148, 309,
    337
Home environment, 272,
    279, 282, 284, 318
Homer, 246, 289
Hope, Laurence, 138, 234
Hot buttons, 106

Hot drinks, 160, 223
Houseplants, 48
Howe, Edgar Watson, 204
How to Make Love to a Man, 80
Hugs, 4, 50, 326, 330
Hull, Raymond, 143
Humanitarianism, 146
Humiliation, 81
Humor, 19, 147, 271

Iacocca, Lee, 213
Ideas, developing, 94, 225, 226
The Iliad, 246
Illness, 152, 286
India's Love Lyrics, 138, 234
Individuality, 83, 321
In-laws, 87, 241
Instant Orgasm, 268
Interdependence, 83, 129
Interests, sharing, 17, 202, 205, 275, 362
Investments, 232, 262, 310
Isha Upanishad, 78
"I" statements, 89, 163
It Takes a Village, 193

Johnson, Samuel, 139
Jolie, Angelina, 43
Journals, 6, 218, 246, 281, 338, 342
Judd, Ashley, 191
Jung, Carl, 6

Kahlo, Frida, 191
Kama Sutra, 49, 61, 65, 179, 181, 189, 298, 319
Karaoke, 315
Katak dance, 168
Kaufman, Margo, 264
Kearns, Robert, 210

Keller, Helen, 127
Kennedy, John F., 74
Kerr, Deborah, 2
Kerr, Jean, 135
Kipling, Rudyard, 347
Kissing tips, 2, 90, 92, 103, 179, 181, 251, 330
Kübler-Ross, Elisabeth, 121

Lacordaire, Jean Baptiste Henri, 363
Landers, Ann, 248, 283
Lange, Jessica, 113
Lao-tzu, 94, 192
Laughter, 19, 147, 271
Law of Attraction, 116, 117, 195, 219
Lawrence, D. H., 16, 53
Lebowitz, Fran, 265
Leigh, Vivien, 2
Lewis, C. S., 116, 269
Liar, Liar, 314
Life as a House, 314
Life goals, 59, 116, 194, 198, 201, 239
Like Water for Chocolate, 57
Lincoln, Abraham, 131, 304
Lingerie, 12
Listening skills, 85, 222. *See also* Communication tips
Living trusts, 180
Longfellow, Henry Wadsworth, 281
Loren, Sophia, 35, 320
Love, altruistic, 5
Love, expressing, 22, 313
Love, rituals for, 276
Love, unconditional, 121, 323
Lovemaking tips, 56, 61, 65, 67, 101, 138, 189, 224, 268, 269, 326, 330

Lovemaking toys, 23, 45, 324
The Lover, 203
The Lower Depths, 208
Loyalty, 317. *See also* Promises, keeping
Lying, 39, 128, 349

Machado, Antonio, 69
Machiavelli, Niccolo, 288
Making up, 90
Man caves, 143
Man of La Mancha, 35
Mansfield, Katherine, 211
Marital discord, 243, 258, 314
Marriage contract, 76, 277, 314
Marriage counselor, 131, 192, 235
Marriage plan, 41, 239
Marriage renewal, 338, 348, 355
Marx, Chico, 319
Marx, Groucho, 89, 306
Massage, 153, 159, 172, 240, 254, 286
Maugham, W. Somerset, 58
Maurois, Andre, 348
McGraw, Phil, 108
Mead, Margaret, 43
Meditations of a Parish Priest, 72
Meltzer, Bernard, 103
Million Dollar Baby, 183
Milne, A. A., 334
Miniature golf, 199
Mitchell, Langdon, 73
Money, commingling, 229, 232

Money issues, 39, 54, 62, 83, 134, 144, 188, 204. *See also* Financial issues
Monroe, Marilyn, 2
Montessori, Maria, 120
Moonlight, 15, 126
Moore, Demi, 2
Moore, Thomas, 75
Moral character, 218
Morley, Christopher, 15
Mother-in-law, 241
Mother Teresa, 96, 130
Movies, 2, 35, 100, 113, 183, 191, 203, 210, 255, 314, 349
Mrs. Doubtfire, 314
Munch-Bellinghausen, Eligius von, 104
Murdoch, Iris, 323
Music, 298, 324
Myss, Caroline, 356
Mystery, 321

The National Parks: America's Best Idea, 95
Nature, 63. *See also* Outdoors, exploring
Negative cycles, 86, 192, 316
Nehru, Jawaharlal, 38
Newlyweds, 54, 75, 321, 328, 333
Newman, Paul, 271
The New York Idea, 73
Nicholson, Harold, 27
Nicholson, Jack, 215, 255
Niebuhr, Reinhold, 235
Nightingale, Earl, 41
Nin, Anaïs, 36, 110, 170, 276
Nobody Knows My Name, 218

Noise, diminishing, 278
Notes, writing, 58
Nutrition, 137, 361

Obama, Barack, 241, 352
Obama, Michelle, 241
O'Donohue, John, 284, 285, 311
Oerter, Al, 254
O'Keeffe, Georgia, 205
1001 Ways to Do Good, 157
Organization tips, 289
Orgasms, 138, 158, 268. *See also* Lovemaking tips
O'Toole, Peter, 35
Outdoors, exploring, 24, 63, 95, 245, 300, 339, 360, 364
Ovid, 55, 101

Pacino, Al, 191
Paintball, 308
Palmer, Arnold, 199
Paradigm, shifting, 47, 81, 183, 270
Parenting skills, 93, 135, 145, 193
Parenting styles, 96, 120
Parker, Dorothy, 174, 200
Parker, Sarah Jessica, 253
Patton, George S., 100
Peale, Norman Vincent, 258
Pearce, Joseph Chilton, 96
Pedicures, 153
Penney, Alexandra, 80
Peppard, George, 2
The Perfumed Garden of the Shaykh Nefwazi, 357
Perfumes, 51
Perret, Gene, 296
Pet names, 71
Pheromones, 8

Physica, 159
Planetarium, 112
Plants, 21, 22, 27, 48
Plath, Sylvia, 32
Plato, 34, 324
Please Don't Eat the Daisies, 135
Poetry, 172, 294
Porter, Katherine Anne, 153
Positive thinking, 201, 316
Possessions, 288, 325
Posters, 121, 175
Praise, 1, 215
Prévert, Jacques, 4, 177
Previous relationships, 122
Privacy, 123
Procrastination, 351
Promises, keeping, 76, 277, 314, 317, 338
Proust, Marcel, 1, 5, 159, 247

Racetracks, 252
Rand, Ayn, 207
Reading together, 31, 160, 172, 211, 357
Relaxation tips, 32, 39, 165, 212, 230, 233, 248, 264, 284, 350
The Remedies for Love, 101
Responsibility, 122, 345, 346, 352
Retirement plans, 296, 310. *See also* Financial planning
Retreats, 192, 291. *See also* Trips
Riley, James Whitcomb, 212
Rilke, Rainer Maria, 230
Rivera, Diego, 191
Rivers, Joan, 33, 88, 187
Robbins, Anthony, 47

Robbins, Tom, 37
Robinson Marian, 241
Rochefoucauld, François de La, 149
Roger, Ginger, 74
Role-playing, 53, 214, 245
Roles, gender, 113
Roosevelt, Eleanor, 81
Roosevelt, Franklin D., 46
Rossetti, Christina Georgina, 3
Routines, 177, 183, 276
Roux, Joseph, 72
Rumi, 22, 111, 332

Sackville-West, Vita, 27, 48
Sade, Marquis de, 179
Sailing, 186
Saint-Exupéry, Antoine de, 8
Sanctuary, 23, 185
Sand, George, 328
Sandburg, Carl, 198
Santayana, George, 92
Sappho, 158
Sarandon, Susan, 43
Satir, Virginia, 4
Savings account, 62, 232. See also Financial planning
Scent of a Woman, 191
Schuller, Robert H., 239
Schulz, Charles, 232
Schweitzer, Albert, 157
Scrapbooks, 246, 281
Secrets, keeping, 9
Seductiveness, 55. See also Lovemaking tips
Self, boundaries, 83, 321
Self, sharing, 10
Selflessness, 5, 261
Self-pleasure, 269
Selleca, Connie, 256

"Serenity Prayer," 235
Setbacks, 200
The Seven Spiritual Laws for Parents, 218
Sex appeal, 320
Sexual fulfillment, 50, 54, 83, 155, 311. See also Lovemaking tips
Sexy dances, 15. See also Dancing
Sexy lingerie, 12
Sexy notes, 58
Shakespeare, William, 8, 85, 233, 275, 326
Shaw, George Bernard, 354
Shopping tips, 166, 221, 274, 283. See also Money issues
Showers, 156, 324
Sickness, 152, 285
Signoret, Simone, 312
Sills, Beverly, 194
Skelton, Red, 341
The Skin of Our Teeth, 277
Skydiving, 365
Smith, Adam, 166
Snuggling, 2, 4, 11, 31, 285, 350
Social networking, 37, 246, 322, 353
Socrates, 100, 114, 349
Some Like It Hot, 2
The Song of Solomon, 90
Spa, 153
Spinoza, Benedict, 122, 221
Spiritual values, 99, 117, 218
Spock, Benjamin, 346
Spooning, 11. See also Snuggling
Sports, 40, 202, 257
Stamp, Josiah Charles, 345

Star-gazing, 245, 336
St. Augustine, 228
Steinbeck, John, 95
Steinem, Gloria, 260
Stepmom, 314
Still Life with Woodpecker, 37
Sting, 359
Storytelling, 69
Stray Birds, 117
Stress, 32, 130, 165, 212, 230, 233, 248, 264. See also Relaxation tips
The Summing Up, 58
Swank, Hilary, 183
Swayze, Patrick, 2, 176
Syrus, Publilius, 144

Tagore, Rabindranath, 117
Tango, 191, 196
Teamwork, 216, 219
Teas, 160, 223, 358
Tennis, 257
Text messages, 16, 115, 173
Thackeray, William Makepeace, 10
Thatcher, Margaret, 113, 250, 262
Therapist, 131, 192, 235
Thoreau, Henry David, 195, 292
Time capsule, 273
Time management, 124, 212, 220, 228, 327
Titanic, 2
Tolerance, 47, 162, 271
Tolstoy, Leo, 177
Toothbrushes, 174
Tootsie, 113
Travels with Charley, 95
Trevino, Lee, 307
Trips, 30, 44, 186, 192, 214, 255, 291, 312

Trump, Donald, 297
Truthfulness, 39, 128, 349
Trysts, 23, 319
Twain, Mark, 31, 39, 165

Ultimatums, 92, 142, 209
Unconditional love, 121,
    323
Unwinding, 39, 233, 248,
    284. *See also* Relaxation
    tips

Vacations, 186, 192, 291.
    See also Trips
Valentino, Rudolph, 191
Values, 99, 114, 117, 218
Van Gogh, Vincent, 44
Viewpoints, 78, 80, 169,
    239, 250. *See also*
    Disagreements
Visualization, 195, 201,
    316, 348, 351
Volunteerism, 43, 47, 146,
    157, 188, 227, 363
Vulnerabilities, 107, 110,
    111, 127

War of the Roses, 314
Washington, Booker T., 43
The Way of Lao-tzu, 192
The Way We Were, 314
Weaknesses, 344, 349, 351
Wealth, 232, 262. *See also*
    Financial planning
Weight loss, 137, 361
Welch, Raquel, 267
Wesley, John, 362
West, Mae, 115, 251
When Harry Met Sally, 13
Why We Love, 41
Wilde, Oscar, 317
Wilder, Thornton, 277

Williams, Robin, 17, 325
Wills, creating, 299
Window-shopping, 287
Winds of Doctrine, 92
Wine-tasting, 237
Winfrey, Oprah, 331
Winslet, Kate, 2
The Woman in White, 223
Woodward, Joanne, 271
Workaholics, 220
Working together, 207, 208,
    216
Workouts, 33, 254, 334,
    356
The Wrestler, 26
Wrestling, 26, 183
Wriston, Walter B., 68

Yeats, W. B., 197, 314
Yoga, 50, 248, 254, 286
"You" statements, 89, 163

ABOUT THE AUTHOR

Meera Lester is happily married to architect/designer Carlos Carvajal. She is the author of more than two dozen books, including *365 Ways to Look—and Feel—Younger, 365 Ways to Live Happy, The Everything® Law of Attraction Book,* and *365 Ways to Live the Law of Attraction.* Read her blog on Amazon.com or find other information about Meera on Facebook, LinkedIn, or on her website at *www.meeralester.com.*

jane
ON TOP

Getting Where Women Really Belong

- Trying to lose the losers you've been dating?
- Striving to find the time to be a doting mother, dedicated employee, and still be a hot piece of you-know-what in the bedroom?
- Been in a comfortable relationship that's becoming, well, too comfortable?

Don't despair! Visit the Jane on Top blog—your new source for information (and commiseration) on all things relationships, sex, and the juggling act that is being a modern gal.

Visit the Jane on Top blog today at
www.adamsmedia.com/blog/relationships